PORTFOLIO

STICK TO DRAWING COMICS, MONKEY BRAIN!

Scott Adams launched *Dilbert* in 1989. The strip now appears daily in more than two thousand newspapers in sixty-five countries. His business books include *The Dilbert Principle* and *Dogbert's Top Secret Management Handbook*, both #1 *New York Times* bestsellers. Adams has published twenty-three books with more than ten million copies in print. He lives outside San Francisco.

D0963318

SCOTT ADAMS

STICK TO DRAWING COMICS, MONKEY BRAIN!

Cartoonist Explains Cloning, Blouse Monsters, Voting Machines, Romance, Monkey Gods, How to Avoid Being Mistaken for a Rodent, and More

For Shelly, Savannah, and Justin

PORTFOLIO
Published by the Penguin Group
Penguin Group (USA) Inc., 375 Hudson Street, New York, New York 10014, U.S.A.
Penguin Group (Canada), 90 Eglinton Avenue East, Suite 700, Toronto, Ontario, Canada M4P 2Y3 (a division of Pearson Penguin Canada Inc.)
Penguin Books Ltd, 80 Strand, London WC2R 0RL, England
Penguin Ireland, 25 St Stephen's Green, Dublin 2, Ireland (a division of Penguin Books Ltd)
Penguin Group (Australia), 250 Camberwell Road, Camberwell, Victoria 3124, Australia (a division of Pearson Australia Group Pty Ltd)
Penguin Books India Pvt Ltd, 11 Community Centre, Panchsheel Park, New Delhi – 110 017, India
Penguin Group (NZ), 67 Apollo Drive, Rosedale, North Shore 0632, New Zealand (a division of Pearson New Zealand Ltd)
Penguin Books (South Africa) (Pty) Ltd, 24 Sturdee Avenue, Rosebank, Johannesburg 2196, South Africa

Penguin Books Ltd, Registered Offices:
80 Strand, London WC2R 0RL, England

First published in the United States of America by Portfolio, a member of Penguin Group (USA) Inc. 2007
This paperback edition published 2008

10 9 8 7 6 5 4 3 2 1

Copyright © Scott Adams, Inc., 2007
All rights reserved

Most of the contents of this book first appeared on the author's blog.

Scott Adams's comic strips are distributed by United Features Syndicate.

THE LIBRARY OF CONGRESS HAS CATALOGED THE HARDCOVER EDITION AS FOLLOWS:
Adams, Scott, 1957–
Stick to drawing comics, monkey brain!:cartoonist ignores helpful advice / Scott Adams.
p. cm.
ISBN 978-1-59184-185-2 (hc.)
ISBN 978-1-59184-230-9 (pbk.)
1. Adams, Scott, 1957– 2. Cartoonists—United States—Biography. I. Title.
PN6727.A3A3   2007
741.5'6973—dc22   2007017177

Printed in the United States of America
Set in New Baskerville
Designed by Kate Nichols

Except in the United States of America, this book is sold subject to the condition that it shall not, by way of trade or otherwise, be lent, resold, hired out, or otherwise circulated without the publisher's prior consent in any form of binding or cover other than that in which it is published and without a similar condition including this condition being imposed on the subsequent purchaser.

The scanning, uploading and distribution of this book via the Internet or via any other means without the permission of the publisher is illegal and punishable by law. Please purchase only authorized electronic editions, and do not participate in or encourage electronic piracy of copyrighted materials. Your support of the author's rights is appreciated.

Contents

Preface

Ⅰf you are reading this, you probably waited for the paperback version of the book to come out. That is a strong testament to your self-discipline and deep appreciation of economics, more commonly known as cheapness.

The paperback version of this book is superior to the hardbound version in several ways. First, if you plan to read it aloud, there's a good chance someone will yank it out of your hands and start beating you with it. That's when you really appreciate the softness.

The paperback version costs less, it's lighter, and the material has a solid track record of not triggering epileptic seizures. But most important, this paperback version includes some new content. I don't know how many extra pages it has because I'm writing this before it is typeset. But my best guess is that it is five reading sessions longer than the original, depending on several factors such as the amount of fiber in your diet.

Feel free to read this book in any order whatsoever. Start at the end, the middle, whatever. It's written in bite-sized pieces for people with tight schedules and short attention spans. I think we both know that is you.

Scott Adams

Introduction

You might be wondering why I wrote a non-Dilbert book. The answer requires some explaining.

First, allow me to confess that I have failed at 90 percent of the things I have ever attempted. Failure rarely bothers me. I always learn something in the process, and the screwups provide a nice backdrop of humility for the few times when things work out. To understand my reasons for writing a non-Dilbert book—other and beyond my natural impulse to create new things—I need to take you back in time.

In a way, this book started when I was a kid. I was about nine years old when I told my mother I planned to win an art contest that was advertised on the back of a cereal box. If my drawing of the famous geyser Old Faithful were judged one of the best, I'd win a prize. Mom tried to explain just how many people would enter a contest like that, presumably so I wouldn't be disappointed when I didn't win. I understood the odds, but I was sure I was going to win anyway, so I sketched my picture and sent it in.

I won a camera.

When I was eleven years old, I was certain I would find the Golden Egg at the annual Easter Egg Hunt in my town. Imagine a field full of hidden eggs, the area is covered with kids looking for those eggs, and only one egg is the golden one. Against all odds, I was sure I would be the one to find it.

Later that week, my picture was on the front page of our local papers. "Scott Adams Finds Golden Egg."

It was about that same time when I first heard the word *valedictorian*. I was surprised to learn that there was an actual name for the best student in the graduating class. I decided to become one of those. How hard could it be?

In 1975 I graduated as valedictorian.

I recall one day in eighth-grade science class when the teacher was giving the answers to some standardized tests we were taking for practice. I raised my hand and pointed out that his answer was wrong. I argued that he was misinterpreting the question. This didn't seem likely to him, given that he was a professional science teacher and I was fourteen. But to humor me, he agreed to go back to the source and check.

I was right. He had misinterpreted the question.

On my first day at Hartwick College I met a large muscular guy named Bob near the communal mailboxes. He was in his early twenties, returning to college to finish his degree. In the course of conversation I discovered that we both played tennis, so we set up a match. He spouted something about being the top player at his previous college and how he would mop the court with me. I had never taken a tennis lesson, but I played often and usually won, so I assured him that he would be annihilated. (Yeah, I was like that.)

He turned out to be the better player by far, but he had a bad day, and I won. He was both surprised and displeased, or at least that's my interpretation of why he smashed his racket to bits in front of me after match point. A few months later he became the top player on the college team. (I never beat him again.)

During my corporate career I attended a mandatory class on problem solving. The first exercise involved a case study that was selected because there were so many factors to consider. Our job was to use the tools they taught us and weed out the unimportant factors until we found the root problem. We were assured that this process would take quite a while, and some groups might never solve it.

I read the case and identified the root problem on the first pass. It was the sort of solution where once you saw it, you knew it was right. The instructor accused me of cheating because he had been teaching the course for years and no one had ever solved the problem just by reading it.

I remember telling my friends and family that I was going to submit some comics to become a syndicated cartoonist. I don't remember even one person predicting I would succeed. Thousands of wannabes submit comics for syndication every year and only a few get contracts. And most of those comics fizzle after a few years. My entire art experience included frequent doodling plus getting the well-deserved lowest grade in art class in college. That was my total preparation for my new career.

I sent my samples to several comic syndication companies. One syndicate helpfully suggested that I find an actual artist to do the drawing for me. United Media had lower standards and offered me a contract for Dilbert. That turned out to be a good move on their part.

When Dilbert was only in about fifty newspapers, and I still had my day job, I got a call from a meeting organizer in Calgary asking if I wanted to give a speech—preferably a funny one—to a bunch of engineers. I had spoken to small groups before, generally at my day job. And I had taken the Dale Carnegie course, but that only involved giving speeches to my forty classmates. It was a long way from stand-up comedy in Canada. But they offered to pay me $5,000 U.S., which got my attention. I figured the worst that could happen was I would embarrass myself in Canada.

So I flew to Canada, showed them some comics that had gotten me in trouble, and told witty stories. They seemed to enjoy the show. That was about three hundred paid speeches ago. I can't tell you my current price, but the biggest offer I ever turned down was $100,000 to do a one-hour speech for a tech company. (I had prior commitments.)

Keep in mind that I'm only telling you about the things that worked out well for me. The vast majority of my efforts, in all fields of life, have ended in failure and embarrassment. But the successes have a pattern to them, and perhaps you are starting to see it.

A few years into cartooning, Adrian Zackheim, an editor for a major publishing company, approached me about writing a humorous business book. I had never taken any writing courses. I hadn't even read many books. But I said I'd give it a try.

That book was *The Dilbert Principle*. It became a #1 *New York Times* bestseller. So I put out a second book right away, and the two of them occupied #1 and #2 on the nonfiction list.

About a year later, after a meeting with my tax accountant in a nearby town, I stopped into a restaurant for lunch before heading home. I knew the manager from her prior job at a restaurant where I had eaten hundreds of times. We chatted and she mentioned that someday she wanted to own her own restaurant. I had always wanted to invest in a restaurant, for reasons that are unclear even to me. So I said that if she was serious she should put together a business case and I'd consider funding it. She did just that. Everyone told me I was nuts to get into the restaurant business with no experience.

The business (Stacey's Café) has been a solid success, and Stacey and I opened a second restaurant (Stacey's at Waterford) a few years later.

Several years ago I was approached by some advisers for people in high places. I can't give you the details of this story, or even tell you why I can't give you the details. But the gist of it was that they needed help squelching some bad ideas that had taken hold in the public consciousness. They thought humor might be one part of the solution, and they were Dilbert fans, so they tracked me down. The challenge was that the bad ideas sounded terrific to the uninformed person. You couldn't kill these particular bad ideas with logic because the arguments against them would be too complicated. You had to go in through the back door.

I suggested a few cleverly designed, hypnosis-inspired phrases that were the linguistic equivalent of kung fu. They were simple (that's my specialty), and once you heard these phrases, they made any competing ideas seem frankly stupid. Think of Johnnie Cochran's famous refrain, "If the glove doesn't fit, you must acquit." In my opinion, O.J. is a free man largely because of that phrase. My phrases worked the same way.

The people in high places tried my phrases. The phrases became world headlines the next day. I could tune the TV to any news channel and hear my words coming out of pundits' mouths. The phrases smothered the competing ideas and just maybe changed the course of world events. (One can never know for sure.)

I mention these stories because over the course of my life, every time I try something different or unlikely, someone says the equivalent of "don't quit your day job." When I venture into areas clearly outside of my expertise, I hear, "You're in way over your head" and, lately, "Stick to drawing comics."

Somehow I have to square that seemingly good advice with the fact that I've so often been successful against long odds, especially when I'm in way over my head. In fact, that's when I do my best work. I gave you several examples, but trust me when I say there are plenty more. Here are two.

I was in way over my head when I used Google to correctly diagnose a sudden and exotic problem with my ability to speak. The first four doctors I visited had been stymied. So I decided to do my own medical research using only the Internet. My correct diagnosis led me down a path to the right experts so I could (mostly) recover my voice. During this process I've met and heard from people who have had this condition for decades, often without ever getting a correct medical diagnosis.

I have a degree in economics, but frankly all I remember is something about lowering prices to increase volume. Yesterday a friend forwarded me a tongue-in-cheek story that ran on a business website about how I might win the Nobel Prize for Economics. The article was based on a list of investment tips I wrote that have been widely reprinted by economists and business publications. My tips weren't anything new—I just figured out how to explain in one page what usually takes an entire book. Economists like brevity.

To put all of this in context, I remind you again that I fail miserably about ten times for every one success. (That's an accurate estimate. I've literally kept score.) The failures always involved activities for which I was completely qualified. Ironically, I couldn't even "keep my day job." On the other hand, my successes have all been in areas in which I had no obviously relevant background or experience whatsoever.

I know that many will say I shouldn't have written this non-Dilbert book, especially since it isn't about business. Non-Dilbert books are not my area of expertise. "Stick to drawing comics" is the advice I will hear more times than I will care to count. You might be thinking it already. I'm used to it.

If I had listened to that sort of advice in the past, I never would have done anything interesting in my life, much less be successful. Was it smart to write this sort of book, or will it turn out to be another in a long list of my failures and embarrassments? Beats me. Thank you for giving it a chance.

I started writing the material in this book at about the same time I proposed to my wife, Shelly. I tested a page or so of my writing each day on The Dilbert Blog, and used the comments from readers to weed out the worst of it. I wrote daily, so you could think of this book as a diary of my thoughts as I transmogrified from a bachelor to a husband. In some cases you might have been sharing similar thoughts, assuming you were also deranged, exhausted, sometimes medicated, and generally riddled with stress.

You'll be happy to know that I didn't write much about my wedding or the planning thereof. I'm a man, and frankly I don't remember details. I think we had flowers. And it was on a boat of some sort. We probably danced.

The one thing I do remember is standing at the altar and watching my beautiful bride come around the corner after we had been apart an agonizing twenty-four hours. That's the only memory I want or need.

Some readers will wonder why I couldn't write a book without all the vulgarity that you will find here. I could. I've written lots of those books. But I always felt constrained because I couldn't write entirely in my own voice, which is, I am not too proud to say, often vulgar. If you have a sense of humor, there's a good chance you know some colorful words yourself. So don't be all judgy.

My Innocent Look

Apparently the airport security people are trained to look at your face to see if you are twitching like a terrorist. They always take a long, deliberate look at me after checking my boarding pass. I figure they must have taken the one-hour course on identifying bad people by their body language. So I try to put on my most natural expression—the one that says "I am not a terrorist. I am just passing through. There is no reason to detain me." I also think those thoughts really hard just in case I'm a Jedi and no one ever told me.

But I worry that a fake innocent look is exactly what a terrorist would use. I'm not a good actor. When I smile to have my picture taken, it looks totally unnatural. It doesn't even look like a smile. It's more of a grimace mixed with a note of surprise and perhaps a dash of intestinal discomfort. So when I act "natural" for airport security, I have some serious doubts that I look natural at all.

Then I start imagining that the security guy is acting natural himself while actually thinking something along the lines of "When this obvious terrorist turns around I will try to kill him with a single blow. I might get some sort of bonus." So the two of us are locked in this Academy Award-losing acting moment where I am pretending to be a guy who is *not* pretending to *not* be a terrorist while the security guy is pretending to be a guy who is not planning to kill me. It's a long moment.

Then the security guy writes something on my boarding pass. It looks like maybe an initial or some sort of code. I worry that this code is what will cause the other security people to swarm me at the metal detector when I am most vulnerable. I sometimes consider modifying the little code while I'm in the next line. But since I don't know the codes, I could end up accidentally changing the "innocent traveler" code to the "Bin Laden KILL KILL KILL" code.

So I don't alter the code. But I still spend a moment before passing through the metal detector wondering what it feels like to be Tasered and beaten with batons at the same time. I figure it's only a matter of time before I find out.

Dangerous Donuts

Did you see my Dilbert comic on August 4, 2005, that featured Dogbert as a police negotiator? When I first submitted it to my editor at United Media, it showed a cop shooting an unarmed suspect who had just surrendered. Here's the original version.

The problem is that there's an unwritten rule in newspaper comics that you can't show a gun being fired. I knew that, but my editor was new on the job and I thought it was the perfect time to try and slip one through. But his alert assistant thwarted my plan and brought it to the attention of an informal committee of executives to decide how to handle it. The group ruled that the gun could not be shown. The concept of a peace officer gunning down an unarmed suspect was okay, but I couldn't show the actual gun firing.

So I submitted an altered version, this time replacing the middle panel with the words *BAM BAM BAM* to indicate a gun firing without actually showing it. The assistant editor showed the new version to the executives and they decided that the comic still showed a gun, and still showed that it was firing, so that wouldn't work either.

Luckily I have sixteen years of corporate experience, and I know how to navigate my way around group decisions. What I needed was a solution that could only appeal to a committee. I suggested a compromise. I would keep everything the same, except the gun would be replaced with a donut... that fires bullets. My compromise was accepted. Without explanation to the readers, this is the actual comic that ran that day.

Interestingly, the executives were right. To the best of my knowledge, no one complained about the donut-related violence. But had we shown the actual gun, it would have been trouble. There is a certain art to this job, and it's obviously not in the drawings.

Time for a New Look

Every now and then, I meet someone who prefers to avoid all sources of news. People say it's an excellent strategy for a stress-free life. But it's not for me. I'm a news junky. In a typical week I watch about nine thousand people get whacked by all sorts of newsworthy tragedies. I can watch the same poor bastard die fifty times from nine different camera angles and still go back for more. But this important "knowledge" comes at a cost—that is, my guts are generally knotted and I suspect that every object in my environment will either explode or fall on me.

Recently I was traveling, and ordered breakfast from room service. The guy who delivered it is evidently the type who avoids all sources of news. I say this with some confidence not just because of his carefree demeanor, but also because he looked exactly like Saddam Hussein. As a general rule, if you look like a brutal dictator, it's time to update your look. Shave the mustache, do something with the hair, get an earring—that sort of thing. But he seemed quite happy with himself. I'm sure he wasn't actually Saddam, but I overtipped him just to err on the cautious side.

I worry that the next newsworthy mass murderer will look exactly like me. I see Scott look-alikes all the time—driving past in cars or at the mall. Often we smile or wave, both of us wondering which one is the "poor man's version."

Statistically speaking, you have to assume that one of my near-clones will someday have a bad attitude and a bazooka at the same time. The best you can hope for is that it will happen on a busy news day and no one will notice. But if I can't have that, I'll settle for nine camera angles and good lighting.

Bad Thoughts

I spend way too much time thinking of excellent crimes I could commit if I were a crime-committing sort of person. Every time I read about hurricane-related looting, I wonder about the best way to do it.

I think I'd get myself a looting boat, stocked with a bunch of camping stuff, in case I got stuck in the disaster area. And it wouldn't hurt to have a big jacket that said FEMA on it. I'd wait until a hurricane started to threaten a particular community and then I'd steal a car and start towing my little pirate boat in that direction, monitoring the news as I went. I'd set up camp near a target-rich environment, tie the boat to a lamppost, up high, and wait for the storm to empty the city. There's a good chance I'd be killed by the hurricane before I did any quality looting, but that's a risk I'm willing to take for free pants that aren't my size.

I might bring my own decoy puppy, in case anyone saw me climbing through a broken store window. I'd just hold up the puppy and yell, "It's okay! I got her!"

After I did my looting—or as we white people like to say: "gather my supplies"—I'd motor my little pirate boat down the main street, out to the ocean, and back to my hidden lair that would be stinking of damp merchandise.

Sometime soon I plan to do some thinking about ending world hunger. But frankly, that seems harder.

Lawyer with a Porpoise

Several people e-mailed to say they noticed that my comic on September 6, 2005, which featured a porpoise killing a lawyer, was published in two different versions. The tame version ran in newspapers and the edgier one ran on my website. What's up with that?

Sometimes I create two versions if I think newspapers will have a problem with the edgy one. It's not censorship per se, just a case of keeping the customers happy. I don't feel artistically stifled because showing the edgy one to 1.5 million people on the Web satisfies whatever tiny molecules of artistic integrity I possess.

Here's the tame one. My editors at United Media had no problem showing the lawyer being killed, but we negotiated the cause of his demise to look this way.

It's amusing, I think, but the original version was punchier. See if you can guess why newspapers would have had a problem with this next one.

Apparently there's an unwritten rule about showing a porpoise with his head in a lawyer's ass.

I still got complaints about the tame version, but only from people who said my drawing of a porpoise looks more like a dolphin. That offended some people.

Dilbert reader Paul Simer saw the comic and helpfully suggested that the lawyer "needed to start living a Porpoise Driven Life."

I wish I had said it.

Mad About the Wrong Things

Maybe it's the way I was raised, but I find that I get mad about all the wrong things. For example, when I hear a news report about some serial killer who buried forty-three victims in an underground bunker that he constructed beneath his shed, my first reaction is *Wow, he built an underground bunker under a shed!* I find myself admiring his industriousness and passion in the pursuit of his dreams. That's clearly wrong.

Then today I read in *Reader's Digest* about Marine engineer Richard James who invented the Slinky in 1943 after a tension spring from a meter used to test battleship horsepower fell off his desk and "walked" end-over-end.

I hate that guy.

I don't know the full story (that's why they call it the *Reader's Digest*), but it sure seems like he was rewarded for being clumsy. I can't respect that.

I've met several people who made fortunes by founding and then selling dotcom companies that soon went out of business. They aren't just rich, they're crazy rich. And all of their heirs will be crazy rich, too, until they drive their Ferraris over embankments and restore my faith in karma.

Well, now that that rant is over, I can get back to reading "Laughter, the Best Medicine" and see how many people got paid $300 for submitting a funny story that they read in the Dilbert Newsletter and claimed it happened to them. I don't know if the *Reader's Digest* intends to fill me with jealous rage, but it's hard to see this as a coincidence.

Fear of Birds

Well, it's official: I'm afraid of birds.

I was already afraid of sunshine, under the theory that a day without sunshine is like a day without melanoma. And I'm uneasy around those plastic things that hold six-packs together; I'm always worried I might get my head stuck in one. I'm afraid of a lot of things.

Now this bird flu business has me worried. I already circle the parking lot twelve times to find a space that isn't under a tree and directly in the crapping zone. If birds start getting the flu, they'll be firing from both ends. There aren't enough squeegees in the world.

I've got my fingers crossed that global warming will kill all the birds before they start hurling on me. With any luck, someday the global warming will make those birds burst into flames in midflight. Problem solved.

But until that happy day, I'm thinking of moving to Florida. I'm no ornithologist/meteorologist, but I'm pretty sure birds don't like hurricanes.

The media always focuses on the negative aspects of hurricanes. They never mention how it helps clear out the birds for a while. Just once I would like to hear a news report with an upbeat take:

"Thanks to hurricane Wilma, nothing has crapped on our Eyewitness News van for hours. Back to you, Bob."

I Love Technology

oday (the day I wrote this) I woke up early because I have a cross-country flight. I fired up my computer and used the airline's website to change my seat assignment and print out my boarding pass.

Well, technically, I spent an hour trying to do that, but the website kept melting down at different points until I finally gave up and called their 800 number and handled my transaction in an efficient manner using their speech recognition system.

Well, technically, I spent fifteen minutes crawling through the automated menus until my cat climbed up on the desk and meowed into my speakerphone. That put the system into a mode where my only two choices were "before the flight" and "during the flight." That's not the sort of question you want to answer without knowing the context, so I bailed out and called again. This time I efficiently handled my transaction using their sophisticated phone system.

Well, technically, I spent what seemed like a lifetime crawling through the automated voice menus until I got an option of talking to a live person. The live person courteously and efficiently handled my transaction.

Well, technically, the system said it was transferring me to the next available agent but it disconnected me instead. On my second try, I got a nice woman in India who helped me change my seat. Then I had a wonderful flight.

Well, technically, the airline's automated message called me an hour later and said my flight was canceled for no particular reason. But I was automatically rebooked to a new and better flight with excellent seats and vegetarian meals. There was a good chance I could get backrubs from attractive flight attendants, too.

Well, technically, they booked me on an overnight flight that would guarantee that when I gave my keynote speech to a crowd of one thousand industry leaders soon upon landing, I would look like a heroin-addicted badger that had stowed away in a jar of mayonnaise.

But no problem. I changed airlines and booked a more reasonable flight. Then I breezed though the security screening and had a wonderful travel experience.

Well, technically, when you make a one-way flight at the last minute, it raises red flags on someone's computer. A potato-shaped woman with unfashionable glasses herded me into the "severe search" line. Someone told me to stand in a high-tech phone booth sort-o-thing that blew air on me, analyzed it, and informed the technician whether I had been in contact with explosives lately. I passed the test, but I spent the whole time wondering how I could get some.

Now I'm sitting in the airport, waiting for the flight that will probably hit an asteroid and plunge into the ocean. But I'm still optimistic about the backrubs.

How Certain Is Certain?

I'd better reduce the font for this entry because it's about the guy sitting next to me on the flight to Chicago.

Before takeoff, we both sat here tapping away on our Black-Berries, sending last-minute messages. But where I interpreted the flight attendant's instruction to turn off all electronics as just that, the high-powered executive next to me had a different view. He interpreted it to mean, *Hide your BlackBerry when the flight attendant is looking. Otherwise, keep working all the way through takeoff.*

On one hand, I'm almost totally certain that a BlackBerry can't bring down an airline. If it could, even in the most unlikely scenario, it surely would have happened a dozen times already. If you consider all the flights in the world and all the cell phones and BlackBerries and laptops and PDAs that have traveled on them, it seems impossible that they could be a threat.

But still. There he was, tapping away, and maybe, just maybe . . . killing me. I thought about doing something, such as informing the flight attendant. But I need to rely on this passenger to move for me at some time during this flight so I can use the restroom. It could be a tense, uncomfortable flight if I get him angry. I had to balance a 10 percent chance of a bursting bladder versus a .00000001 percent chance of a fireball-related death.

So I just sat there, staring at the rule-breaker thumbing his little death machine while the pilot gunned the engines and headed sky-ward. Could this be the one time when a BlackBerry causes a jet to plunge into the Rockies? How certain was I that this was safe? Can you ever be sure enough in these situations?

My only solace is that if this puppy goes down, the headlines will read "Plane Crashes. Dilbert Cartoonist Is Turned into Charcoal." That's Top Billing, baby. So in a way, I'd win, unless this scofflaw is the new chairman of the Federal Reserve or something impressive. It would suck if I died in a fireball and only got mentioned in the sidebar.

It Doesn't Hurt to Ask

Yesterday I gave a speech to a large industry group. Afterward, people were gathering around me to ask for autographs, make small talk, and whatnot. A big guy with a huge moist hand the size of an unidentified corpse, the sort that you find along the Interstate while collecting cans, shook my hand and asked, "Can I have one of your foils?"

"What?" I asked, confused.

"Your foils . . . that you used in your talk. Can I have one?"

"Um, no. I use them for my talks."

The transparencies (or foils) are used on a digital video system as part of the presentation package I use whenever I speak. I'm thinking that if I give him one, I have to replace it. That means finding the original comic file, finding where I keep the transparencies I use for the printer, printing off a new one, keeping my cat from licking the wet ink off it after it prints (big problem), and finding where it fits back in the presentation. And this is if I remember to do it, which is iffy at best.

I'm also worried about the twenty people hearing the foil request. If they sense weakness, they'll demand their own foils, or bits of my clothing, perhaps toiletries from my travel bag, and so forth. I didn't want to start a precedent.

"Dave Barry gave me one of his," argued the corpse-handed man.

"Well, you can't have mine. I need them," I said, feeling cheap.

The best part of the story is the face he made when it became clear I wasn't going to change my mind. It looked like someone had taken his dog and shoved it up his grandmother's ass, put them both on his driveway, borrowed his SUV, and used his gas to run over them repeatedly in front of the kids.

He closed with "It doesn't hurt to ask," although it obviously did.

Hi Jean

I s it just me, or do you think of the word *hygiene* whenever you say hi to someone named Jean?

Speaking of hygiene, I just visited an airport men's room that only had warm air blowers to dry your hands—no towels. They might as well just hang up a sign that says "We Encourage You to *Not* Wash Your Hands."

Personally, I'm so afraid of cooties that I wash my hands about forty times a day. But even *I* had to pause and wonder if the time commitment would be worth it. I know there's some scientific principle involved whereby the movement of the warm air will, in theory, hasten the drying process. In practice, I'm fairly certain it's nothing but evaporation plus the placebo effect combined with a process I call "giving up" and walking out with wet hands.

In the end, my fear of cooties trumped my distaste for inefficient men's room technology and I went for it. As I stood there for what seemed an eternity, my thoughts drifted to my highly absorbent pants. Would it be so wrong to cut sixty seconds off this process and just wipe my hands on the sides of my pants, carefully avoiding the crotch area?

So I picked two strategically unimportant pant areas, finished the job that the placebo started, and went on my way. But I couldn't feel good about it.

Test Your Editing Skills

Did you see my Dilbert comic on November 3, 2005, where the Pointy-Haired Boss is interviewing for a new Boss's Pet? Here it is again in case you missed it.

It's mildly amusing at best. But the original version, which didn't make it past my editor, was a bit edgier. It looked like this.

Can you guess why it was rejected? I'll give you a minute to think about it before I tell you the answer. Hint: It's not as obvious as you think.

Waiting...

Waiting...

Waiting...

Time's up. You probably guessed that it was too sexual because of the inference that the Pet is being asked to hump the Boss's leg. That's close, but not precisely right. The problem was that it smacked of sexual harassment.

I was blind to that interpretation when I drew it because the Boss isn't expecting any sexual gratification out of the deal. It's just his leg, after all. All he's doing is seeing how well qualified she is for the job. And I would have done exactly the same joke if the interviewee had been a guy.

But I think my editor is right. It could be interpreted the inappropriate way for sure.

Did you see it as sexual harassment, or are you, like me, a sociopath?

Getting Away with Murder

Did you see the story about the convicted murderer who escaped prison by using a fake ID and a set of civilian clothes? The guards just opened the door and let him out.

The authorities described the escapee as narcissistic. That's the fancy way of saying he thinks he's better than other people.

I have to admit, if I made a fake ID using nothing but a pack of Marlboros and a spoon, and made a set of civilian clothes out of pillowcases, then walked out of jail, I'd be feeling pretty good about myself, too. I know for sure that I'd feel superior to the idiot who let me out. And that's not even counting the part about getting away with murder.

I feel sorry for the guard who checked the ID, saw the picture of Joe Camel, and thought *looks good to me*. Plus, you'd think one of the guards would notice the skort* made from a pillowcase.

The murderer won't last long on the outside. The fun of being a narcissist is telling other people how wonderful you are. The media is all over this story, so now he's a *famous* narcissist, and that's no prescription for a cure.

He'll probably start out slowly, just bragging to people he plans to whack anyway. But eventually he's going to tell someone who can outrun him. Or he'll forget to tie someone securely. I just hope he gets sloppy before he comes after the people who mock him in humor books.

---

* For the benefit of the men reading this, a skort is a cross between a skirt and shorts. It's the perfect clothing for people who are indecisive and/or narcissistic murderers.

Narcissistic Murderer Update

Police caught the escaped narcissistic murderer. Apparently they found him standing outside a liquor store, drunk, making no effort to hide his identity. This has caused some observers to conclude that he wasn't so smart after all. But you aren't thinking like a narcissistic criminal mastermind.

My theory is that he left something in his cell, say a pair of good sunglasses or a pack of cigarettes, and he wanted to go back and get them. He knows he can escape anytime he wants. But this time, just for the extra challenge, he wants to do it while drunk.

On some level, I admire his attitude.

Writer's Block

One of the most common questions I get is "Do you ever get writer's block?"

The thing I love about that question is that it reveals a wonderful optimism in the person who is asking. I suspect that the people who ask this question believe they possess deep wells of creativity and talent that are inexplicably blocked. All they need is the secret unblocking spell from a cartoonist and then a geyser of bestselling books will spray forth.

I wish I had that kind of optimism. I imagine myself asking an NBA player how he deals with jumper's block, under the theory that if I can learn how to unblock my jumping skills, I will no longer need a car. I'll just jump wherever I want to go, like the Hulk, but less angry.

Unfortunately, I'm too literal to answer the writer's block question in some useful way. I can't get past the common sense that I always have writer's block up until the moment I have an idea. It's sort of a binary situation.

The better question would be *how* I get past writer's block. The quick answer—and maybe the only legitimate one—is that I'm just wired that way. There's a fine line between creative and goofy, and believe me, you wouldn't want to spend time in my head. Let me give you some real-time examples. I'm on a plane as I write this. Allow me to write down my thoughts as they happen, just so you get a sense of it. I haven't planned this:

I wonder if you could make gigantic noise-cancellation headphones to put on the outside of the plane so all the passengers don't need them on the inside?

Damn, this was a stupid idea to write down my thoughts. Now I don't have any, except for my thoughts about not having any thoughts. Oh, God, I'm stuck in some sort of loop.

Wait, now I have a thought about the drunken lady's glass of wine on the seat divider next to me. It's rocking wildly from the turbulence.

It's going to land on my keyboard. Oh, God, I know it is. Uh-oh, I think she looked over here and read that I called her a drunken lady. My hands hurt from typing. I have to pee again but the seat belt sign is on. If she dozes off, I might have to top off her chardonnay.

Okay, that's enough of that. My point is that you should be glad you're not me.

Immortality Plan B

I used to say that my goal was to live to 140. I have confidence that medical science can improve enough to make that happen. People tell me that it's a stupid goal because no one wants to be old and decrepit. These naysayers are forgetting about the likely breakthroughs in mood-enhancing drugs. The best mood enhancers available today either have horrible side effects or they're illegal or both. But over the next thirty years or so, I expect those problems to be solved. When I'm 120 I'll be grinning from ear to ear and so "vital" that my pants will need orange warning cones around them.

That *was* my goal. But lately I'm thinking it's too conservative. If you've been watching the news, you know there's reason to think that gene therapy and the like will be able to keep wealthy cartoonists alive for hundreds of years.

There's one wrinkle in this plan. I just visited my parents in Florida and I noticed that they are shrinking as they age. My dad has lost about four inches so far, with no end in sight. This suggests a more realistic goal. My new plan is to live long enough to slowly disappear. It will be a lengthy process, I hope, but within the next five or six hundred years, I hope to fit inside a matchbox and have a pet beetle named Skippy.

I'll still travel the world, probably from inside the shirt pocket of my faithful servants Mandrake one through forty-seven. I'll instruct each Mandrake to cut a hole in his shirt pocket so that it lines up with the picture window on my matchbox home. From there I will run my Dilbert empire and write humor books until I shrink to the size of a neutrino and fall into the center of the earth to live for eternity in the molten core.

Unless I forget to feed my pet beetle Skippy and he eats me. Then I will become beetle poop and forever be the punch line in a cruel Yoko Ono joke.

That's my plan. Let me know if you see any flaws in it.

Awkward Situation

Prior to giving a talk to a business group in Atlanta, I was waiting in a tiny concrete dressing room, passing the time by reading the *Atlanta Journal-Constitution* and using my Black-Berry. It quickly became apparent that the backstage crew uses the bathroom in the dressing room because it's nearby and rarely occupied by speakers.

One of the AV technicians came rushing in and was startled to find anyone sitting there. He recognized me from the earlier sound check. Now he had a dilemma. I could tell from the look on his face that this visit wasn't going to be the brief kind. The dressing room is tiny and concrete, with little privacy from the business area of the bathroom. I could practically see the gears going in his head.

Do I just act nonchalant and go pinch out a steamer in this tiny airless dressing room? How professional would it be to leave the keynote speaker marinating?

He hesitated. He said hi. He continued to the bathroom, then paused, put his head down, and shuffled out as fast as he could, as if maybe he had only gone in to use the mirror to check his beard for anomalies.

A few minutes later, another technician came rushing in. Surprise. Hesitation. But he decided to go for it, since it was only the quick kind.

The third guy was the funniest. Surprise. Hesitation. Then he did the "just here to wash my hands" fake before scurrying away.

It made me wonder what I would have done in their situation. I think I would have gone for the hand-washing fake, possibly mumbling something like "Just ate an orange." That lends a suggestion of both cleanliness and fresh citrus to the otherwise awkward situation.

Sometimes that's the best you can do.

Things I'm Not Worried About

I know there's something wrong with me because I worry about all the wrong things. For example, I spend a lot of time worrying about the shielding on my microwave oven. Whenever I stand within ten feet of it, I'm sure I feel my spleen heating up. And when the microwave is turned on, I'm even more worried.

On the other hand, I can't generate any healthy fear about Iran developing a nuclear bomb. I realize that's exactly the sort of thing I *should* be worried about. But for me, something is missing.

Iran's highest religious authority—I think he's called the Grand Ottoman, or whatever—issued a fatwa saying that his followers are prohibited from building a nuclear bomb. It seems to me that if the Iranians wanted to lie about their secret program, they'd let their politicians do it. After all, that's their job. There's no reason to get the Grand Ottoman into the lie and erode his credibility. Because later, when he issues a ruling that, for example, everyone must bang his head with a porcelain unicorn, the citizens will wonder if this is one of the real fatwas or the kidding type.

Now if you'll excuse me, today is laundry day and I need to make some new shirts out of aluminum foil.

Nature and Other Annoyances

s I write this, I am pedaling a recumbent exercise bike, listening to CNN in an air-conditioned room, and typing on my BlackBerry with my thumbs. Some might say that I am no longer in touch with nature.

Personally, I feel that I have way too much nature in my life now. There are still bugs that make it in through the cracks, and dangerous sunlight assaulting me through windows. And don't get me started about the ragweed, malaria, and bird flu barf that's looking for an unlocked door.

In my perfect world, I'd have some sort of prophylactic outer barrier around the entire building in case any nature tried to penetrate to the inner core. Every minute or so the inner space between barriers would be flushed and the contents piped directly to the pup tent of some flannel-wearing person who appreciates an occasional infected mosquito. It's a win-win scenario.

I'm not technically a cyborg, but I'm working toward it. Already I draw comics to earn money to power the machines that are at this moment (a) in my hand, (b) under my buttocks, and (c) sending news to my ears. I have a symbiotic relationship with these devices no different in principle from the agreement I have with my liver. My mind does its part, and my liver, BlackBerry, exercise bike, and TV do theirs. I don't want to say that I prefer the technology to my natural body parts, but it's worth noting that only my liver complains if I drink too much.

I look forward to a day when I can leave my body behind and transfer my mind into a robot that already has all the features I need. You might wonder how happy I would be in a robot body with no genitalia, but I figure that by then the scientists will know how to send an electrical stimulation to the part of my brain that makes me think Carmen Electra is humping my leg for foreplay. I'd have all the benefits of genitalia with none of the disadvantages.

And if I wanted to have genitalia anyway, for some aesthetic reason,

I could get a snazzy unit installed at the local robot parts store. I'd probably want something chrome, about the size of a Honda Civic muffler. And I'd want it to be detachable in case I needed it for odd jobs, such as clearing away cobwebs from the corners of ceilings.

As a robot, I would be indestructible and live forever. This would be totally cool, at least until the sun exploded and destroyed the Earth. Then I would be floating in space for eternity, trying to flap my arms to fly. That part might get boring.

Writing Under the Influence

Today I am whacked out on pain killers because yesterday I had surgery to correct my deviated septum. I didn't ask a lot of questions about the procedure, but I can deduce most of the details based on the way I feel today. Apparently doctors shove a starving wolverine into one nostril, where it scratches and eats until it hits brain. Then they pull him out by his tail. Nurses stop the bleeding by packing each nostril with a queen-sized mattress that is carefully wrapped around a wino.

I wasn't worried prior to the surgery, at least until I had an unfortunate nose-related dream. In my dream, the surgery was finished and I was admiring my highly functional nose in the mirror. It processed air perfectly but it looked somehow different. At first I couldn't put my finger on it. Eventually I noticed: I had one huge nostril where before I had two smaller ones. Call it a uninostril if you must.

Now I sit here, my brain half functional, my lower ganglia stinking of wolverine breath, wondering if beneath the bandages I have one nostril or two. In my dream, the uninostril looked sleek and modern. The only downside I could think of is that this is exactly the sort of thing that can earn you a nickname for life, such as Nostrildamus or Snout Adams.

And if anyone ever used the phrase "I need that like I need a hole in the head," I would just tilt up my head, flare my huge nostril, and say, "You got that right." Then I would laugh at my own joke until I snorted an entire sandwich and a bag of chips out of my nose hole.

I really shouldn't be operating a keyboard.

Expensive Water

The other day I was doing some grocery shopping and picked up a case of bottled water. A woman who evidently works for a competing bottled water company noticed my choice and insisted on knowing why I wasn't picking her lower priced water instead. The clear inference was that I'm not too bright. Water is water, she noted.

The first defense that came to mind went unsaid, but it would have gone something like this: "If I'm dumb enough to buy water, I'm certainly dumb enough to pay too much for it!"

But that didn't feel right. My second impulse was to say something along the lines of "Do you know who I am??? I'm the creator of the world famous Dilbert comic strip that runs in two thousand newspapers in sixty-five countries. I buy overpriced water because I *can*. And by the way, this is just the water for my cat."

That didn't feel right either.

My third option was just as wrong, and it would have gone like this: "Well, since you asked, I assign an economic value to the use of my mind for price shopping versus the alternative use of imagining you naked right now."

Too risky.

After I left, I thought I should have said something like: "As any bottled water professional should know, research has shown that the color of a container influences the perceived taste. Your company's bottles send the subliminal suggestion of day-old puddle water with a hint of excrement."

But I didn't say any of those clever things. Instead, I mumbled something about being in a hurry and shuffled away.

I still drink overpriced water, but I no longer enjoy it.

Cartoonist Kills Thousands

The toughest part about being a cartoonist is that every now and then I accidentally kill people. I claimed my first victim in the mid-nineties, after an author put his name on a chapter from one of my books and submitted it to a magazine. During the ensuing legal wrangling, he had a heart attack and dropped dead. I heard from one of his angry friends that it was my fault because my complaints about his theft caused him unnecessary stress. I felt bad, but I also saved a bundle on legal bills. And it's nice to know that if I ever get mugged I have a nonzero chance of disabling my assailant simply by complaining about him until the stress kills him.

Recently I killed thousands more people. I don't have exact numbers yet. The problem stems from my comic that ran on November 20, 2005, implying that retail stores might harvest organs from bad customers and sell them on eBay.

I've received dozens of letters (long ones!) from very angry people who assure me that the Dilbert comic will reduce the number of organ donors. The concern is that people will think their parts will end up on eBay and so they won't be inspired to donate.

This would only have an impact on exceptionally dumb potential organ donors. But as you know, that's a large block of the general population. Now, I have to wonder how many people are smart enough to read an entire Dilbert comic and still dumb enough to think that the first person on the scene of an accident might be there just to harvest organs for eBay. It can't be more than 1 percent.

Let's see, we estimate that 150 million people read Dilbert, so 1 percent would be 1.5 million. And only 10 percent of them might have donated an organ anyway, so I'm probably killing 150,000 people.

It's times like this when "oops" doesn't seem sufficient. Normally, I try to limit my killing to people who have it coming. But the people who need transplants often don't fall into that category. So allow me to recommend that you fill out an organ donation card now.

Otherwise, you might be killing someone, too, you bastard.

Peeping in My Window

My temporary home, a rented apartment, has its largest window facing other apartments across the courtyard. When I first moved in, I was careful to keep the blinds closed so as not to flaunt my pendulum of naughty parts as I pranced to the shower and back. (Yes, I prance. There's nothing wrong with that.) But over time, it just seemed like too much work to be opening and closing those blinds all the time. So my standards began to relax.

Before long I was content with holding a bit of clothing or a towel modestly over my private zone as I passed the window. But soon that, too, seemed like too much work. So I just picked up my pace and fast-pranced sideways to the window, hoping that the one-second exposure wouldn't blind any innocent onlooker.

If you guessed that fast-prancing started to seem like too much work, you know me well. Fast-prancing became prancing, then walking, and now outright dawdling. In fact, if I drop a sock in front of the window, I'll bend right down and pick it up. And I won't hurry about it.

You might wonder where I will draw the line. Well, the great thing about my line of work is that I embarrass myself in front of millions of readers every day. Consequently, I've developed a high tolerance for that sort of thing. Obviously I wouldn't do anything in front of the window that's scatological or reproductive, or suggestive of either. But I'm giving careful consideration to twirling.

Try This at Home

Kids, are you tired of hearing adults say, "You can't know that you don't like something until you try it"?

Yes, you *are* tired of it.

When my older brother, Dave, was about twelve, he developed the only known defense to the "try it" position. It's guaranteed to work. And it goes like this.

ANNOYING PARENT: Why won't you try these peas?

DAVE (twelve years old): I don't like peas.

ANNOYING PARENT: You don't know you don't like something until you try it.

DAVE: Good point. Why don't you go out to the backyard, find a nice frozen dog turd, and use it as a popsicle? You can't know you don't like it unless you try it. Or are you willing to admit that there are some things you know that you don't like before you try them?

As a kid, time is on your side. You have plenty of it. Parents are always busy. Once you have taken the yes/no question of eating peas into the more philosophical realm of frozen dog turd analogies, the smart parent will surrender. The only downside to you as the victorious kid is that you'll eat more unhealthy foods and die a slow and horrible death before your time. But that's a risk your parents are willing to take on a wiseass like you.

Cloning

I don't have to tell you that there are plenty of good reasons to want your own clone:

1. Spare parts.
2. Slave labor.
3. Decoy in case of assassination attempts.
4. Source of excellent practical jokes on the spouse.
5. Reasonable doubt when you kill someone.

And that's not even counting if you're gay. But on the other side, there's really just one reason you can't have your own clone: It's immoral. Sure, it's illegal, too, but that's mostly because it's immoral, so it's really just one reason.

I always wonder who gets to decide what's immoral when it comes to brand-new things that aren't anything like old things that we all agree on. It's exactly this sort of question that makes me unfit to hold any kind of elected office. I always lean toward the practical approach that doesn't make a good sound bite. For example, my political platform would include "Let's make a few human clones just to see if any of them become soulless zombies intent on eating our flesh before descending to the bowels of Hell." See what I mean? It makes a crappy bumper sticker.

The big question with clones is how they get their souls, assuming souls exist. If God gives them brand-new souls, then they aren't actually clones at all. They'd be fundamentally different. But it also makes God more of a soul gumball machine than the omnipotent creator of the universe. The scientist who makes the clone would, in effect, be controlling God by making him pinch out another soul to inhabit the clone. That's disturbing on many levels, not the least of which is the way I phrased it.

But maybe your clone gets half of your soul, say 10.5 grams worth.

That would suck, too. I have enough trouble dancing with the little bit of a soul I allegedly have. If you cut that in half, I'm polka dancing.

If each of your clones has a new and different soul, but everything else is the same, we'd probably start assigning letters to keep them straight—A, B, C, and so on. And that suggests the one best reason to not clone yourself: Everyone would call you an A-soul.

Thieves Everywhere

Today my wallet was stolen for the four hundredth time, and frankly I'm sick of it. I don't know what bothers me more— the crime or the fact that the thief always sneaks back into my home an hour later and puts the wallet back in a hard-to-find place such as the top of my dresser.

There's never anything missing from the wallet, so I know the thief isn't especially good at his job. It might be the same idiot who keeps stealing my car every time I park it at the airport. He always refills the gas tank and parks it somewhere in the general vicinity of where I know I left it, but still it's rude and unsettling.

My parents are having a similar problem. They spend winters at their little town house in Florida, and this year when they came down from New York my dad noticed that something was terribly wrong. As he explained it, there "wasn't enough dust on the furniture." After six months, you expect a good layer, enough to leave your initials. But this year, suspiciously, there was almost no dust at all.

My dad could have investigated in a scientific manner, such as checking the *Farmer's Almanac* to see if it was supposed to be an especially dustless year. But why bother when you know the house has been invaded by people who dust your stuff without asking?

The worst of the home invading pranksters is the one who keeps screwing with my laundry. It's always the same stupid trick and I am not amused. It works like this: I return to my closet with a warm basket of freshly laundered clothes, only to notice one sock on the floor halfway between the clean laundry in my arms and the hamper from whence it came. Now I have to ask myself, is that a clean sock that just now fell from my basket, or is it a dirty sock that fell an hour ago when I was taking the dirty stuff from the hamper?

I know the prankster is hiding somewhere in the closet, watching as I inspect the sock, checking for radiant heat, flexibility, and freshness. I sniff it, give it the dangle test (to see if it is still shaped like a foot), and then make my decision. I'm never entirely comfortable that I made the right one. That's why I often walk with a slight limp, just so I don't spend so much time putting weight on what might be a dirty sock.

Well-Informed Super Geniuses

Y ou've probably noticed that opinion pollsters go out of their way to include as many morons as possible in surveys. That's called a representative sample. And what it means is that the opinion of Einstein, for example, counts as much as the opinion of the guy who thinks The Family Circus comic is sending him secret messages via Little Billy.

I think it's dangerous to inform morons about what their fellow morons are thinking. It only reinforces their opinions. And the one thing worse than a moron with an opinion is lots of them.

The only polls I want to see are ones that exclusively include the people in the top .01 percent of intelligence, and who are also highly informed on whatever topics the polls include. Let's call those people the Well-Informed Super Geniuses. If most of the people in that group have the same opinion, and it's different from mine, I'm willing to change my opinion. After all, I don't tell my doctor where to find my appendix. Why would I tell a Well-Informed Super Genius what to think about the global socioeconomic implications of a particular foreign policy or monetary decision or whatnot? (The exception would be if I didn't trust him because he had some financial interest in the outcome.)

But what if the Well-Informed Super Geniuses have wildly divergent opinions on a particular topic? That's just as good to know. It means that being smart and well informed doesn't help as much as you'd think. Then I could keep my squirrelly opinions and bask in the smugness of knowing that at least a few Well-Informed Super Geniuses agree with me.

In all seriousness, when the next presidential election rolls around, I'm considering funding some polls that only include the Well-Informed Super Geniuses, assuming they can be found. Wouldn't you want to know what they think before you try to remove your own appendix, metaphorically speaking?

How to Dance

There was a time when I considered writing a self-help book. But then I realized it's logically impossible. If you think about it, a self-help book is really just an author trying to help your sorry ass. It's not as if you wrote the book yourself. It's not even close to being "self help." So stop taking credit for other people helping you. That's all I'm saying.

But speaking of helping you, today I will attempt to teach the dance-challenged among my readers (okay, the hetero guys) how to move on the dance floor in a way that does not invite spectators to do any of the following:

Point
Snicker
Spray for fleas
Post a video of you on YouTube under the humor category
Grab your tongue so you don't swallow it

If you are an incompetent, random dancer, I feel your pain. For many years I desperately wanted to know how to dance in a less frighteningly spastic manner. I knew there must be some formula to dancing, and if I could just learn it, I would be the king of the dance floor.

I approached this problem the way I approach most things, by asking questions of those who have talent. I wanted to know the tricks and techniques involved. Predictably, the selfish dancing bastards would give me useless suggestions, such as "Try to feel the rhythm" or "Just do what comes naturally." This advice, plus large amounts of Grey Goose, produced in me a movement that could only be described as Turbo-dork.

But I am observant if nothing else. And so I made it my personal project to closely observe the best dancers, hoping to discover what separates the movers from the flailers. One day it hit me. There is indeed a simple secret, and when I employed it, I transformed instantly from a Turbo-dork to a mildy uncoordinated guy. It wasn't a clean win—I will grant you that—but it was enough to reduce the pointing and laughing to which I had grown accustomed.

The secret is this: hip movement.

That's it. End of story. So simple, yet so powerful. You can test my secret formula for yourself. First, try dancing in front of the bathroom mirror by *not* moving your hips. Feel free to wave your arms and legs in whatever fashion seems most dancelike to you. The horror that you observe will likely scar you for life.

Now try it again, but this time move your hips to the beat, and don't pay much attention to your arms or legs. Yes, you should be moving those arms and legs, but you'll find that they don't matter. Now look in the mirror and behold: You are dancing less dorkishly then ever before. It's all about the hips.

At this point, you also look totally gay, and that's another advantage because it might attract some hot women who are looking for a safe guy to dance with. The only downside of being a hetero guy who dances like a gay guy is the occasional surprise grinding by a shirtless guy in chaps. But you'll get used to it. As my grandfather used to say, anything worth having is worth letting another man rub his package on you.

It's the Thought That Counts

I asked my fiancée what she wants for Christmas and she was nice enough to e-mail me a specific suggestion for a hard-to-find item.

I copied the product name from her e-mail, pasted it into the Froogle search engine, and found the cheapest one on the Internet. That took about twelve seconds. It took another minute to enter my address and credit card information.

When it comes to gift-giving, they say it's the thought that counts. So far, I had seventy-two seconds invested in my future wife. I wondered if that was enough.

I knew that my fiancée's job of shopping for me wouldn't be so easy. I have the deadly combination of not caring much about material possessions plus a high disposable income. In the unlikely event that I decide I want something that's small enough to fit in a box, I buy it that same day. I figure she's spent about two weeks shopping for something for me. And I'm not much help. When she asks what I want, I say stuff like, "Well, I need some shoes. But I have weird feet, so don't get those." As I write this, she's frantically shopping for something that fits the category of "not shoes" and "doesn't already have."

Grudgingly, I knew I had to close the "gift thought gap." So I went to the tennis store and shopped as slowly as I could for a nice bag to hold her tennis racket. I probably lose some points for shopping in my own favorite store where I get a contact high by touching tennis rackets and giving them practice swings. I picked out a nice bag, but as it turned out, not as nice as the one I saw in her car the next day. That's probably something I should have noticed a month ago. Minus two points for being unobservant. And minus another two points for yelling an obscenity when I saw it.

Now I have to think of some more shopping ideas that have the single virtue of taking a long time. The actual gift doesn't matter that much because all it will do is sit around on the floor for a few weeks and then, when I'm away on business, get moved to the crawl space under the house.

Unfortunately, gifts are too easy to buy these days. Nothing takes long enough to showcase my diligent thought and hard work. My fall-back plan is to create a spreadsheet where I can log the time I spend "thinking about" her gift. I'll have a column for comments, in case she audits it later. The comments will be things such as "Thought about how much she likes eating crab. Didn't think of any good crab-related gifts."

Here again, as is often the case with me, I am penalized for being a fast thinker. I'll have to have a footnote that says I round everything up to the nearest fifteen-minute increment.

The Problem with Being Clever

All things considered, being clever is better than being dense. But cleverness has its downside. For one thing, no one believes a clever person. I spend about half of my day explaining to people that I'm not hatching a plot. You'd be amazed how often I have to preface my comments with: "I know you think this is the beginning of a practical joke, but this time it isn't."

Recently I developed a speaking disorder for some mysterious reason. The best medical guess is that it's something called a spasmodic dysphonia—a problem that causes the vocal cords to go nuts for no particular reason. The net effect is that while I can give a speech to a crowd of five thousand people, I generally can't utter more than a hoarse whisper to someone one-on-one. It's like a stutterer who can sing okay but can't talk normally.

It's bad enough to find out that I'll probably never speak normally to another person for the rest of my life. But to make things worse, my notorious cleverness makes people think I'm joking when I explain it. The following scene has been played out about a hundred times in the past week.

> ME (hoarse whisper): Hi. How . . . are . . . you?
> OTHER PERSON: Ooh, sounds like you have laryngitis.
> ME (hoarse whisper): No . . . it's a . . . speaking disorder. It's . . . permanent.
> OTHER PERSON: Ha Ha Ha Ha! You're funny.

I worry that someday I'll be injured in a bad accident and the first person on the scene will think I'm kidding. He'll see blood spraying from an artery, recognize me from some speech I once gave, and say, "That's cool! How are you doing that?" I'll try to correct his misconception, but my voice will be inaudible unless he happens to bring along five thousand friends and a microphone. Then I'll bleed to death.

No, seriously.

Intelligence Is Overrated

I recently coined the phrase philosotainment. It's philosophy for the sole purpose of entertainment, as opposed to enlightenment. With philosotainment, there's no pressure to be accurate or right in any way. It's just a fun diversion. What follows is a prime example of philosotainment.

With all the debate about intelligent design, I started to wonder if intelligence is overrated. In particular, are intelligent people happier than unintelligent people?

If you were to rank the following two hypothetical individuals by happiness, what order would you put them in?

1. Bob the dentist
2. Snowflake the dog

Dentists are generally smart, and yet they have one of the highest suicide rates of any profession. In stark contrast, dogs are goofy and they always look happy. You almost never hear about a dog trying to shoot himself.

I know you want me to make a joke along the lines of "Dentists would be happy, too, if they could lick themselves." But this is a serious discussion and I won't have it. Plus that's why dentists have office assistants.

Anyway, if intelligence doesn't help make you happy, what good is it?

You might argue that survival of the species is a good enough reason for intelligence. After all, most people prefer being alive even if the highlight of their day is hosing the shareholders by reading Dilbert comics on company time.

I think you'll agree that the usefulness of intelligence in humans is that it improves the odds of survival. We need all the help we can get.

But this raises an even more interesting question: Why would God need to be intelligent?

And by intelligent, I mean in some fashion that people recognize. For example, right now I'm using my intelligence to write this chapter while eating a delicious meal at my restaurant. There's an ex-employee eating lunch across the room and I can't recall her name. I'm worried that she'll say, "Hi, Scott," and then I'll say, "Hi . . . you there." I'm already planning to exit through the kitchen so I don't have to walk in her direction. And this is a good example of something God would not be worrying about.

In fact, I can't think of a single thing that my intelligence helps me do during the day that God would also need to do. I'm reasonably sure that the same could be said of you.

If God exists, and he has intelligence, I feel safe in saying that it's entirely different from the sort of intelligence that people have. He wouldn't need intelligence to make him happy, and he has no risk to his survival, so what type of intelligence would an omnipotent being possess?

To answer that question, let's start with the overblown human definition of intelligence and subtract out all the things God doesn't need. First, throw out all the human intelligence associated with desire, greed, sex, fear, frustration, politics, scheming, remembering quotes from Monty Python, and anything else that has no purpose for God.

Now get rid of love, as humans understand it, because that's obviously the opposite of intelligence. I don't mean that in a cynical way. I mean that if you could "think yourself" into falling in love, you'd be doing more of that, and less falling in love with the Safeway cashier who, you keep forgetting, is paid to act friendly.

We're not done yet.

What about consciousness? You'd expect God to be conscious as we understand it, right? But that wouldn't make sense for an omnipotent being. Our own consciousness is mostly about imagining what can happen next and comparing that imagination to what does happen so we can adjust accordingly. That's useful for survival, but only for creatures that are made of meat and surrounded by carnivores. God wouldn't need that sort of imagination because omnipotence means that your preferences are by definition the same as reality. There's no point in being almighty if you have to sit around imagining what you want and then waiting for it. So God would have no use for consciousness.

All that's left of our notion of intelligence, that is consistent with an omnipotent God, is the ability to do things that require planning and intention.

Atheists say the universe was built without the need for design. And by that, they mean some sort of design as humans know it. But how important is that sort of design anyway? Humans need to design things in advance to do them right, but would an omnipotent being have that constraint?

If humans could build great things without the need for user specifications, and timelines, and to-do lists (in other words, without design), we'd do it that way. Design is necessary if you are operating on a tight schedule with a limited budget and resources. God has no schedule or resource limitation. So why would he design in the same way a human would? When we impose the need for humanlike design processes on an omnipotent being, we're selling God short. He'd do it his own way. An omnipotent being's method of design might involve a relatively short list of physical laws, a bunch of matter, and a lot of time. And at the end of that process, God's design would resemble art, with all its flaws, compared to anything a human would design. (Compare your finely engineered car to a messy sunset. Which one is a better design?)

If you accept that God's design process wouldn't be the same as human design processes, and intelligence for God doesn't mean the same as intelligence for humans, then it's hard to argue against intelligent design. No one can know what the words *intelligence* or *design* would mean for God. And you can't rule out what you can't even define.

But does God even exist? It depends how you define Him.

God, by any definition, is not part of our natural world. He's supernatural. And yet, believers say, he exerts an all-powerful force upon the natural world. Is there anything in our common experience that meets that test?

Absolutely: concepts.

Allow me to explain by analogy. We believe that love exists, yet it is little more than the sum of the biology and situation that evoke it.

Love itself is simply an umbrella concept that contains all of those chemical reactions and environmental happenings. Love is supernatural in that sense, as all concepts are. You can't scoop up a bucket of love. Love influences the physical world while not being a part of it. Just like God is alleged to do.

Even the biggest atheist would agree that God exists as a *concept*. And that concept is undeniably the most powerful one in existence. It influences virtually every human activity from procreation to war.

The universe, by definition, is comprised of all the matter, and energy, and the rules that hold it all together. In sum, those things form a concept that atheists say created the Earth and all its creatures.

Is the universe, thus described, both intelligent and a designer? As I already explained, that depends entirely upon how you define those terms for an omnipotent being.

I can't bring myself to believe in a God with a personality that is anything like my own. I base that on the paucity of lightning attacks on people who deserve it. But the universe can be said to have both intelligence and design if you remove the parts of the definitions that would only apply to a human being and not a God.

What about intention? Doesn't God need intentions in order to be the God we imagine? I don't think so. Intentions are for creatures who don't already have everything they want. For an omnipotent being, reality and intention would be indistinguishable. Otherwise, if God had intentions, it would imply that he didn't already have what he wanted. And how can you be both omnipotent and unsatisfied at the same time?

When I've made this argument in the past, the left-wing nuts came out of the woodwork and accused me of being a proponent for the creationists and intelligent design arguments. I'm not in those camps. I'm just a philosotainer who thinks atheists believe in God.

How to Be a Marketing Genius

Several years ago, I found myself nutsack deep in flaming e-mails for my prediction that illegal downloads of music would lead to lower sales of CDs. It seemed obvious to me. But scores of illegal music downloaders and self-proclaimed marketing geniuses argued vehemently that these "free samples" would lead to *increased* sales of CDs. That didn't happen, of course, because it turns out that people prefer "free and instant" over "overpriced and later," especially if the risk of getting caught is vanishingly small. This experience reinforced my belief that my MBA gave me a better understanding of markets than my verbal sparring partners got from doing bongs and thinking as hard as they could.

Recently I offered my book *God's Debris* for free on the Internet, under the theory that the people who like it might be inspired to buy the sequel in hard copy. 170,000 people downloaded it in the first two weeks. Many of them presumably e-mailed it to other people who e-mailed it to yet other people. I'm guessing half a million people read it in the first month. It's a love-it-or-hate-it kind of book, so let's say 250,000 people loved it. That seems about right, based on the reviews on Amazon.

Now for a test of your marketing savvy: How many of the people who loved the free sample went ahead and purchased the sequel? The answer is in the next paragraph, so make your guess before reading further.

Okay . . .

I don't know the exact number, but it appears to be less than a thousand. An alarming number of readers were confused about this whole process and wrote to ask if they could also have the sequel for free.

I don't regret making *God's Debris* available for free. I had nothing to lose, since the hardcopy version was published five years ago and had run its course. I was happy just to know that I authored one of the most read books on earth for a month. It was worth a shot. But I think

I demonstrated one marketing truth: When something is free, that's what people expect to pay for the next one. So maybe my MBA *isn't* that much better than doing bongs and thinking as hard as I can.

I learned a similar lesson, but apparently it didn't sink in too far, when I was taking classes years ago to learn to be a hypnotist. My teacher explained that people will believe they are getting more benefits from hypnosis if they are required to pay for the experience. The explanation, in my words, is that your brain tells itself, in effect, that hypnosis must be good stuff or else you wouldn't be paying for it. Your ego won't let you be the sort of person who feels like you got scammed by some witch doctor sort of thing. You're too smart for that. So you rationalize that the hypnosis works, and that belief actually helps it work.

I co-own two local restaurants. There's a question I like to ask non–restaurant owners who think they are experts in the business based on their vast experience at eating: What are the most important factors for a successful restaurant?

People usually guess it's the food or the service, maybe the overall value. That seems fairly obvious, doesn't it? But it's way off. The most important factor in a restaurant's success is the physical ambience, including lighting, noise, seating, colors, and location in an interesting area. The best restaurants do *everything* right, but if all you have is good food and good service, you're in trouble. In my local area, unless the food is inedible, the restaurant will be packed, as long as the ambience is good.

The reason ambience is so important is that it makes your entire body feel good. The right lighting can make your date look more attractive. And the ambience can make you want to drink more than you normally would. Put it all together, and you might not remember what you ate, or how long it took to arrive, but you'll remember you had a great time. Your dinner companions could be hideous morons, but the right lighting, music, and alcohol can totally fix that. Good service won't.

In other words, if your date insists on going to a dark place with a full bar, he thinks one of you is ugly.

You Look Fabulous

Fashion is essentially dressing in a way that makes other people less likely to say behind your back any of these phrases:

"It looks like The Gap crapped on him."
"Not bad for a homeless person."
"Hey, it's Rosie O'Donnell!"

At the highest level of fashionableness, people will hate your guts for looking too beautiful. I will spare you that fate, and only teach you how to look exactly as good as well-dressed normal people and no more. However, I can't do it alone. This is a group effort and will require technology, venture capital funding, patent infringements, and more.

I call it Dilbert's Closet. It's a hypothetical website that shows the fashion-challenged exactly what to buy and where to buy it online. It works like this:

Any person can publish his own "closet" of items he thinks look good on him. He provides his clothing sizes, several digital photos of himself modeling each item, and a link to the online store that carries it. As a shopper, you would search the site for people who look like you, including height, weight, age, coloring, glasses, hair, and more. Then when you buy something, you know it looks good on people who look like you. In the real world, whenever I see a guy who looks like he could be my clone, only slightly distorted, the first thing I do is look at his shoes for ideas. Dilbert's Closet is the more efficient form of that.

You probably won't live anywhere near the guy who looks like you, and is publishing his closet, so you can buy every item that looks good on him and not worry about running into him at a party.

If you don't feel like buying his clothes, you can steal his photos and pass them off as your own on dating websites. It'll make you look like a snappy dresser without spending a dime.

The operator of the Dilbert's Closet website, and the people who run the individual closets, would get a small referral fee from each transaction completed, like Amazon's referral program. Over time, the people with the best closets would make fortunes.

And here's the cool part: Every item of clothing you publish online becomes a business expense and tax write-off. At least until you get audited and have to explain that you get your tax advice from cartoonists.

Usually when I write about an idea, hundreds of people gleefully tell me it already exists. If that's the case here, let me know. I need some pants that look good on a guy who looks like Tom Petty after chemo.

Adopting

When I hear about people such as Angelina Jolie and Madonna adopting African orphans, it makes me feel like I'm not doing enough. But I have to be honest: Adopting a baby seems like a lot of work, especially when you consider the "flying to another country" part. I want to be nice, but in a way that involves fewer flies. I was on the lookout for an easier way to show the world that I'm a good person, and thanks to President Bush, I think I've found it.

The president asked people to adopt the embryos that can't be legally used for stem cell research. An embryo would be the perfect adopted child. I'd just keep it in the fridge, claim a tax deduction for my new dependent, and fend off the advances of Brad Pitt, who would, in all likelihood, become turgid by my caring attitude.

If my embryo gets lonely, I'll get a few dozen more to keep it company. Embryos are small, so there would be no problem with storage, at least until the next power outage.

Embryo babies are not as cute as regular ones, I grant you that. But when you consider the convenience and economics of the situation, it's hard to argue against them. You'd never need to buy clothes for an embryo. It never talks back, and it couldn't have premarital sex in the refrigerator no matter how hard it tried, despite easy access to condiments.

I'm not sure if I'd need to feed it. It probably comes with a pamphlet that tells me that sort of thing. I hope I get an embryo that isn't a fussy eater. I want one that eats the stuff you sprinkle in aquariums. Again, I'm lazy, so if the food doesn't come in something that looks like a salt shaker, I'll probably neglect my embryo.

The hard part is naming my embryo. It needs to be a cool name or else the other kids will tease it. I'm thinking along the lines of Emery the Embryo, or maybe Dot.

Billionaire's Money Question

Here's a horrible little game that you can play at your next family gathering. I call it the Billionaire's Money Question, and it's a real eye-opener. All you do is pose the following hypothetical question to your family:

"Suppose you found a thousand dollars in cash that you knew had been lost by a billionaire. Now, because this is a hypothetical question, let's assume that the billionaire would never be aware that he lost it, and there would be no way that anyone else would know if you kept the money. And let's say you knew there would be no reward or other indirect benefit in returning the money. Would you give it back?"

If you ask this question in a group, I suspect a lot of people will say they'd give it back. But if you ask people privately, you might be surprised to discover that many of your family members are crooks.

The best-case scenario is that your family wouldn't give back the money because they are just too lazy to bother. Either way, it's going to be tense if you misplace your wallet at the family reunion.

In my experience, most of the people who say they'd give back the cash are the ones who don't need an extra thousand dollars. The ones who say they'd keep it usually have a good idea how they'd spend it, as in "I'd keep it because I need a plasma TV." Based on my limited sampling of this question, people who need a new TV are not as generous as those who already have one.

A certain percentage of the population believes that God is watching them, with one hand on a lightning bolt and the other on the trapdoor to Hell. I've found that about half of that group will also keep the money, under the theory that if God wanted the billionaire to have it, he never would have let him lose it in the first place.

Party question: Would you keep it?

We Influential Management Thinkers

everal people e-mailed to tell me that I was ranked as the #12 Influential Management Thinker in the world.

No, seriously. It was on a website, so it must be true.

My first reaction was to feel sorry for the poor bastards who ranked thirteen through fifty. I imagine they would have felt pretty good about making the list until they were topped by the guy who wants to adopt a frozen embryo, name it Dot, and keep it in the fridge.

I'm not entirely sure who I'm influencing with my world-class management thinking, but it can't be a good thing. I do get a lot of e-mail from people who say that Wally has become their role model. That's not helping the ol' GDP. And I like to think that my Alice character has given women permission to punch people. I never imagined that advocating workplace violence would win me any prize. But I guess placing twelfth isn't much of a prize when you think about it.

Still, I have to admit I'm feeling quite heady from this honor, and already planning my next management influence. I think I'll see if I can influence all managers to dress as clowns, based on the theory that a happy workforce is a productive one. If this doesn't put me in the top ten Influential Management Thinkers by next year, I can honestly say that I don't know what will.

Mysteries of the Universe

There are many fascinating mysteries in this universe. I choose to ignore all of them and instead focus my sense of wonder on the following question: Why do female real estate agents have bizarre hairstyles?

You know what I'm talking about: poofy, disturbingly large, a death rattle from the sixties. If you saw photos of these hairstyles and were asked to do free association you might say: "Liberace ... Montana ... mushroom cloud ... Kaiser Wilhelm."

Real estate agents put their photographs on advertisements and even on their business cards. I assume this practice started years ago when hot women entered the profession and needed a marketing advantage. This advantage turned out much better than they hoped because ugly Realtors jumped on the bandwagon and started publishing their own pictures. Now a prospective client doesn't need to choose between the adorable and the unknown. He can choose between the adorable and Quasimodo. That removes all the ambiguity.

I've been photographed about a trillion times since I started Dilbert. And I can tell you with authority that the only difference between Larry King and Hillary Duff is distance and lighting. And *still* most Realtors look unattractive in their photos. If you see a Realtor's photo and she looks less than stunning, there's a good chance she has the sort of face that would make Stevie Wonder even blinder. His eyeballs would retract so far into his brain he'd forget how to play the piano.

If I were to sell real estate, I would use my ugliness to my advantage. No one trusts beautiful people anyway, especially when large sums of money are involved. My real estate motto would be "I'm hideous and I haven't starved to death yet, so you know I must be good!"

Ideals

In debates about one thing or another, people often argue that we shouldn't abandon the ideals of the Founding Fathers of the United States. So I started wondering what those ideals were.

Before I go on, let me say that I'm highly patriotic, despite what you read here. Please don't ask me to move to Venezuela.

As you know, the Founding Fathers had a lot of time to write things down because they didn't have television, and there are only so many hours that you can spend whittling new teeth. But I don't believe they ever got together and created a document called the Bill of Ideals. To understand their ideals we must look to their actions. Here are a few of the ideals they apparently shared:

1. Slavery—excellent source of poontang
2. Women voting? That's crazy talk!
3. People who don't own land suck.
4. A good way to change tax policy is through violence.
5. It's not really cross-dressing as long as you also wear manly boots.
6. Treason is okay if you have a good reason.
7. It is fine to be fat if you are also witty and invent things.

Moments ago, as I was searching the Internet for some Founding Father tidbits upon which I could wittily comment, I came across this historical fact about the Louisiana Purchase:

> *Though the transaction was quickly sealed, there were those who objected to the purchase on the grounds that the Constitution did not provide for purchasing territory. However, Jefferson temporarily set aside his idealism to tell his supporters in Congress that "what is practicable must often control what is pure theory." The majority agreed.*

Jefferson later admitted that he had stretched his power "till it cracked" in order to buy Louisiana, the largest single land purchase in American history. As a result, generations of Americans for nearly two hundred years have been the beneficiaries of Jefferson's noble vision of America and his efforts at expanding the continent.

I found it at this website in case you want to check for yourself: http://earlyamerica.com/earlyamerica/milestones/louisiana/

As I suspected, the Founding Fathers were a practical bunch of dudes. That's an ideal I can get behind.

Who Is Holier?

Here's some more ammo to stir up things at your next gathering of inebriated relatives. Ask the question: Who is holier—Mother Teresa or Bill Gates?

Set the scene by pointing out that on Mother Teresa's side of the ledger is her lifetime of spiritual inspiration and helping the poor. Not too shabby.

On Bill Gates's side, we have his targeted philanthropy—for vaccines and whatnot—that will probably end up saving the lives of 100 million people. And he already convinced his good friend Warren Buffett, and perhaps others, to do similar things with their own fortunes. So let's add another 100 million people saved by Bill Gates's secondary effects. You could talk me down to an estimate of 10 million eventual saved lives, but still, it's a big number.

This should get the adults jabbering. Once they're preoccupied denouncing Bill Gates as the Devil's henchman (oh, it'll happen), slip away and find where the smaller kids are playing. Round up the ones in the range of five to eight years old and ask them: "If Santa Claus fought Jesus, who would win?" Tell the kids that Grandpa will give five dollars to whoever comes up with the best answer.

Then leave the house as quickly as possible.

I asked the same question on my blog. My favorite answer was this:

And as for Santa and Jesus fighting, the winner would be Jesus. Because he can walk on water, so he could drag Santa to the middle of a lake and hold him under while staying pleasantly dry. Now if you were to include the nine reindeer and twelve apostles then the fight might get more interesting.

Gambling

One of the downsides of interacting with other people is that they keep uncovering defects I never knew I had. For example, I recently discovered that I can't learn to gamble. Sure, I can put coins in a slot and push a button with the best of the grizzled old casino hags, but when it comes to the more exotic forms of gambling, I have some sort of mental block. Craps? No way. Pai Gow? Nope. Even blackjack eludes me.

In order to learn something, you must have enough interest to activate whatever brain chemistry it takes to first concentrate on the subject and then to burn the rules into your long-term memory. Apparently this is easy for people who believe their gambling decisions have a strong influence on whether they win or lose. To me, every casino game except the slots looks like an annoying set of rules layered on top of what should be a simple process of taking your money and giving you nothing in return.

Apparently, when other people hear the rules of card games they think *This is how I will become rich. I must pay attention.* My brain just activates the fight-or-flight response. I don't know whether to run away or start punching the dealer.

I can't tell you how many times well-meaning people have described to me the simple steps involved in casino blackjack. It always sounds to me exactly like this:

> "It's easy. If the dealer gets at least (I'm drifting off by now) and you have (Jesus, will this explanation ever stop?) then obviously you would (Is my soul leaving my body? No, phew, it's just cigarette smoke). But if you get dealt a (mwuwahah) then you want to double down. That means (Hey, that guy behind you has a funny shirt. I wonder where he got it). And of course you can always bet on the (Nahnahnah-nahnah), and that means (I'll be at the slot machines)."

I wish I were one of the people who get an adrenaline rush from gambling. But not so much that I'd eventually need to sell the kids to a Thai businessman. There's an ideal sweet spot for addiction, and I envy those who have it. These lucky people have all the incentive in the world to learn complicated gambling rules. In stark contrast, I get only a modest psychological buzz from the slot machines, mostly because of the blinking lights and seductive noises. But after about an hour I start regarding my remaining money as a filthy thing that I must shed as quickly as possible. One way you can know for sure you'll never be a professional gambler is if you have ever had the thought *I wonder how quickly I can get rid of this last forty dollars.*

Your Body Hates You

You might think that the various parts of your body are all on the same team. Not true. Your back, for example, hates your guts.

The way you can tell that your back is evil is that it never warns you when it's about to give you a painful, life-altering sprain that will make you envy the dead and, most of all, the dead people with good backs.

Your back accumulates and stores slight injustices in the same way a camel's hump stores water, or figs, or pus, or whatever the hell is in there. Then your treacherous back watches and waits for the right opportunity to strike.

If you have ever had a severe back sprain, you can answer the following with no problem. Which activity is most likely to result in the worst back pain of your life?

1. Skiing to outrace an avalanche
2. Lifting a car to save a baby
3. Kickboxing competition
4. Bending over to pick up a piece of Pringles you spit out while laughing at your own joke

The last thing your back wants is for you to have an excellent story to mitigate some of your discomfort. Your back will not be happy until you are not only painfully debilitated but also a pathetic bore in the eyes of others.

> OTHER PERSON: So, how'd you end up in the full body cast?
> YOU: Well, it's a funny story. I was tying my shoe . . .

The Future of Shirts

What's the longest you've ever worn a shirt backward without knowing? I don't mean inside-out. That happens all the time, and you can go all day like that. People might even think it's intentional. I'm talking about backward, where the little label in the collar ends up under your chin.

I usually catch myself after the first five minutes of wearing a shirt backward. I call that my mean-time-to-backward-shirt-awareness, or MTBSA. I monitor that because once it hits fifteen minutes I know it's time to start wearing a fishing hat and driving slowly in the passing lane.

My tennis partner once showed up for our match with his shorts on backward. It didn't make much difference except when he tried to put his balls in his pocket. [Insert your own joke here, but don't use "That's gotta hurt" because I just did.]

I can no longer count on other people to alert me to the fact I'm wearing a backward shirt. Not since I became invisible. And by invisible, I mean I'm an adult male over the age of thirty-five. Beyond that age, no one has any reason to look at you. People are neither aroused nor curious about my existence. I'm pretty much just taking up space. I would give up on clothing entirely except I know I would take far too long applying suntan lotion to my private parts.

Anyway, in the future, I believe shirts will be omnidirectional. You'll be able to wear them forward or backward and it'll all be the same. It won't even matter if you poke your head through the armhole. The fabric in the shirt will have sensors that detect what a raging dork you are and adjust the shirt accordingly.

By the time that happy day comes, I'll be more invisible (i.e., older) than ever. And I'll also be old enough to violate all social norms with impunity. I plan to wear shirts as pants. I'll just put my legs through the arms and let my junk dangle out of the head hole. If anyone bothers to pay attention to me, which seems unlikely, I'll just shout, "I'm old!" and shuffle away, enjoying the breeze all the way.

It's always wise to have a retirement plan.

Silent Words

Words in the English language often have silent letters for no good reason. I think the extra letters should be donated to other languages that don't have enough. The Hawaiian language comes to mind. I wasn't paying close attention when I visited Hawaii, but I think the native language only has three or four consonants. But that's okay because there isn't much to talk about over there. Here's just a sample of things you never need to say in Hawaii.

Where's my snow shovel?
I wish we had some good scenery.
Look out for that snake!
Nice shoes.
I wish we were in North Dakota.

The list goes on and on.

If we have no choice but to keep all the silent letters, let's extend the concept to entire words. It would be handy to have silent words inserted in all of my sentences. That way I could secretly be honest while outwardly being polite.

Me: That's an attractive baby you have there (silent: assuming it's supposed to be a proboscis monkey on crack).

I'd also like to proclaim here and now that all future sentences I utter are appended with the silent disclaimer "but of course there are obvious exceptions." The abbreviation is BOCTAOE.

This is important because about half of my time spent interacting with people involves me staring dully at them while they point out the obvious exception to whatever I've just said.

Example:

ME: Nice weather.

OTHER PERSON: Not everywhere on Earth. Plus, the day is young. It could still get cloudy later.

ME: Nice try, but I append all of my statements with a silent BOCTAOE.

OTHER PERSON: Damn the silent disclaimers!!!

Good and Bad Problems

Not all problems are equal. For example, if you have an arrow through your head, that's the bad kind of problem. If you have too many customers to handle in a timely manner, that's the good kind.

Another good kind of problem is one you didn't know you had. Let's say that the back of your head was especially ugly but you were otherwise okay-looking. That wouldn't be a problem to you because you wouldn't necessarily know it (BOCTAOE). Then some idiot would say, "What's wrong with the back of your head?" And suddenly that's all you'd be able to think about. The problem wasn't a problem until you knew it was a problem. Ignorance is underrated.

Yesterday I went to a speech pathologist because I thought I had one problem (speaking). I left with two problems. As I was practicing saying, "Many more men on the moon," she squinted at me and said, "Did you know your face twitches?"

"What?"

"Your face twitches. Sometime your eyes twitch and sometimes your face twitches next to your nose."

I immediately asked my fiancée if she had ever noticed my face twitching. She said, "Yes, you've done that since I've known you. You do it when you're thinking."

"And you never mentioned it?"

The only thing worse than finding out that I have a twitch is finding out that it happens "when I'm thinking." Because it turns out that I think fairly frequently. And thinking about *thinking about* the twitch makes it worse, I think.

Anyway, it made me wonder about some other bad things you could say to people to make them self-conscious for the rest of their lives. Maybe . . .

"All I can say is that incandescent light is not your friend."

Or

"I have a nickname for your nose. Do you want to hear it?"

Or

"Is that the way you usually walk?"

Coiner of Phrases

According to the Internet, I have become a prolific coiner of phrases. You can do a Google search on any of these gems I created and get all kinds of hits.

The Dilbert Principle
Dilbertian
Catbert
PHB
Rat Dance
Frooglepoopillion
Elbonian
Induhvidual

And more recently, BOCTAOE and YSLE. If you haven't been paying attention to everything I say or write, those mean "but of course there are obvious exceptions" and "you stupid lemon-eater."

On one hand, it's fun to add words and phrases to the popular culture. But on the other, I can't help feeling bad about further bloating an already wordy language. I'm worse than that guy who invented the phrase "on one hand, blah blah blah, but on the other hand, blah blah blah." I hate him. I also hate the guy who decided we should use three blahs when one would do the trick.

Inventing words feels hypocritical because I believe we should trim the existing supply of redundant and unpleasant words. I have my reasons. For example, some words are unattractive simply for the way they sound:

Talc
Moist
Cleaver
Spittoon

Then I'd get rid of words that no one can spell:

Toboggan
Broccoli
Picnicking

And when it comes to the following trio, I say we keep just one and get rid of the other two. I don't care which one we keep. Having all three just begs trouble:

Their
There
They're

Then I'd get rid of words that you can't get out of your head after you hear them, such as osso buco and Mary Steenburgen. In fact, the worst sentence I can ever imagine hearing would be something along the lines of "Mary Steenburgen thought the osso buco tasted like moist talc."

Try living with that today.

My Irrational Beliefs

Have you ever marveled at how many things you believe without evidence? It turns out to be most things. I rarely have time to consult the peer-reviewed scientific literature before doing something such as, for example, shaving and whistling at the same time. I've never seen any evidence that doing those two things simultaneously is dangerous, but I can't rule it out. So I believe, without conclusive evidence, that it's safe.

When you don't have conclusive evidence, you have to rely on common sense. That's the same method employed by the first guy who died from eating a poison mushroom. I believe his last words were something along the lines of "All the other mushroom types were fine, so it's just common sense that this one would be . . . Gaaaaaak!"

Mostly I believe whatever people tell me, as long as it sounds somewhat reasonable or until someone else tells me it's wrong. For example, I believe that the theory of evolution is useful for geologists searching for oil. Many people have told me so, and I've heard no argument to the contrary. It certainly sounds like one of those things that could be true. But it makes me wonder if creationist geologists are worse at finding oil than atheists. Somewhere in Calgary I imagine a conversation between a creationist geologist and his boss:

BOSS: Matthew, why haven't you found any oil? All the other guys have.

MATTHEW: Well, I've been looking everywhere, but all I find are these stupid fossils that the Devil put there to fool me.

BOSS: Find oil or you're fired.

MATTHEW: Oh, great. He got to you, too.

Traditional Values

Have you ever wondered why some people brag about their "traditional" values when they obviously mean "superior"? It's because "traditional" is a more flexible word. It implies an inherent goodness without the need to defend the details. I plan to start using "traditional" as my adjective of choice in all sorts of contexts where I want to infer ambiguous goodness without obvious lying.

> PARENT: Here's a picture of my family.
> ME: That's one traditional looking family! [Translation: They look like dustbin trolls on crank.]

Or

> FIANCÉE: Which blouse do you like better?
> ME: I like the traditional one. [Translation: You pick one and I'll agree as if it was my opinion all along.]

Or

> ECONOMIST: Do you support higher interest rates to fend off inflation or would you prefer a more pro-growth policy?
> ME: I prefer a traditional approach. [Translation: It's your turn to be baffled.]

I also wonder how long you'd need to age a crappy set of values before they became desirable via the process of traditionalization. If it's not too long, I recommend that we make an investment in the future and start incubating some future values now. For example, I think our descendants would thank us for making it a tradition to get sloppy drunk and pass out whenever in-laws come to visit. We could give it a cool name, such as "hibernation," so it sounds more like a tradition than a character flaw. It would be awkward for a few generations, but eventually it would be as natural as hanging a big sock over the fireplace and waiting for Santa.

What's in a Name?

Not long ago, the covers of both *Time* and *Newsweek* featured Olympic skier Bode Miller. A big part of their stories is that he likes to drink. This is no surprise to me because I believe people become whatever their names imply. A bode bag is a leather container used to carry booze in settings where a bottle would be inconvenient, such as while skiing. Miller is a brand of beer. Bode Miller's name implies "a leather container full of beer, often seen on ski slopes." He's reportedly living up to that name.

I once worked with a woman whose name was Ann Kratabol. It sounds just like you're saying "incredible" with a funny speech defect when you say it fast. Every time she introduced herself she would say, "Hi, I'm Ann Kratabol." Her career was doing just fine. I don't think it was a coincidence, what with all the positive affirmations.

I'm told that there was a guy in my hometown named Jack Cass. I assume he ran for Congress, but I don't know.

True story: I once got an e-mail from a guy named Richard Head. I wonder what his friends call him.

I also worked with a woman whose last name was Beavers. Her first name wasn't that interesting but I always wondered about the rest of the family. I'm betting there was a Harry in there somewhere.

Jet-Lagged Baby

Many of you noticed that my comic about the jet-lagged baby that ran on January 25, 2006, had two endings. One version ran on the Internet and the other ran in most newspapers. I sometimes offer alternate versions (a naughty one and a harmless one) when I know newspapers will have heartburn over a particular topic. Here's the harmless version that actually got published.

Now here's the way it was originally written. I think it's a bit snappier.

It's not censorship per se. It's just a case of the editors deciding what their local readers would prefer to see. That's their job. Unfortunately for them, my job often involves making their job more difficult. If I can give you one piece of career advice, it would be this: If you have the choice of working as the guy who craps on the carpet, or the guy who has to clean it up, only one of those jobs lets you read a magazine at the same time.

My New Catchphrase

When you're a big-time cartoonist with a blog and a public e-mail address, getting criticized a hundred times a day is part of the package. Luckily I'm blessed with an unnatural level of tolerance for criticism. Often the criticisms are well thought out and entirely accurate, and my reaction is "Yup, you nailed me." That happens about half the time. The rest of the criticisms are from stupid lemon-eaters and they amuse me no end.

My favorite criticism of late came after I said on my blog, "If you know the history of the Great Wall, it was highly successful in keeping out animals. But invading armies just bribed the guards and walked through the gate."

I got this criticism:

Mr. Scott Adams, you ought to apologize for calling nomadic tribes of ancient "animals." Read history and have a little respect for others. Chinese G.wall was a border between sedentary and nomadic peoples, and what will be left out of China if you let supressed Inner Mongolia, Uigur and Tibet or even Taiwan go independent? Map of China will get reduced to 1/4 th of its size. So who is agressor animal?

From now on, whenever I make an especially good debating point, I plan to drive it home by adding, "So who is aggressor animal now?" It won't make sense, but I hardly think that matters. I know a good phrase when I hear it.

Inappropriate Responses

I'm often in my own little world. Usually no one can tell. One of the ways I give myself away is that I respond to what I assume people should be saying instead of what they actually say.

The FedEx guy just delivered a package. When I answered the door I expected him to say something along the lines of "How are you?" So our exchange went like this.

> FEDEX GUY: Here.
> ME: Good, and you?

He just walked away.

I also get myself into the "how are you" loop. It works like this.

> ME: How are you?
> OTHER PERSON: Good. How are you?
> ME: Good. How are you?
> OTHER PERSON: Um . . . still good.

That's pretty much a signal that you weren't listening and don't care.

I also have a habit of closing a conversation with inappropriate trivial sayings. That works this way.

> OTHER PERSON: My entire family ran away and I have a terminal disease.
> ME: I'm so sorry. Well, I gotta run. Have a nice day!

Interesting Factoids

Yesterday I learned how to determine which one of the wall outlets is controlled by the wall switch. The controlled outlet is installed upside down, and only one of the two plug holes is controlled. At least that's true on new construction where I live. BOCTAOE. This is the sort of marginally useful information that one feels the need to share with the world.

An hour ago I discovered another helpful fact. My radio/alarm puts off heat while sitting there waiting to wake me up. I had carelessly tossed a sweatshirt on top of it and later found the garment warmed precisely to my liking. On cold days, I plan to leave my sweatshirt on top of the radio/alarm when I go to sleep so it's all toasty when I get up. Mmm-mmm.

I also plan to train my cat to wear my underpants at night to keep them warm. It's called innovation. Deal with it.

Whale Watching

As I write this, I am on vacation in Maui, sitting on a sectional sofa in a cozy rented condo, overlooking the ocean. Whales are plainly in view, breaching and spouting and carrying on. Every time I see one, I feel as if I'm watching something special. It never seems to get old.

I can't figure out why the hell I want to spend so much time staring at whales. I'm generally hard to amuse. But if a whale spits some water out of a blow hole (I like saying *blow hole*) half a mile away, I think I just witnessed the birth of Jesus. And if I see 10 percent of a whale's back, I practically achieve a full climax.

This puzzles me because I don't even respect whales that much. They eat too much and they're too dumb to breathe underwater like the fish they ought to be. They are essentially cows that like water.

This morning at about dawn, I was sipping some green tea and looking for more whales from the comfort of my condo. Suddenly I spotted a whale down on the beach. It appeared to be dead. This excited me because I've always wanted to see a dead whale up close. I couldn't wait to finish my tea, grab my flip-flops, and take a better look. But in time, the light of day informed me that it was only a large rock.

The bottom line is that I spent a good thirty minutes being entertained by a rock impersonating a dead whale. Tonight I plan to drink some Grey Goose and stare at that rock again. It's hard to say what is my best vacation ever, but this one is a contender.

The WCM Method

The biggest relationship mistake you can make is to assume that because you have some special training or knowledge on a topic, that your opinion should be extra important. You could be the world's most respected expert on insects, for example, but if your mate insists that caterpillars grow into chipmunks, there will be no talking him or her out of it. You could try saying, "I have a doctorate in bugs, I know what I'm talking about," but your mate will hear, "I am an overbearing ass pimple who doesn't know a fly from a suspicious mole."

So forget about how much you know, or how smart you think you are, or how much extra information you might have recently collected. That will not help you. Instead, I offer you the only solution: the WCM Method.

WCM stands for Who Cares Most. If you want your relationship to have a chance, defer all decisions and interpretations of fact to the person who cares the most.

In practice, this will mean that women will make 98 percent of all the decisions and be "right" 98 percent of the time. Compared to men, women care more passionately about just about everything. Men mostly scratch what itches and call it good. BOCTAOE.

Many women and some men who read this will sharply disagree with my gross generalization. To you I say with all sincerity, "You're right. I don't know what I was thinking."

See how easy that is?

Oil My What?

Yesterday I got a massage at a hotel spa. As I was disrobing I noticed a big bottle of massage oil sitting near the sink. It was labeled "Nut Oil."

My first thought was "Gee, they have a different type of oil for every body part." My second thought was that I might enjoy this massage more than I imagined. But my bubble was burst when I noticed there was only one bottle of oil. No "Elbow Oil" or "Shoulder Oil," just the one bottle of nut oil.

Then I thought perhaps they detected something about me on the phone when I made the appointment, as in "Don't use the normal oil on this one. Get the nut oil."

For the record, I am not a nut. I am an optimist. That's exactly like a nut except with a better attitude.

Optimistic Cynic

People are often surprised to learn that I consider myself an optimist, albeit an optimist with cynical tendencies and a dark side that Lucifer himself would find a little creepy. (Perhaps you've noticed.) I'm actually named on a website that lists famous cynics. You don't normally associate cynicism with an upbeat attitude. But I have exactly that combination and will defend it.

I've always been an optimist. Every time I enter a contest or play a game, I fully expect to win, regardless of the odds. Every time I go to the mailbox, I expect to find a check. It's just that sort of irrational optimism that caused me to enter cartooning with exactly zero experience and no artistic talent to speak of. (That worked out okay.)

While I've had some notable successes, the vast majority of things I've attempted have been flops. But I shake them off and keep on plugging. I always learn something from the flops that helps me later. For example, failing at my corporate careers made me a better cartoonist. And I always expect that the next thing I try will work, so I see no point in dwelling on past failures.

I'm also optimistic about humanity in general. I think we'll solve the problems of terrorism, war, poverty, and most diseases in my lifetime. I really do. And I think the next generation is better than every generation that came before, including the so-called Greatest Generation.

I'm optimistic about myself and about humanity in general. My problem is with the average asshole who I often assume is a self-destructive miscreant, already circling the drain and trying to take me with him. This view is no more "true" than my irrational optimism, but I find it useful to think that way. It keeps me on my toes so I can recognize the most dangerous scams and traps before it's too late. And it helps me write comics, of course.

Despite my dismal view of many individuals, as a matter of personal preference, I give people my trust before they earn it, so long as the downside of doing so isn't too deadly. But that has less to do with those other people and more to do with who I want to be. I find that trust changes people. They become what you tell them you expect. Likewise, you become what you expect of yourself.

As a human being, you are a collection of many things: skin, bones, brains, experience, and emotion. But more than all of that, you are your expectations. That's why I choose to be an optimist.

Some Guy Told Me

There are many ways to learn things. You could read a book, take a class, perhaps do your own experiments. My favorite source of knowledge is called "some guy told me." When you consider that my other favorite source is hallucinations, the "some guy told me" method of knowledge acquisition is relatively reliable.

Recently I was wondering how whales have the time to suck in enough oxygen through their tiny blow holes during the fleeting moments they are above water and not exhaling. That's when "some guy told me" that he had asked the same question at a place I can't recall but will refer to as the Institute of Whale Experts, or IOWE for short. The guy at the IOWE, or it could have been a woman, said that the people in his organization don't know the answer to that question either.

This made me feel rather smug, being nearly as smart on this particular question as some guy, or it could have been a woman, at the IOWE.

I also asked the naturalist on my whale-watching cruise how whales sleep, since they need to frequently surface for breathing. This is important because I know from experience that getting up at night to pee even once will make me tired the next day. I can't imagine needing to wake up and go someplace every time I needed some oxygen. The naturalist guy, or it could have been a woman, informed me that whales don't exactly sleep. They just sort of meditate now and then. I didn't ask, but I assume that killer whales do not meditate as much as they should.

By far, the most important thing I learned about whales, aside from the fact that their blow holes are not involved in foreplay, is that some whales have two of them. That's right, two blow holes.

Now you might say that a whale needs a second blow hole like he needs a hole in the head. But it wouldn't be funny. My point is that a whale with two blow holes is for all practical purposes a giant nose. And that is why I don't swim in the ocean: It's full of noses.

Revealing Looks

Have you ever been in this situation? You're negotiating with a friend on the question of what time to get together. You want an early time and your friend is pushing for something later. The two of you agree on a time in between and then your friend gives you *the look*.

It's the look that says "I plan to show up late, at precisely the time I originally suggested, but I'll make it seem like an accident." The look is characterized by what could best be described as a temporary coma. The person's face goes cold and lifeless for a fleeting moment, like a bad poker face, followed by a forced smile and the "Okay. Right. See you then." His sentence might even trail off into a mumble. That's a dead giveaway.

You know you're hosed, but you can't really accuse your friend ahead of time. "You filthy weasel! I know you plan to show up late!" And you can't show up late yourself on the off chance that your friend actually shows up on time.

It makes me wish I were one of those people who can't read faces— I think they're called engineers. But I'm not one of those. In fact, I studied hypnosis years ago, and one of the unexpected side effects is that I have an unusual skill for reading people and seeing hidden motives. It comes in handy, but it's a mixed blessing because I often see the train heading my way and I can't always jump in time.

Here's one face-reading tip that you can use right away. When people look at something or someone they like, their pupils widen. It doesn't matter if they're looking at puppies and rainbows or porn. If they like it, their eyes try to get some more. It's even true of your pet. When your dog or cat looks at you, or at some favorite toy, check out the eyes.

Note: If your dog's pupils don't widen when he looks at you, he's planning to kill you in your sleep.

Inebriated Hillbillies Are <u>Not</u> Funny

I once featured an inebriated hillbilly in a Dilbert comic. Dogbert kicked him off a log and into a ravine. Apparently this comic was insensitive to hillbillies. Here's the comic, and below it is a letter objecting to my depiction of hillbillies.

And here's the letter I received.

Dear Mr. Adams,

I am writing in regards to the "Dilbert" cartoon that was published in the Gazette-Mail *in Charleston, West Virginia, on Saturday, February 18th. I have long enjoyed your cartoon strip, having spent eight years at Marshall University confined to a tiny cubicle (even though I was a full professor) and having to track the amount of paper I used due to budget constraints.*

I am currently the co-director of the Center for the Study of Ethnicity and Gender in Appalachia and teach in the Appalachian Studies graduate certificate program at Marshall's graduate college. One of my interests is the ways in which stereotypes of Appalachians in the general culture have rationalized and justified the historic mistreatment of Appalachians as an ethnic group.

Your cartoon "killed" an inebriated hillbilly. He was lying on a log with a jug at his side (probably moonshine?) and wearing bib overalls. He was booted off the log into a chasm and a certain fate. Now, let me ask you a question. Would you have drawn that cartoon of a drunk Irishman, a Jew, a black person, an Hispanic person? I doubt it very much. Most Americans are by now sensitized to the damage that such stereotypes represent for minority groups. And yet you, as well as many others, still feel free to picture hillbillies (translate: Appalachians) in this way.

I would like to urge you to look at the most recent issue of the National Geographic. *There is an article there on mountaintop removal and the ecological, cultural, and social damage that it is visiting upon the mountains and their people. I would argue that most Americans have ignored this disaster-in-the-making for so long because there is a general agreement that hillbillies are of less worth—"useless" human beings. Your cartoon confirms that sense.*

I would be the first to acknowledge that some Appalachians are alcoholics and wear bib overalls. But I suspect that there are many other people in this country that would fit that description as well. We are a proud people—closely tied to our land—who have given this country music, literature, and social movements that raised the standard of living for all of us. Why is it that television and the print media are so focused on only our social problems? Or see us only negatively?

I appreciate your taking my comments under consideration. This is not meant as a personal attack, but hopefully will be educational for you. I would be glad to recommend a reading list for you or email you some material

Sincerely,

Lynda Ann Ewen, PhD

Professor Emerita of Sociology, Marshall University

Co-Director, Center for the Study of Ethnicity and Gender in Appalachia

Editor, Series of "Ethnicity and Gender in Appalachia," Ohio University Press

In my defense, the hillbilly in my comic wasn't killed. He landed softly in a bush made entirely of Styrofoam peanuts. But I didn't have enough room in the comic to show that. You'll have to take my word for it.

Second, I thought that being a hillbilly was a lifestyle decision, which would make it fair game for humor. If you like bib overalls, enjoy using the word *'taint,* as in " 'taint fittin'," and have ever eaten a rodent or sipped dandelion soup, then I think it's fair to call you a hillbilly no matter where you grew up.

Third, it's crazy to think that growing up in the Appalachian Mountains is what makes you a hillbilly. I grew up in the Catskill Mountains, a section of the Appalachians. We weren't no dang hillbillies! We just thought we had a colorful way of talking:

> CLASSMATE: I shot me a woodchuck.
> ME: Why?
> CLASSMATE: I had a gun. It had fur. Case closed.
> ME: Did you barbecue it?
> CLASSMATE: Hell no. I put it on a fence post as a warning to the others.
> ME: Warning of what?
> CLASSMATE: Don't matter.

Unlike hillbillies, we always wore shirts. Unless it was warm outside. Or it was spaghetti night. Only crazy people eat spaghetti with a shirt on. And I admit I have eaten my share of rodent stew (woodchuck) and dandelion soup. Neither one tastes as much like chicken as you would want.

Too Many Coincidences

Have you ever noticed that coincidences come in clusters? Every now and then I hit a cluster of coincidences that make me question my delusions about reality. I'm tempted to concoct an entirely new set of delusions just to make it all square up.

My current view of reality is that I'm in a coma someplace and what appears to be my life is actually my dream. It's not so crazy if you compare it to the alternative explanation that I really did become one of the top-selling cartoonists of all time with no experience whatsoever.

In my coma theory, the little runs of coincidences are the defects in my otherwise perfect delusion. For example, the other day I was at the health club, walking past the tennis reservation desk on the way to the lockers. The woman at the desk answered her phone, looked up, saw me, and said, "It's for you." And it was. The pro shop was calling at just that moment to figure out some billing issues on a racket I had purchased months before. They didn't expect me to be walking past at that moment; they were just calling to ask the tennis desk which Scott Adams I was so they could bill correctly. I interpreted the experience to mean that the real me, the one in the coma, was getting a sponge bath.

Okay, it gets weirder. As I write this, I'm sitting at the bar of my restaurant (Stacey's at Waterford, in Dublin, California) having lunch. My secondary mission today was to pick up a gift certificate that my fiancée asked me to get. I had totally forgotten about that task until a woman sat down next to me and asked for a gift certificate.

Now, I might see someone buying a gift certificate here maybe once every two months, tops. So I'm writing about coincidences as a lucky coincidence happens that totally saves me. I interpret this to mean that the real me, the one in the coma, is being sponge-bathed again, this time in my favorite spot.

Am I a Libertarian?

People keep asking if I'm a Libertarian. Chat sites and websites and blogs have devoted considerable time to this ultraimportant question. I thought it was time to clear up things. The answer: I haven't really looked into it.

I have some vague idea that Libertarians are big on personal freedoms and keeping government out of their pants. My philosophy is more nuanced. I believe all people favor what they think is in their best interest and then rationalize it with absurd philosophical arguments. Or worse, they join a "team" and agree with whatever the leader tells them.

If my philosophy had a name, it would probably be Ignorantselfishertarianism. When it comes to anything complicated, I'm too ignorant to have a useful opinion. For example:

> SOME GUY: Scott, do you think we should return to the gold standard?
> SCOTT: Um . . .
> SOME GUY: Should the United States stay in Iraq and be bled to death or leave now and let the bad guys get a foothold from which they can better try to destroy us?
> SCOTT: Um . . .

Frankly, I'm suspicious of anyone who has a strong opinion on a complicated issue. But when it comes to social questions, those are usually simple. I take sides with whatever viewpoint is good for me personally.

For example, I favor legalizing anything that is relatively victimless, especially if the alternative involves paying to keep strangers in jail while they learn how to better steal my identity when they get out.

Take smoking in public; I favor banning that because I don't like to be around it. Secondhand smoke is like litter in my nose.

On the issue of motorcycle helmets, my first choice would be to make them mandatory, but only for people who I think deserve to be alive. Unfortunately, it would be too hard to keep the list current. So my second choice is to force all bikers to wear helmets. That would have the economic benefit of keeping the supply of tattoos artists, hit men, and crank chefs high, in case I ever wanted any of those services. BOCTAOE.

On gun control, I favor whatever laws allow me to get one easily in case I ever want to shoot someone. I figure that the person I want to shoot probably already has one. But I don't mind having to wait a few weeks for my gun. That might be the only thing that keeps me out of jail someday.

Being an Ignorantselfishertarian isn't as bad as it sounds. Usually what's good for me is coincidentally good for most of the people in the world, too. That's why I call myself good people.

Streamlined Dating Site

If you had to design a dating website that matched people on just two criteria, what would those criteria be?

I think about this sort of thing all the time. And by "this sort of thing" I mean worthless questions. And I don't give up until I have an answer.

My answer to the question is this:

1. Sense of humor
2. Ass size

Remember, you only get to pick two criteria for this worthless exercise. So no matter what you pick, there will be plenty of exceptions. I'm just looking for the *best* two-criteria predictor.

Sense of humor is tops on my list because people who laugh at the same things are almost always compatible on a personality level. The second criteria—ass size—is based on my observation that people end up with mates who have the same approximate ass size. But of course there are obvious exceptions, including rich fat guys with skinny supermodel girlfriends, and Marc Anthony and J. Lo. But in general, unless one of the two has a lot of money, people end up with mates of the same approximate ass size.

Party question: What two criteria would match people better than sense of humor and ass size?

Flying to Orlando

'm traveling today and writing this chapter on my BlackBerry while waiting at the airport gate. I just realized that the enormous lump in my pants was my keys. (This time anyway.) Somehow I got through the metal detector with a wad of keys the size of a small beaver, and I apologize for the disturbing imagery.

This raises an interesting ethical question. Should I inform security that their metal detector is defective, thus shutting down the entire airport while they rescreen everyone? Or should I assume that my keys are all made of plastic?

And what if it turns out that a beaver-sized set of keys aren't supposed to set off the alarm? In that case, should I start packing heat when I fly, under the theory that I might have to take down a hijacker who got his own gun through security?

The public announcement system just told me to report any people who "look suspicious." This is a big category. I need clearer guidance. I just saw an incredibly hot woman traveling with an ugly guy. That looks suspicious. And a maintenance guy just walked by wearing one glove. What's he up to? Am I to believe it's only cold on one side?

I'm going to keep an eye on him. If he makes a move I'll take him out with my beaverkeys.

Wedding Costs

Irecently got engaged. I am learning many things about this process, each more shocking than the last.

I recently learned that, in addition to sending out wedding invitations, sometimes you also send out preinvitations telling people to hold the date. This offends all of my nerdish sensibilities, especially since every person who will get a preinvitation also has e-mail. "Why not just e-mail them?" I asked. That question will ensure that I have a very small role in future wedding planning.

Another big shock is that weddings are not cheap. If you had asked me a year ago to estimate the cost of a great wedding, I probably would have said something like "Hmmm, maybe $3,000, unless it's potluck, and then you could shave off a bit. Do you have to bribe the priest or is that service free?"

My first choice for the ceremony was the Britney Spears method: get drunk in Vegas and wake up with a Budweiser pull-tab ring on my left hand. But it turns out that my friends and family are expecting to wear freshly pressed clothing and attend some sort of event with flowers and cakes and whatnot. There's a lot of pressure to do this thing the usual way.

Luckily I have stashed away a few acorns so I can afford this shindig. Still, I feel some inner need to keep the budget under control without appearing cheap. My current strategy is to frame all wedding decisions in terms of how many African villagers could be saved from starvation with the equivalent amount of money. For example:

> FIANCÉE: Do you think we should have a big cake or a little one?
>
> SCOTT: Well, the difference in price seems to be ... about twelve Rwandans. It's up to you, honey.

Can You Hear Me Now?

Last May I started having trouble with my voice. I figured it was allergies. But it didn't get better when allergy season ended. Eventually I went to the doctor and he told me it might be acid reflux. I popped the antireflux pills and waited for the cure. But it only got worse. On the next trip, my doctor diagnosed it as bronchitis, which I think it probably was at that point. No problem. I popped the antibiotics and waited for the cure. But my voice kept getting worse.

After a few months of worsening, I could only talk in certain situations. I could speak perfectly when I was alone. And I could speak perfectly when I gave a speech to a crowd. But I couldn't speak intelligibly on the phone or in one-on-one conversations. I'd try to talk and literally nothing would come out. The best I could do was a whisper. Obviously I was nuts.

So I consulted my doctor again and he referred me to the "obviously you're nuts" doctor, who said, essentially, "Obviously you're nuts." She thought maybe Paxil would help, since my problem seemed to have a social trigger. I said "no thanks" and continued down the specialist trail.

My trip to the ear, nose, and throat doctor was an adventure. His job was to look for polyps. My gag reflex was too strong for the "direct route," as he put it, so he said he would need to look via the "indirect route." He pulled out a two-foot-long tube thing with a camera on the end and started greasing it up. At the sight of this device, and not knowing exactly what the "indirect method" involved, my sphincter slammed shut and I started yelling "Nooooo!!!" But it turns out you can get to the throat via the nose. This is not pleasant, but compared to the alternative I was delighted.

There were no polyps in my throat, and so that possibility was ruled out. However, my nasal passage was described as "ten miles of bad road," so I had surgery to straighten that out just for good measure. That hurt a lot, but it worked out great as far as breathing. Unfortunately I still couldn't speak, and it was getting worse. And I had a bunch of speaking engagements upcoming. Could I still speak in front of a crowd? I didn't know for sure because my voice had worsened since the last time I tried.

I don't know how many of you fear public speaking. It normally doesn't bother me. But when you're standing backstage while a thousand people are waiting to hear you speak, and you don't know whether you'll be able to utter a peep, that's some scary shit. But amazingly, I would go from barely able to whisper backstage to normal voice onstage. Obviously I was nuts.

That's when Google saved my sanity. I was taking a shower one day—that's where all my good ideas are born—and I started to wonder if my bizarre throat problem was related to my bizarre hand problem. My right pinky goes into spasms when I try to draw on paper, yet I have no problem drawing on a computer even though I hold the stylus just like a pen. I knew from experience that this, too, had seemed like I was nuts until I found the right doctor to diagnose it.

I dried off and Googled "dystonia"—the name for my hand problem—plus "voice." Bingo. There's a rare neurological condition called spasmodic dysphonia, with voice symptoms identical to mine. When I played the online voice samples of people who have it, they sounded just like me. The symptoms are amazingly specific, as in "can speak clearly while yawning but can't speak on the phone." And "can sing but can't speak in normal voice." There's even a propensity for this condition to pair with another dystonia, like the one in my hand.

Now all I had to do was convince my doctor(s) that I wasn't nuts and that I had a very rare condition. As you might imagine, when you tell a doctor that you think you have a very rare condition, that doctor will tell you that it's very unlikely. Your first impulse might be to point out that "very rare" is a lot like "very unlikely," but you don't do that, because doctors have wide latitude in deciding which of your orifices they will use for various medical apparati. So you go with the protocol that involves systematically eliminating all the things that are more likely.

The next speech doctor had access to better technology than the first and determined that I almost certainly did not have the rare neurological disorder that both I and Google insisted I did. She based her opinion on how I sounded and the fact that it was very unlikely that I would have a very unlikely condition. But she did notice a facial tick that might indicate a brain tumor as the culprit.

So off I went to the neurologist who tapped me in various places with a rubber hammer and stared at me for a while and didn't see any ticks. But she thought maybe an MRI was in order just to eliminate the possibility of a brain tumor. That test came out clean.

By that time, I don't mind saying, I was fighting off a powerful cloud of depression, partly because so many people assumed I was nuts, and partly because I couldn't have any sort of normal social interaction. It was like observing life as a ghost. I was there, sort of, but I couldn't speak in most situations. My entire personality depends on being witty and charming. Relying instead on my good looks isn't a good Plan B. I learned that loneliness is only solved by speaking, and not by listening. I was dying inside. If this problem wasn't fixable, and so far my doctors were stumped, the quality of my life was going to plunge about 80 percent for the next hundred years that I planned to live. I'm an optimistic guy, but there's no amount of positive thinking that can fix that sort of thing.

Eventually, as the medical protocol worked its way out, I found my way to a neurologist who specializes in my alleged rare neurological disorder. She listened to me for about thirty seconds and said essentially, "Yup. That's it." Google was right. The good news is that I wasn't nuts. The better news is that there is a well-established treatment. The bad news is that the treatment is not fun.

The treatment involves Botox injections to the vocal cords several times a year. Botox temporarily deadens the muscles that cause the spasms that choke off the voice. Apparently those muscles aren't good for much besides misbehaving, so you can stun them with minimal side effects.

If you're squeamish, skip this paragraph. I'm going to describe the process. The neurologist sticks two electronic sensors on my neck so she can determine when the needle is in the right spot. Then she gives me a local anesthetic on the neck below the Adam's apple. This is just preparation for the bigger and nastier needle that will deliver the Botox. The Botox needle goes through the front of the neck and then she works it toward the inside back of the throat where the vocal cords are. When she's near the right spot, she tells me to say "eeeee." Then, when the needle touches the right place, her electronic gizmo goes all static and she plunges in for the first shot. The needle stays in the front of my neck as she maneuvers it to the other side of the inside of my throat and repeats. It doesn't hurt as much as it would seem, but the creepy factor is through the roof. You can feel the needle inside your neck the whole time. The "bad part" takes about sixty seconds, and believe it or not, you can actually get used to it. Kind of.

A week after the first shot, and right on schedule, the nerve endings in my neck took a holiday and my voice returned. My voice isn't perfect, and I need regular booster shots, but the treatment works, especially when giving speeches. I've given two speeches since starting the treatments, including one this afternoon, and everything was terrific.

I learned that different parts of your brain process speech depending on the context. My telephone speaking context is still a challenge, but my giving-a-speech context works well. I'm not so nuts after all.

On my follow-up appointment, my doctor asked if the Botox worked and I just hugged her.* Speaking seemed redundant. Now when I speak to people, for any reason, I am so freaking happy I can't even describe it. And when I speak to a packed ballroom, like today, I feel reborn. It is pure joy, and I feel like the luckiest guy in the world. Every day feels like a gift now. And that, my friends, is the rarest neurological disorder of them all.

---

* My voice worsened a bit in the months that followed, and I stopped using Botox. But I learned to speak okay without it in most situations.

Constitutional or Not

I keep hearing the argument that some things are constitutional while other things are not. The idea is that we should be in favor of all the things that were decided over two hundred years ago by a bunch of slave-owning cross-dressers who pooped in holes. (Those so-called constitutional things we consider "right.") And we should be against anything else regardless of our common sense and current knowledge. (Those so-called nonconstitutional things we should consider "wrong.") This bothers me because the hole-poopers didn't intend the document to be used as a substitute for thinking.

I recommend a new standard for deciding right and wrong. We have lots of opinion polls, and they seem reasonably accurate. I say that anytime two-thirds of the citizens have the same point of view on an issue that that point of view is automatically called "right" and the alternative is called "wrong." My reasoning is that two-thirds of the adult citizen population would be enough to amend the constitution, assuming they all voted and lived in the right places. (BOCTAOE.)

Sadly, there is no snappy media-friendly name for "two-thirds of the adult citizens who could vote." Plurality and majority aren't specific enough. TTOTACWCV is hard to remember. "Might makes right" is close to the point, but it has a negative connotation.

I recommend just referring to this situation as a 667—a short and oh-so-cool way of indicating that at least 66.7 percent of the population agrees with you, and therefore you are "right" by definition. This would be a big time-saver at parties. Proper usage:

> OTHER GUY: Blah, blah, blah, it's unconstitutional.
> YOU: I have to toss you a 667 on that one.

I tried out this argument on my blog before this book was published and got lots of angry responses. I enjoyed this more than I expected.

People assumed that because I want to label the majority opinion "right" and the minority opinion "wrong" that I would also favor mob rule. No way. I still favor the traditional system where rich people run the country and convince the morons who live here that the voters are really the ones in charge. It's not a perfect system, but no one has come up with a better one. And it's fair in the sense that anyone could become rich and abuse the poor.

My question in this screed was about how "right" and "wrong" are decided. There aren't many good ways to go about it. You're either trusting ancient hole-poopers who wrote something down and told you it was inspired by God, or you're trusting your instinct. And let's face it, you know what a clueless goober you can be. There's no good option.

Personally, I use a modified version of the Spock test for morality. First I try to figure out what is the greater good. Then I compare it to what is good for me personally. If the two things are the same, I label it "right." And if the greater good conflicts with my personal benefit, I call that a tie.

Again, it's not a perfect system, but no one has come up with a better one.

Losing Weight

I have taught you many things, but for some reason I forgot to tell you how to lose weight. To correct this oversight, I give you my very own diet plan. The key to this plan is taking tiny incremental steps that sneak up on you. With this plan, no week is appreciably more difficult than the one before.

First, buy a scale and use it daily. As soon as you find yourself three pounds over your target weight, begin the Scott Adams Diet.

Week 1: Stop eating after 9 p.m.

Week 2: Stop eating after 8 p.m.

Week 3: Stop eating bread and white rice and potatoes. Eat all the vegetables you want. Pasta is good, too, because it doesn't spike your sugar like other carbs.

Week 4: Adjust your schedule to allow exercise every day at a set time. When that time comes, no matter how tired you feel, put on your athletic shoes and workout clothes. Then exercise as much or as little as you feel you can handle. The idea is to make it a routine. There is no other objective at this point. Once it's a routine, you'll automatically start doing more of it just to keep from being bored. That part takes care of itself.

Week 5: Leave about 25 percent of your food on your plate.

Week 6: By now you will have lost approximately zero weight. But there's a good chance you haven't gained any.

Week 7: Experience a wrenching personal problem, such as a relationship disaster, financial setback, or major health problem. This will take five pounds off you in no time.

If you are the sort of person who eats more when you have personal problems, my advice is to buy stretch pants or grow a goatee.

Are Men Just Defective Women?

've noticed that men generally believe they are "different" from women, whereas women generally believe men are "defective" women. You can see that perspective in almost any discussion of gender differences.

Ninety percent of the gender difference seems to be the male preference for compartmentalizing thoughts, while women think everything is somehow connected. Here are some phrases you rarely hear from women:

"I didn't wrap your present because you'd just throw away the wrapping anyway."
"Let's skip Valentine's Day this year so we don't miss *CSI*."
"Your personality is grating, but I'd do you in a heartbeat."
"Bob died? That's a shame. What's for dinner?"

No guy would ever say those things around a women either, but not because he isn't thinking them. We guys have learned how to blend in and talk like women when it's necessary. It feels like being a German spy during World War II and you're always worried someone will ask you a question about the Yankees.

If you're male, you have to do a lot of internal editing before you let anything fly out of your mouth. The best way to filter is to ask yourself how a woman would react to what you're about to say. Here's a little test to see if you know how this works.

Suppose a male sees a car that's a hideous shade of green and he blurts out to a friend, "That is one ugly-ass car!" Now, using the Theory of Gender Compartmentalization, which gender would utter which response?

1. "Holy $%#*&, that color is just wrong for a car."
2. Silence, while thinking "He hates my green sweater."

BOCTAOE.

Winning

Recently there was a tennis tournament in Indian Wells, California. It's one of the biggest tournaments each year, not counting the four Grand Slam events. Because tennis is an individual sport, there are always great stories within the game. This year's biggest story was James Blake's comeback.

If you don't follow the game, let me give you some background. Blake is the son of an African-American dad and an English mom. He was raised in Connecticut and had to wear a back brace for years when he was a kid. He took up tennis, excelled, and went to Harvard for two years before going pro. He looked promising, along with a number of other young Americans, but not top ten material. He was most noted for his sex appeal and great personality.

I became a fan after watching him play Lleyton Hewitt a few years ago. After some calls that went against Hewitt, the Aussie singled out an African-American linesperson and complained to the chair umpire. Hewitt used a poor choice of words that led observers to think he was complaining of racial favoritism. Hewitt says he didn't mean it that way, but nonetheless it became the story. And the media tried hard to get Blake to bite. They wanted him to complain about racism, maybe get a little mad about it. That's good TV. But Blake didn't take the bait. He politely pointed out that people say things in the heat of the moment, and whatever Hewitt said was Hewitt's problem, not his. It seemed to me the perfect response. Sometimes trivializing is the best strategy.

Blake's ranking bobbed up and down, peaking at 22 in the world. He shaved his dreadlocks and gave up his sex symbol image along with millions in potential endorsements. (I'm guessing his hair was prematurely thinning.) Then in 2004 he had the year from Hell. He ran into a tennis net post and broke his neck. Then he got a shingles virus in his face that paralyzed it on one side. Then his dad died.

There was some doubt that Blake would ever play tennis again. He watched the major tournaments from his couch and wondered about his future. In time, his body recovered, and he felt that he had been given a second chance. He grabbed it by the throat.

I don't know what kind of training he did, but oh my God. I watched him play in person during the first week of the Indian Wells tournament and thought it couldn't be the same guy. There was ferocity to his strokes. He wasn't just hitting the ball, he was punishing it. His court speed was breathtaking. His shot selection was brilliant. His backhand, previously a weakness, had become a rocket.

You only needed to listen to the court sounds to know that Blake was heading deep into the tournament. When a tennis racket strikes a ball perfectly, it creates a sound wave that spectators can feel in their entire bodies. If you play tennis yourself, you can practically close your eyes and know who is winning.

Blake blasted through the field of world-class tennis players and found himself in an unlikely semifinal with a Spanish force of nature named Rafael Nadal. Nadal is the number 2 player in the world. He hits with brutal topspin. It's a relentless attack that less than a handful of elite players have been able to withstand in the past year.

Nadal brought his best, but Blake blew past with a combination of game and gamesmanship that surprised almost everyone, not the least Nadal himself.

Now it was time for the championship match against Roger Federer, the best player in the world. Correction—make that the best tennis player who has ever lived. That's not just my opinion. If he stays healthy, many people expect him to hold every important record in tennis.

Against all odds, Blake blazed to a 4–1 first set advantage against the all-time greatest player on Earth. It seemed as though nothing could stop him.

And then something happened. The momentum shifted. The rest of the match was all Federer. Blake seemed to fade away, settling for runner-up, but his effort that week was enough to put him in the top ten in the world.

At the trophy ceremony, Blake spoke to the crowd. He said that in 2004, when he was in the hospital with a broken neck, only one tennis player sent him a note to wish him well. It was Roger Federer.

I wanted Blake to win that match, yet somehow, by losing, he found perfection.

Life in the Universe

Scientists have calculated that it's likely there is life on other planets simply because there are so many planets, and evolution would have had time to do its thing. I disagree, but not for any good reason. I wouldn't rule out the existence of bacteria, for example. But I doubt there are any other humanoids doing crossword puzzles.

One of the interesting things about getting older (or experienced as I like to call it) is that you can detect a problem before you know why. Have you ever been in a situation where someone says, "Let's do it this way," and you get an immediate little stomachache because you know damned well that it won't work? And then someone asks why you think it's a bad plan and you really can't explain it. All you know is that the last ten plans that sounded kind of like this plan all fell apart.

I understand the argument made by the scientists. The universe is so large that even the amazingly unlikely sequence of events that theoretically caused our existence must have happened plenty of other times, too. And I guess it follows that if there is enough life out there, some of it is bound to be advanced.

It makes perfect sense, but to believe that, I'd have to believe that some goober with Excel actually calculated the probability of alien life and got an answer that was within a hundred trillion percent of being accurate. It's possible, sure. But compare it to the other possibility:

People want to believe there is intelligent life out there. The media loves that kind of crap. A good way to get attention is to claim you proved aliens exist.

If you believe that scientists can really calculate the odds of intelligent life, you might be, um . . . young. I think there's at least a 50 percent chance that scientists have grossly overestimated the odds. I used to earn my living making financial projections for big companies, and the only correlation between my estimates and the actual cost of those projects is that they both involved "numbers."

I don't know the odds of intelligent life on other planets. But I have to think it's about the same as the odds that this alleged intelligent life is winged monkeys that flew out of my ass when I wasn't paying attention.

A Moving Experience

Have you ever noticed that you can't remember how painful it is to move to a new home until you are actually doing it? I mean, conceptually you know it will be "hard," but you never fully appreciate the fact that your entire soul will be waterboarded for about four days. At some point during the middle of the process you start thinking, "I will never move again until I die and other people have to carry me." But a few months later, the memory of the horror fades. I assume there's some evolutionary advantage to this relocation amnesia. Otherwise our predecessors would have stayed in their second caves forever, just pooping and fornicating until it became so crowded they had to do both at the same time.

I bought a model town house to use as my office, and sold off all the grandma furniture that came with it. I only kept one rug. I didn't need it for decorating purposes, but I figured it might come in handy someday for disposing a body. Granted, it's unlikely I will ever kill anyone at the office, but if the situation comes up, I don't want to go rug shopping first.

When it comes to evidence disposal, you need a container that's long enough to handle the entire cadaver. Otherwise you waste an evening trying to get it into small enough pieces to fit in Tupperware containers or Hefty Bags or what-have-you. It's bad enough that you're a murderer, you don't want to be a time waster, too.

I spend a lot of time thinking of the best way to dispose of a body. Eventually I assume someone will invent a product for that purpose. It will be a small one-corpse boat that fits in the back of an SUV. It would be programmed with GPS to motor out to deep water and then sink itself. The body would be in a sealed container so it can't bob to the surface. Let's call this product the Abra Cadaver, because it makes the body disappear.

The great thing about the Abra Cadaver is that it would be totally legal to own one. It's only illegal to use it. You could just keep your Abra Cadaver in the corner of your office, leaning against a wall. It could help during difficult negotiations. While it would be illegal to threaten to kill someone, it's totally legal to let them know you could get away with it if you did.

Success Formula

Recently I was asked to give a talk to a class of high school kids. It got me thinking about what it takes to be successful in business. Assuming hard work, and good health, and no crushing personal or personality problems, here's the weightings I would give to the various other success factors.

30 percent brains (including talent)
30 percent luck (being in the right place at the right time)
20 percent looks (including hair, height, weight, gender, and ethnicity)
20 percent reputation of the school you attended

The way to interpret the weightings is to recognize that if you don't have one of those elements working for you, you'd better try to maximize the ones you do have. For example, if you graduated from Lou's College of Fertilizer and Cosmetology, you probably need to be extra street smart, or beautiful, or lucky to compensate. BOCTAOE.

If it's extra luck you need, you can help it find you by trying lots of different ventures, as opposed to grinding along forever in some job that has no upside potential. You usually need to trade your comfort for extra luck.

According to some recent research, you can influence your *perceived* luck by being optimistic. Optimism increases your field of perception, allowing you to better notice opportunities. (See a book called *The Luck Factor* by Richard Wiseman, for details on that research.) This passes the sniff test for me, because it seems as if lots of successful people have, somewhere in their story, a part where they say, "and then I noticed something." The best part about the research on optimism and luck is that you can teach people to act optimistic and get the same results as if it had been innate. So don't worry if you were born dreary. Faking it works just fine.

Optimism also helps you try lots of new things, which, as already mentioned, helps luck find you. You wouldn't try anything new if you didn't expect it to work. Optimists try more things than pessimists. I once made a list of all the business-related things I tried, just to see what my batting average was. I had twenty-nine failures and three successes. (I'm counting Dilbert as one success even though it spawned lots of other things that also did well.) You have to be an optimist with that sort of track record. I am.

Obviously you can also optimize your appearance, by fixing your hair, losing a few pounds, hitting the gym, and updating your wardrobe. I'm sure there is a company somewhere in the world in which the attractive employees don't have an advantage, all other things being equal, but I haven't found that company yet. And I wouldn't want to. Something tells me it would be a serious freak show, or a call center.

All of this was too complicated for the students I was speaking to. So I had the kids stand in a line and then I sorted them into two groups: attractive and ugly. Then I advised the ugly ones to study extra hard and be optimistic despite their appearance.

Okay, I didn't really do that, but only because schools don't allow useful advice. So I told them to work hard and maybe someday they can become firemen.

Dancing

Last night my fiancée and I took a beginner's dance class as sort of a first step toward not frightening children at our wedding. The instructor began by asking who in the class had *never* taken a dance class. I was the only one to raise my hand. This was my first warning sign. Indeed, most of the class had taken *this* beginning class several times.

Luckily, the instructor ignored those novices and adjusted his instruction for the one true beginner in the class. And by that I mean he singled me out with hilarious comments about my lack of ability.

For those of you who have never taken a dance class, it goes something like this. First, the instructor demonstrates some footwork a bit too fast for you to have any frickin' idea what he did. Then he repeats the demonstration several times, each time differently as far as you can tell. And often you can't see the demonstration at all because a big guy named Tim is standing in your way.

Armed with this lack of information, you take your partner and proceed to humiliate yourself by moving randomly and hoping that this flailing somehow turns into dancing over time.

The instructor offers many helpful hints, such as, "Lean over your foot; don't just stick it out." As it turns out, if you don't know where that foot is supposed to go, the leaning doesn't help as much as you would hope.

Then you have the issue of "leading." Apparently that is something a guy with a tin ear and no frickin' clue is supposed to be doing. This problem is compounded if your fiancée is an excellent dancer who can hear the beat. The Seeing Eye Dog does not like to be pushed into traffic by the blind guy.

The instructor tried to teach me the beat by repeating 1-2-3 over the music in a way that prevented me from hearing the music because he kept saying 1-2-3 really loudly. Sometimes he would throw in a 4-5-6. Sometimes he said I should move my foot forward on the 1, sometimes the 2, occasionally the 4, all without explanation. Let me tell you, if you start throwing numbers at a guy like me, they better have some &%$@* explanation to go with them. Is the beat on the 1 or the 2 or the 3, or are there three beats and then some silence? And why do you need the 4-5-6 sometimes and not other times? What the hell is the algorithm? I don't know if rage is what most dance students feel, but my Fist of Death was starting to clench and the instructor had a near-death experience without ever realizing it.

Toward the end, the instructor helpfully suggested that this beginner's class was way over my head. Someday I hope to take a class to raise my level up to beginner.

But first I must find the beat. All I know is that it has something to do with numbers.

Pleasure Unit Theory

I don't believe in free will. That's partly because it's indefinable in any sensible way—that is, you have to assume that the rules of cause and effect are optional for your brain chemistry. Second, it doesn't do a good job of predicting behavior. No one would choose to be a drug addict or a pedophile, just to pick two examples.

I prefer my own theory. I call it the Pleasure Unit Theory. It does a much better job describing behavior, and it goes like this:

> *Pleasure Unit Theory: People organize their lives to get their minimum required units of pleasure. While individuals vary in terms of how many units of pleasure they need, everyone is striving to reach their personal minimum.*

I just saw a picture of Eva Longoria on a magazine cover. She has nearly zero body fat and a perfectly toned body. If you believe in free will, you might be puzzled as to why celebrities can be so thin when regular people can't come close. BOCTAOE.

Your first thought might be that celebrities have more to gain by being thin. For them it's a job, and they can afford to have private trainers and put in the gym hours. That's part of it. But I guarantee that Eva Longoria also eats fewer calories than you. How does she get the willpower?

If you subscribe to the popular superstition called free will, you probably think she has unusually strong willpower when it comes to resisting food. I look at it this way: She already exceeds her minimum level of pleasure with fame, money, and humping a professional athlete who has, and here I am just guessing, a penis that would scare Ahab back to land.

When Eva looks at a piece of pie, she knows it might increase her total happiness for that day by only 1 percent, at the price of losing all the other things that bring her pleasure. By contrast, when you look at that same piece of pie, eating it might be the only good thing that happens to you all month. You *need* the pie to get close to your minimum pleasure units.

My theory explains all the following:

1. Why poor people are fatter than rich people.
2. Why people with crappy lives do drugs that are sure to be destructive in the long run.
3. Why you are reading this book instead of working.

Science has plenty of evidence showing that free will is an illusion. For example, we know people make decisions before the area of the brain responsible for rational thought even gets activated. In other words, you rationalize after the fact while remembering it as if you had made a conscious choice in advance of the action.

There is zero scientific evidence that free will exists. In fact, I doubt you can even define free will without using other indefinable terms like *conscious* and *choice*. You end up in the loop of indefinable terms: [begin loop] Free will is conscious choice. And . . . choice is when you consciously use your free will to choose. [end loop]

I can't tell you how many times people have argued with me that free will exists because "I can choose." But that just substitutes the word *choose* for *free will*. All it demonstrates is that people perceive free will in themselves, and no one has ever argued that point. And a coin-sorting machine can "choose," too, in the sense that it puts the nickel in the right slot.

Here's a question that will kill a party fast: How many of you believe in evolution because you accept the scientific consensus, yet also believe you have free will despite the scientific consensus against it? If so, explain your reasons.

According to the theory of cognitive dissonance, those who believe in both evolution and free will probably experience dissonance and will therefore offer arguments that appear humorously nonsensical to observers. Try it at home and see for yourself. If you can get some sucker to argue for both evolution and free will, watch him flounder for a few minutes, then call him a meat puppet and walk away. You will find this more entertaining than you could imagine.

Helpful Critical Guy Syndrome

Over the last fifteen years I have received approximately one e-mail per week saying, in effect, "You used to be funny. But something has gone horribly wrong." This e-mail, written by a different person each time, is long, and passionate, and often detailed in its argument. These helpful critics make it clear that their tough love is intended to snap me out of whatever steaming hole of mediocrity I have shoved my head so that I can get back to my past ways of excellence.

All of these e-mails are from males who seem, based on their well-written letters, above average in intelligence. That's 780 nearly identical messages from men, and zero of this type from women. I call it the Helpful Critical Guy syndrome, HCGS for short.

I recognize this syndrome because I have it myself. I can't tell you how many times I have thought—quite seriously—that if I could just sit down with this or that famous person for about twenty minutes I could "straighten everything out." Rarely does it occur to me that my thorough lack of knowledge about the subject matter is a handicap. I fantasize that what matters most is the incredibly succinct and Mark Twainish way that I explain my suggestion—for example, "If you want to end world hunger, you have to give people food." I realize it doesn't sound all that persuasive here, but I imagine that when I say it in the Oval Office, I come up with better phrasing that makes all the difference. When fantasizing about being smart and helpful, I find that it's best to leave out the details.

Respecting the Beliefs of Others

People keep telling me that I should respect the beliefs of others. That sounds entirely reasonable, at least until you think about it. The problem is in knowing where to draw the line. I can understand why, for example, Presbyterians should respect the beliefs of Methodists. They're practically the same thing.

But what about those Heaven's Gate guys who believed they should kill themselves so their souls could follow a comet? Am I obligated to respect those beliefs, too? How about the people who give away all of their possessions because they have determined the exact date that the world will end? Do I respect their opinions up to the predicted end-time and then, after it passes, keep on respecting their opinion while they are begging the neighbors to give back their crap?

I respect the Mormons for doing a great job of creating good citizens. Whatever they're doing seems to be working. You rarely hear about a gang of violent Mormons terrorizing a town. But must I also respect their practice of wearing special underpants to ward off evil? Is it a package deal, no pun intended?

I suppose you could argue that we should respect any religion that is peaceful and has good intentions at its core. And I certainly agree with treating all people with respect even if you're not feeling it on the inside. But it seems to me dishonest to display respect for all beliefs equally. Surely there are beliefs that deserve slightly less respect than others.

This has to be an even bigger problem for those of you who have a religion of your own. You're thinking something along the lines of "My prophet talked to a real angel whereas your prophet was evidently taking a drunken forest whiz and thought a tree stump was talking back to him."

I also wonder if showing respect for all beliefs is causing more problems than it is avoiding. The only thing that prevents most people from acting on their absurd beliefs is the fear that other people will treat them like frickin' morons. Mockery is an important social tool for squelching stupidity. At least that's what I tell people after I mock them. Or to put it another way, I've never seen anyone change his mind because of the power of a superior argument or the acquisition of new facts. But I've seen plenty of people change behavior to avoid being mocked.

Many of our biggest world problems are caused by different religious views. But it's not socially acceptable to even discuss whether those views originate from the almighty or a drunken guy whizzing on a tree stump. At a bare minimum, just to pick one example, either Christianity or Islam is completely and utterly wrong. The beliefs are mutually exclusive. Muslims believe all Christians will burn in Hell. Christians believe that the Koran is fiction. They can't both be right. (They could obviously both be wrong if the Heaven's Gate guys turn out to have it right.)

I fantasize about becoming president one day and insisting on settling the question of which religion is "right." I'd assemble all the experts on history and religion and science, and televise them arguing the merits and evidence of their sides, with cross-examination and, most important, mocking. There would be no stop date for this debate. It would continue until even a child could recognize which positions are the most easily mocked. Sometimes that's as close to wisdom as we can get.

Income Gap

I keep hearing pundits whining about the growing gap between the rich and the poor. I have difficulty empathizing with that viewpoint for two reasons: (1) Poor people can vote, and (2) There are more poor people than rich people.

In theory, those unhappy poor people could vote to tax the living piss out of the super rich. Why don't they do it?

I know you'll say the system is rigged in favor of big money, and the voters are manipulated into voting against their own self-interests. That's all true of course. Still, if you're looking to place blame, it has to be on the low-income people who don't vote. If ever there was an appropriate time for the phrase "It's your own damned fault," it's now.

Senior citizens vote like crazy (sometimes literally), and look at all the loot they get. Younger generations are paying those lazy Greatest Generation bastards more social security money than the retirees ever paid into the system. That's because seniors bother to vote. They're smart!

Personally, I don't vote. That's partly because I know there isn't enough information available for me to make an informed decision, and partly because the rich white guys in power (my peeps) are doing a good job of taking from the poor and giving to me. I don't have much to gripe about.

But if I were poor and planned to stay that way, I'd certainly take a free hour off of work every few years to vote for any goobers who planned to screw the rich and give me free stuff. And if that didn't work, I wouldn't be angry at Bill Gates. I'd be pissed at the moronic poor people who didn't bother to yank a handle so we could all get free stuff.

My Pet Peeves

People often ask me about my pet peeves. Here's a few that spring to mind.

Ambiguous Tipping Situations

I once gave a speech on an island that doesn't allow tipping. Gratuities were already included in the charges. This concept made me happy. But when I showed up, a guy took my bag from the car and loaded it onto the ferry that was going to the island. Was this part of the no-tipping zone or was he the last guy I have to tip before being *on* the island. *Gaaa!!!* I don't think the owners of the resort meant for my first impression of their island paradise to be rage, but I'm surprising that way.

Wrongly Accused Dumbass

One of the drawbacks of being unusually smart is that I rarely do things the way other people think those things should be done. This often makes me look like a dumbass. In theory, if I had infinite time, I could explain all of my actions to anyone who cared to listen. At the end of this explanation they would probably say, "I understand, now that you've explained it for the past three hours." But I don't have that kind of patience. Consequently, even my closest friends think I'm a dumbass half of the time, when I know it couldn't be more than a third of the time, tops.

Unclear Queues

It bugs me when I can't figure out who is next in line. I always blame the second person who arrived. The first person is blameless because one person can't form a line even if he tries. But that second bastard can doom twenty people to incurable tension by refusing to stand directly behind the first person in an obvious "this is the line" fashion. That second idiot will start drifting to the side, perhaps checking out nearby merchandise or reading signs. That's when the trouble begins.

The third person arrives and has no idea where to stand. It's starting to look random. By the fifth person, the odds skyrocket that I will be accused of line-cutting no matter what I do. I spend my entire time in line rehearsing my imaginary defense for how I really was behind the guy who keeps wandering around.

I know I should be worrying more about global warming, and less about tipping, and unclear queues, but I'm a dumbass. As far as you know.

German Cannibal

Did you hear about the German cannibal? It sounds like the beginning of a joke but it's not. A German guy had a lifelong fantasy of eating someone. So he ran an online ad for a volunteer. This is the funny part: A guy volunteered.

So the cannibal and the volunteer get together and they fulfill their mutual fantasies. The cannibal films the entire thing so we know for sure that the volunteer really did volunteer.

Anyway, the cannibal recently got convicted. He got a life sentence. Interestingly, eating people is not illegal in Germany. It's only the killing part that is prohibited, even if the guy volunteers to be killed.

This is all a long way of saying that I spent a good deal of yesterday wondering how the following conversation would have gone if the cannibal had gotten the death sentence.

> WARDEN: What do you want for your last meal?
>
> CANNIBAL: Did you save any of the guy I was trying to eat? I hardly touched him.
>
> WARDEN: Well, yes, his body is in a freezer in the evidence room. But that would hardly be appropriate.
>
> CANNIBAL: Why not? Cannibalism isn't illegal. And he's already dead.
>
> WARDEN: Yes, but I don't think . . .
>
> CANNIBAL: And you know he gave me his body to eat. You saw it on the videotape. So it's legally mine to eat.
>
> WARDEN: Um . . . technically, I suppose that's true.
>
> CANNIBAL: And the condemned man gets to eat anything he wants, right?
>
> WARDEN: Okay, okay. What do you want on the side? Maybe some broccoli?
>
> CANNIBAL: Broccoli? Yuck!

Wedding Registry

One of the curses of wedding planning is the whole gift-giving dilemma. This is especially acute for people like my fiancée and me because for us all material goods fall into one of these categories.

1. Already have it
2. Don't need it
3. Too expensive for a gift
4. What the hell is it?

We could tell people "no gifts," but that would cause them to fret about whether other people will give us gifts anyway. Or they'll have to think twice as hard to come up with a gift that is thoughtful and not a gifty gift. That piles uncertainty atop inconvenience and expense. That doesn't seem fair.

My friend Josh advised me that it's easier for everyone if we simply register at some store so people can choose from the list. This process involves spending many hours online selecting merchandise that we don't need and won't fit in the house. And that brings me to the biggest problem.

Two kids and a fiancée planted flags on all the good space in our home before I moved in. I have complete domain over three horizontal feet of closet space, three drawers, and the front left corner of a nightstand. I park my car at my office a block away. I managed to tuck my tennis bag between the dresser and the TV stand but I don't expect that to last.

Consequently, any new item that enters the house either has to be nailed to the ceiling or—and this is the part I fear—I have to throw away something. As the person in the household who has the lowest attachment to possessions, I figure my stuff will be the first to go. That means that when my fiancée and I shop for stuff to include in our gift registry, we have entirely different feelings about each potential item:

FIANCÉE: Hmm, this toaster is 2 percent better than the one we have. Let's add it to the list. And we'll keep the old one as a backup.

ME: There goes my tennis bag.

Wedding Favors

My fiancée, Shelly, and I are in the process of picking "favors" for our wedding. Allow me to explain the term *favors* to those of you who are foreigners, hillbillies, igno-ramuses, or me one week ago. A "favor" is a small gift for the wedding attendees. It's an allegedly useful item that's usually made of glass or metal. (Plastic and cardboard don't seem weddingish enough.) There might be a ribbon or a candle involved and it probably has some inscription to commemorate the event.

"Favor" is one of those great ironic names. To my way of thinking, you're not doing a guy a favor by giving him something he doesn't want and can't throw away. That's more like a penalty. In fact, I could imagine exactly this sort of penalty for minor crimes.

> JUDGE: You urinated in public. Your sentence is that you must keep this functionless knickknack somewhere in your home for the rest of your life.
> URINATOR: Noooooo!!!!

We plan to have alcohol at the reception. I worry that I'll guzzle a few Grey Gooses, corner some elderly relative, and say, "Heeyar. Pack thish liddle peesh of crap very carefully and then take it back and display it wiff your glass turtle collection. It's a little favor from ush to you."

I tried to deduce the purpose of wedding favors but came up dry. Obviously the gifts will not be chosen based on any need that is shared by the attendees. It is unlikely that anyone will get watery-eyed and say, "My life was a tragedy until I got this one champagne glass with some-one else's name on it. It completes me!"

Apparently the point of the wedding favors is to avoid embarrass-ing ourselves in front of the pope or Martha Stewart or whoever else we invited. Off the top of my head, I can't think of any of my friends or family who would judge us by the quality of the wedding favors, as in "I kind of liked them until the whole bottle-opener-with-a-bow incident."

I assume the judgmental invitee is one of Shelly's family members that I haven't yet met. There must be a picky aunt in the mix that's ruining it for everyone. Otherwise the attendees would be getting something useful like backscratchers or those cool flashlights that wind up.

My theory, already judged unhelpful, is that we should simply agree on a price-per-favor that is nonembarrassing and buy from the catalog-o-favors whatever is nearest that price. I'm thinking that anything below seventy-five cents apiece would be shameful, and anything over a hundred bucks would cause my relatives to start stealing.

Somewhere in that range there has to be a vase or a bottle stopper that doesn't look exactly like the ones at Costco. That plus a ribbon is all we can ask.

Flying Monkey Butt

Apparently some newspaper chose not to run this Dilbert comic from May 15, 2006, because it features a winged monkey emerging from a lawyer's butt.

As you might have noticed, I enjoy trying to figure out what I can get away with. I thought this one cleverly avoided the classic no-no categories. It's not sexual because the attorney isn't enjoying the monkey coming out of his butt. And it's not violent because the monkey is coming out of a preexisting body opening. It's not bathroom humor because technically the monkey is not a turd. And the lawyer's pants never come off so there is no nudity. I thought I covered all the bases.

I wasn't worried about defamation even though the lawyer looks exactly like my real life lawyer, Jeff. That is a total coincidence. And my deep understanding of the law is that he would have to prove that monkeys do *not* fly out of his ass. My defense would be "Let's just wait and see. It doesn't happen that often."

Most Optimistic Guy Ever

My favorite news story recently is about Louisiana congressman William Jefferson. The FBI allegedly videotaped him accepting $100,000 in cash from an informant. When the authorities searched his house they reportedly found the cash in his freezer, wrapped in food containers and aluminum foil. The serial numbers allegedly match the money the informant gave him.

That's not the funny part, although it's a good start. The funny part is that he's claiming he's innocent. I'm trying to imagine him on the witness stand explaining all of this away.

PROSECUTION: Congressman Jefferson, why did you put the money in food containers and store it in your freezer?

JEFFERSON: Well, I like my money to be chilled.

PROSECUTION: What?

JEFFERSON: Yes sir. I find that if I cool it to about sixteen degrees Fahrenheit, it doesn't stick together. You should try it.

PROSECUTION: Why did you think our informant was giving you $100,000 in cash? Didn't it seem like a bribe?

JEFFERSON: Heck no. You'd be surprised how many times people have given me $100,000 for no reason whatsoever. I had to put a second refrigerator in the garage just to keep it all chilled.

PROSECUTION: You have a second refrigerator?

JEFFERSON: Um . . . I'll say no.

PROSECUTION: You just said you do.

JEFFERSON: You can't prove that.

Anyway, the point is that I have to admire his optimism.

Pragmatic Party

Ioften fantasize about how I would fix everything if I were president. My fantasy is unfazed by the fact that the voting public is not keen on candidates that are unqualified, unattractive, godless, and morally bankrupt.

In my fantasy I form what I call the Pragmatic Party. All of my policies would be based on what is most practical. I would accuse my opponents of basing their policies on superstition—that is, the belief in supernatural beings. That's called framing the debate. It's also why I could never be elected. Well, that plus the parts about being unattractive, unqualified, and morally bankrupt. I'd get a ding for those things, too.

You need one Big Idea when you run for president. I would explain that our current system of government was conceived prior to the Internet, electronic mass media, and sophisticated polling methods. Two hundred years ago the only practical form of government involved voting for a small group of individuals who would pretend to represent you. Now we have better tools and we should use them. I would thus infer that my opponents are hole-pooping cavemen desperately clinging to the past. Again, that's called framing the debate. I'd get lots of TV time because the media would consider me a loose cannon. They like that.

The Pragmatic Party platform would always mirror the majority opinion of the country. When the majority opinion changed, so would my platform. I would be immune from accusations of flip-flopping because change would be built into the platform. I would say that electing a candidate that is unwilling to change is the same as electing a lamppost. During the first debate I would turn to my opponent and say, "Senator, explain to the people how you are different from a lamppost." That's the only sound bite the media would play all the next day.

Although my party's platform would mirror the majority for all "mature" issues, as president it would be my job to protect against the potential evil whims of the majority. I would rarely need to use this power to thwart the majority, and when I did I would explain it in pragmatic terms.

Example: "I know that the majority of you voted to kill all flute players and divvy up their wealth, but I think that doing so would be a bad precedent. Remember that every one of you is a minority of some sort." People would understand the reasoning even if they really hated flute players. It's hard to hate the practical.

There would be situations where the public's knowledge would not be adequate for the decision, such as national defense situations, especially those that develop quickly. I'd make those decisions, consulting with Congress and the relevant experts, and explain to the public later. At some point, when the public is up to speed, they can get involved. That's practical.

I would explain that the president shouldn't be leading the people, especially in moral questions. Presidents don't have a great track record of obeying the laws and keeping their trousers up. I say let the people decide what is moral. Getting your moral direction from politicians is like getting health tips from Keith Richards.

As president, I would refer to myself as the Chief Flashlight. I would shine light on whatever the citizens needed to know to form their opinions. I'd order the government to publish on the Internet continuous debates on all important issues. And I'd let the proponents of each side manage their sides of the debate. I'd order a team of independent researchers to attach links to any factual claims so you citizens can see for yourselves who is trying to hoodwink you. Both sides would be free to make any claims they like. But the independent team would always point the reader to the facts. Over time, the compulsive liars would lose all credibility and be pushed aside by their own people.

As president, I would rarely take sides on the major issues. My job would be to bring the best arguments on all sides of every issue to the citizens and help them make up their own minds. My administration would make it a top priority to improve how the government communicates with its citizens. And that might require making the information more entertaining or at least easier to digest. As a general rule I would say that if the citizens don't understand both sides of all important issues, I have failed as president. If the people need simple charts and graphs, I'll provide them. If they need puppet shows, I'll stick my hand in a tube sock and hide behind my desk. Whatever it takes.

My administration would not employ a White House spokesperson. Speaking to the press about American policy is the president's job. And I'd have a press conference daily. It wouldn't be difficult because virtually all of my policies would be based on the majority opinion. When people asked me why I had a certain policy, I'd point to the poll numbers and say, "Duh." If I did something to thwart the majority, as the president occasionally must, I would point to the majority of experts who advised me, and explain to the citizens how they can read up on the reasons for the decisions. I'd invite them to get involved when they are up to speed.

When the press tried to make me say I was 100 percent sure about my positions, I would say I wasn't. I'd explain that only an idiot is 100 percent sure of anything.

I would also keep a top twenty-five list of the biggest threats to the country. Threats would be categorized by both current and future potential. That list would form the basis for resource allocation policies. Even my budget proposals would be subject to direct input from the public. I'd insist on a running opinion poll for every major expense category. Those polls would not be binding, but Congress would have to explain any deviations from public opinion. Those deviations would be one of the main foci of the Big Flashlight.

As president I would support unlimited campaign contributions from any domestic source. But I would make it easy for citizens to see both the source of the contribution and the voting record of the recipients. I would fully expect the lobbyists to influence votes, and I'd condone it as long as the informed citizens preferred it to be condoned.

I would also publish all terror risks and natural disaster alerts on an ongoing basis. In the short run, there would be panic every time the government said, "Osama is targeting your town." But in the long run the citizens would see that there are so many threats that they can't judge them all to be real. And if some people want to leave town for a low-level threat, I say that is their right. I would help the citizens by requiring that all threats be given a ranking for likelihood. If you think a 2 percent risk of getting nuked is too high for you, it's your right to know that and to leave town.

I would do away with closed-door meetings, at least as far as the president is concerned, with the exception of defense issues. If the citizens can't see the thought process leading up to a decision, they have a legitimate reason to be concerned.

I would push for a constitutional amendment that allows two-thirds of the states to fire the congressmen from any other state. This would get rid of the guys who are crazy, flagrantly corrupt, or excellent at screwing the entire country by inserting pork benefits for their local constituents.

I would spend no time campaigning after being elected the first time. My methods would speak so loudly for themselves that there would be nothing to add. If the citizens wanted another four years, they know exactly what they'd be getting.

That is my fantasy.

Asok's Underpants

Here's another Dilbert comic that didn't make it past the editors at my syndication company, United Media. They felt that many newspapers would object.

As you can see, the image clearly shows Asok's naked buttocks. I don't doubt that newspapers would object; surely some of their readers would complain. It's a business decision, and I respect that.

But what exactly is there to complain about?

The image isn't sexual. It's difficult to imagine a minor looking at that image and deciding to become a gay hooker.

The objectionably naked part of Asok is one curved line. Should we also avoid the letter *C* because it looks too much like a butt crack? And don't get me started with the letters *OO*.

The image of Asok isn't scatological because I specifically drew his buttocks to be nonpooping. So unless a turtle head pops out (to quote Austin Powers), it's innocent on those charges, too.

Still, I do agree that people would complain. So I redrew him wearing huge underpants, and that seemed even funnier to me.

And then I redrew his butt crack on the underpants. No one complained.

Relativity

We humans generally assume that reality is fixed and objective. Therefore we assume that the reason other people view reality differently is because they are ignorant and/or irrational.

The problem with that view is that there are more well-informed and rational people opposing your worldview, no matter what your view is, than there are on your side. For example, lots of brilliant and well-informed people support my view that God is a delusion. But if we took a poll of the brilliant and well-informed people of the world, the majority would disagree with me. They'd be worshipping Allah or Jesus or Buddha or waiting to reincarnate. Likewise, every one of the brilliant and well-informed people in any of those groups is vastly outnumbered by people who disagree. This has always bothered me. So I came up with a theory to explain it.

Einstein's great insight was assuming reality was not fixed, and that everything was relative to the observer. If the observer moves at nearly the speed of light, not only does reality appear different, it actually *is* different. You would literally age at a different rate than your twin that stayed in place relative to you. We don't notice the differences in our tiny, slow-moving life. But it's there. The universe simply doesn't exist as a single objective reality. It's smeared all over the place.

I have extended that thinking to people. Let's imagine for the sake of my new theory that people are always rational within their own reality. It only seems as if they are not because we all live in our own bubble of reality, with our own rules of what makes sense. Within any given bubble, everything is perfectly rational and logical and all the dots connect. It's only when you try to send an argument from one bubble to another that the logic breaks down.

In my theory, it could be completely true for a Muslim that Allah exists in that individual's bubble of reality, and completely true for the infidel skeptic that Allah doesn't exist in his bubble. This is an extension of the old argument about whether people perceive the color red the same. For all practical purposes it doesn't matter for questions of color because we're all happy with our own perceptions and we can't see what other people see. But for questions of God, it matters, because when you describe the reasons for your belief, and those reasons leave your bubble, they arrive as complete nonsense when they enter my bubble. And if I feel the need to point that out, you might feel the need to bore me or kill me.

As with Einstein's theory of relativity, our different views of reality aren't relevant for most of life. We only notice the difference with a few topics. For example, in some bubbles of reality, the following reasoning makes complete sense:

> *The Earth couldn't create itself. Something had to create it. Therefore, God exists.*

In my bubble, and in many others, that line of thinking is indistinguishable from nonsense. It is the height of irrational and ignorant thinking, but only within my bubble and those like mine.

Now, to be fair, my thinking sounds equally irrational and ignorant to believers even though it makes perfect sense in my bubble. For example, I think this explanation seems sensible even if wrong:

> *The Earth couldn't create itself. Therefore the universe must have always been here, even if compressed into a singularity so that time as we know it doesn't have meaning.*

When I make that argument to religious people, they look at me like I just took a whiz on the couch while announcing that I plan to marry their daughter. My reasoning makes absolutely no sense after it leaves my bubble of reality and enters theirs. Somehow it turns into nonsense on the trip. When I try to explain my reasoning, it's like yelling English to a guy who only speaks Chinese and hoping the extra volume will help.

When I hear people say that they know God exists because he healed their aunt's cancer, it sounds to me exactly like "Rocks are liquid because five is greater than six." It sounds like utter nonsense when it leaves their bubble and enters mine. But I know it makes sense in their bubble. So something must be different in there.

In this theory, our brains are nothing but rationalizers for a reality too complex to understand. When I see cars driving down the street, perhaps you see kangaroos. If we take a cab together, I think we're sitting in the backseat and you think we're in a kangaroo's pouch. I think I'm leaving the cabbie a tip and you think I'm giving a treat to the roo.

If you doubt that reality differs for all observers, try watching some of the French Open tennis tournament on TV. Notice how many times the players see a line call one way, only to have the umpire point to the mark in the clay and prove them wrong. Then the TV commentators turn on the Shot Spot technology showing that both the player and the umpire missed it by a mile.

I welcome you to send your logic to my bubble, but don't be surprised if I react like you're a frickin' moron. It's nothing personal. It's a bubble thing.

What's My Lion?

As a rule, I don't like to laugh at the misfortune of others. The exception to that rule is if it's really, really funny.

Did you see the Reuters story about the man that jumped into a lion's habitat at the Kiev zoo and yelled, "God will save me, if he exists"? One of the lions, apparently an atheist, mauled him to death.

You might assume that the lion wanted to eat him. But I think the lion just wanted to shut him up. And when you are a lion, you don't have many tools. Here is the complete list of lion functions:

Napping
Killing
Eating
Pooping
Fornicating

There's only one thing on the list that was guaranteed to make the guy shut up, although that last one might have gotten him to change the subject to something more along the lines of "Nooo! Please! I was saving myself for the monkey habitat!"

This story presents more questions than answers. For example, was the guy a true believer trying to prove his faith, or was he an atheist who was tired of no one understanding his arguments? If he was a believer, was his faith too weak? Or was he unlucky and caught God on a break? Maybe God just turned to one of his cherubs and muttered something like, "I don't roll like that," because it seemed funny. If he did, the cherub would not laugh, because cherubs are basically babies with wings. So God would either have to resort to a poop joke or a miracle to make that baby laugh.

All we can hope is that people learn something from this tragedy. For example, the next time a believer jumps into the lion habitat, he should yell, "If God exists, he will order this lion to kill me!" That way, everyone wins.

Best Gift Ever

One of the best gifts I've ever received was a losing lottery ticket. My brother bought it for me. I realize that doesn't sound like a great gift, since it only cost a dollar, and it lost. But the way he did it was pure evil genius.

No one wants to buy a winning lottery ticket for someone else. You'd bang your head on the wall for the rest of your life, yelling, "Why oh why didn't I keep that one??? Whaaawhaaaawhaaaa!!!" That's bad for the wall.

My brother solved that problem by buying for himself two additional lottery tickets with the same numbers as the one he got for me. He explained that in case my ticket won, he wanted to be twice as rich. It's the thought that counts.

That happened years ago. Since then, I've told that story about a hundred times, always to good effect. Now it's a book chapter on a day when I had no other ideas. It's the gift that keeps on giving. Almost every other gift I've gotten has been worn out, outgrown, used up, lost, broken, stolen, or thrown away. But the lottery ticket story keeps chugging along.

In its own way, it was the most thoughtful gift I've ever received.

Night of the Living Ant

O ne of the perks of being a big-time celebrity cartoonist involves using a vacuum cleaner to get rid of ants in the kitchen. Before I made it big, I couldn't afford a vacuum cleaner. I had to shout at the ants to scare them away. In retrospect, I don't think ants have ears, because yelling never worked. Sometimes I had to keep my snacks in a wooden bowl floating in the bathtub. Eventually, when the ant army built up to the point where they could lift me in my sleep, but before they could get me down the ant hole, I would give notice on my apartment and find another.

Now I can afford high-tech vacuum weaponry. It's sweet. I'm not allowed to use the "good" vacuum cleaner, obviously. That one is only for the carpet. I use the one that no longer stays locked in the upright position. So I suck up a few ants, then the vacuum cleaner falls over and impales my thigh. I curse, return the vacuum to its unlocked upright position, and repeat. Suck-ow-%$&*#. Suck-ow-%$&*#. Suck-ow-%$&*#. Someday I hope to buy a new vacuum cleaner exclusively for ants.

Eradicating ants in the kitchen is exactly like being attacked by zombies, except the zombies are very small and the worst thing they can do is walk on your crackers. As you know, when zombies attack, you can kill several hundred of them with your automatic weapons and flamethrowers and stabby things, but additional zombies keep on coming as if they hadn't noticed. Ants are just like that. They really aren't good at pattern recognition. You can vacuum six hundred ants in a straight line and yet ant six hundred and one won't see it coming. He'll be all "Hey, why am I suddenly in this bag full of dust? Carl, is that you?"

I get a perverse pleasure out of every ant that goes down the hose. It would bother me if they screamed in pain or begged for their lives, but they don't, so it's all good. Every time a new ant appears on the cabinet door, I delight in sending him to dustbag heaven. Ahhh, good times.

The only other household chore I enjoy as much as ant eradication is cleaning the cat box. It's like panning for gold, except the gold is cat poop. That inconvenient fact doesn't detract from the thrill of the find as much as you'd think. There's something in our basic DNA that likes to find free stuff, even if the stuff is turds. Arguably, I paid for the cat food, so the nuggets aren't really free. But as long as there's some time lag between the paying and the prospecting, it's still a low-grade thrill.

Fecalruba

angered the entire population of Aruba with this comic on June 14, 2006:

Man, did I get angry e-mail from Aruba when that comic ran. Apparently the Arubans, or Arubians, or Arubitarians—whatever they call themselves—think Fecalruba is my way of mocking Aruba. Apparently they're still quite touchy about the bad press when American Natalee Holloway disappeared there. If there are two things you could say to hurt tourism, they are:

1. When you visit our country, we might let someone kill you and then not solve the crime.

Or...

2. The island and all of the structures are made of fecal matter.

Neither of those statements is 100 percent true of course, but the Arubatheenians are worried that tourists might come to think of their island as a turd-scented murder pit when in fact it is quite delightful and pleasing to both the nose and the eye.

I must confess that my knowledge of geography stops just short of "tiny islands that are somewhere." So I don't know if they are developing nukes, or they have a crack team of hit men controlled by the board of tourism, but I no longer feel safe. I have this mental image of a small pod of genetically engineered Arubistanians swimming toward California like porpoises, all menacing-looking.

So let me say right now that Fecalruba is a totally different country from Aruba. In Fecalruba, they have an excellent track record of solving crimes.

Brushes with Fame

One of the benefits of being easily frightened is that I avoid a lot of potentially painful experiences via a process I call "running like a scared rabbit." That came in handy today on the plane during the boarding process. I was already in my aisle seat when a klutzy guy tried to stuff his carry-on bag in the overhead bin directly above me. I heard the flight attendant yell a warning and the next thing I knew I was diving toward the window seat while the luggage bounced off the top of the seat where my head had been. I believe I screamed like a little girl being mauled by a crocodile. It just sort of slipped out.

Normally my cowardice would not be so embarrassing, but as luck would have it, the next three passengers in the aisle—the ones most closely observing this ugly situation—were soldiers in full army fatigues. They laughed and complimented me on my ducking abilities. Then they probably went to Iraq and battled insurgents. I'm just saying that the contrast wasn't lost on anyone.

But that's not my point. I often wonder during these random encounters with strangers if any of them are Dilbert fans. The guy that almost nailed me with his luggage had that "I work in technology" look about him, if you know what I mean. There's some nonzero chance that he's a Dilbert reader and has no idea he almost took me out. I wanted to tell him, just so he'd have a good story that no one would believe. "You know that Dilbert comic? I almost killed the guy that does that."

I was once on a business trip, in my corporate days, and noticed that Grace Slick and the Jefferson Starship were on the same flight. My coworker had a camera bag slung over his shoulder and wasn't controlling it as he worked his way down the aisle. He turned to say something to me and his camera bag whacked Grace in the back of her noggin so hard that she never again had a successful album. It might be a coincidence, but I like to think it wasn't.

When I tell people I grew up in Windham, New York, I'm surprised how many people say they have skied at the Windham Ski Slope. Sometimes they skied there during my high school years when I worked in the ski lodge on weekends, 1974–75. I ask if they remember buying a hamburger at the snack bar. If they did, there's a good chance I was the guy who cooked it.

And if your family ever vacationed at the Sugar Maples resort in the Catskills from 1975 to 1979, there's a good chance I carried your bags or poured your coffee. However, if your daughter told you stories of getting drunk and dirty dancing with a member of the staff, that was a lifeguard named Ted.

My Self-Absorbed Arrogance

Here's the quandary, as I see it. There are three qualities I want to have: (1) success, (2) honesty, (3) humility.

At most, logically, I can only have two of the three. It's impossible to have them all. For example, if your life is a complete disaster, it's fairly easy to be humble while being honest, as in "To tell you the truth, I'm a worthless pimple on the ass of society. You could strangle me with my own putrid bedsheet and no one would notice I was gone."

Things get tricky with success. Suddenly there are huge chunks of your life that you can't mention without appearing to brag, even though they are nothing more than a description of what you did today. And omitting them seems somehow dishonest. In the old days, pre-Dilbert, when someone asked me about my day I would simply recount what I did in the wittiest way I could. Now if someone asks me what's new, I have to say things like "not much" or "the usual." Other times I just complain about how busy I am without offering details. If forced to talk about myself, I have to focus on some story that shows how unlucky or incompetent I am. Anything else would sound arrogant. Nowadays, if I step in a huge pile of dog crap, my first thought is, "Excellent. Now I have something to talk about if someone asks me how my day went." I'm not complaining; being a minor celebrity is a great deal. But there is a strange sort of loneliness that comes with it, and I never would have expected it.

I owe my current understanding of this phenomenon to my ex-friend Amy who taught me that no one likes an honest successful person. She taught me this lesson by not liking me after success "changed me." And by changed I mean I acted exactly the same as I always did, but that honesty seemed grotesque when things started going my way. Any mention of what I was thinking or doing during these successful times automatically sounded arrogant and braggy.

Let me show you how this works. I just got back from giving a speech in Miami, at the Jackie Gleason Theater. The "honest" story is so full of celebritylike experiences that you'd want to punch me if I described it. So if any of my friends ask how it went, I'll tell them the following true story:

I walked out of the hotel to meet a car that would take me to the theater at seven a.m. to check the AV setup. As I walked toward the waiting car, two supermodel-looking women in their early twenties, wearing practically nothing, noticed me walking past. One was behind the wheel of a nice car and her friend was talking to her from the side. The driver flashed me a huge smile and said in a flirty-pouty voice, "Are you leaving us so soon?" My response was, and I quote, "Uhh, blpshdph amsp fphr wah." You see, supermodel-looking women wearing next to nothing rarely strike up conversations with me, so I wasn't prepared. Nor do they represent my target demographic for Dilbert, so I was confident they didn't recognize me.

The supermodel-looking driver reacted to my unintelligible mumble by smiling seductively. When I got in the car and looked back to get my last "bonus" supermodel glance, the woman behind the wheel was looking directly at me, with an obvious "I want you now" expression. Again I was caught off guard, because no supermodel-looking woman has ever looked at me when she could be looking at something else, such as a lamppost or the sky. I thought to myself, "I must look good in this shirt."

But there was one other theory that I couldn't rule out. I asked the driver, "Are those women high-priced hookers?"

"Yeah," he said. "They're probably just getting done from last night."

Still, I do think I looked good in that shirt.

A Tail by Any Other Name

Wouldn't it be great to have a tail? It would come in handy for so many different household chores. For example, when I iron a shirt, I want to hold the shirt, the iron, and the electrical cord to keep it out of the way. There's no way you can do that without a tail. That's why I keep all of my good shirts balled up in a heap in the back of the closet. There's no point in even trying.

That's also why I read with great jealousy the news report of the former handyman who won more than $400,000 in a lawsuit over a penile implant that gave him a ten-year erection.

He must have been the fastest handyman ever. When I do home projects, I never have a good place to keep the roll of duct tape. I'm all "Where did I put that duct tape? Is it under the cardboard?" Not this guy. He'd have his various types of tape, coils of wire, and, depending on how lucky Mrs. Handyman was, several more items right there when he needed them.

And I can imagine him up on his ladder, needing to hammer in a nail and realizing he forgot to bring his hammer.

"Hmm, I could climb all the way down and get my hammer . . . or . . ."

Looks left. Looks right. *Ziiiiiip. Bam bam bam bam.*

Problem solved.

According to the article, the only downside is that it was embarrassing to hug people. If I were him, I wouldn't do any hugging. I'd put a glove on it and keep one arm behind my back all the time. And I'd shake hands with everyone I met. You can't tell me that would ever get old.

A Dilbert reader alerted me to the true story of a man in India who was born with a thirteen-inch tail. People think he's a reincarnation of the Hindu monkey god Hanuman. The man claims that people are cured of severe ailments when they touch his tail.

According to the press, he also likes climbing trees and eating bananas. Seriously.

Doctors have offered to remove the tail. They don't think he is a monkey god at all. The tail seems like more of a congenital defect to them. This raises an interesting question: How can you tell the difference between a reincarnated monkey god and an ordinary tree-climbing, banana-eating guy with a disease-healing tail?

For that matter, how do we know for sure he isn't just an extraordinarily well-endowed guy who realized that if he tucked his unit behind him, diseased people would want to touch it? I'm assuming he gets lots of free bananas in this arrangement, too, so it's a sweet deal.

And this brings me to one of my little rules in life. I have many rules that apply to many different situations. Some of the rules are used more often than others. Here's one I rarely use, but it seems relevant:

Rule 472: Before you touch a monkey god's tail to cure your leprosy, make sure the tail doesn't have a little hole in the end.

Night of the Living Doormen

Yesterday I gave a speech at a hotel in San Francisco. Afterward, the hotel valet was retrieving my car as I waited out front. I guarded my tiny carry-on-sized bag against the two drooling doormen as their eyelids made cha-ching sounds. You could almost hear them thinking, "If I can touch his bag, he'll have to give me money."

Just to be clear, I am a generous tipper. I tip for good service, I tip for putrid service, and sometimes I tip just because someone is dressed as a person who expects to be tipped. Long ago, I also worked for tips, so I have no problem with the tipping system in general. And I figure that the people who can afford to tip well have some obligation to keep up the average. I'm fine with that, and happy to do my part. But there are exceptions.

One exception is a doorman who takes the bag from my hand, then turns around and puts it in my car. This is an unnecessary service that usually just slows me down. It takes about the same amount of time to hand a guy a bag and have him put it in the trunk as it does to put it there myself. And I have been opening doors by myself for years. I'm good at it. If I have to stop while the doorman lunges in front of me to get my door, it just kills my momentum. It's like the homeless guy who washes your windshield at the stoplight; the service is useful, but you still feel vaguely mugged.

My rule is that if I can prevent the doorman from touching my bag, I can avoid tipping and still maintain a clear conscience. "What kind of car do you have?" asked the doorman, obviously planning to make his move when the valet arrived. I thought about giving him a fake car model so I could get the advantage. My plan was to unlock my trunk with my right hand while holding my tiny bag with the left, using my body to shield the bag from the doorman.

That's when I got distracted. The valet pulled up with my car and I made the mistake of tracking it with my eyes before grabbing my bag.

The doorman lunged. He was a pro. He did a reach-around, snatch-and-go, and headed for my car. Shit, I thought, there goes two bucks.

Then the valet jumped out of the car. He lunged for the trunk in an effort to maximize his tip, but the doorman beat him. I wondered how many times a day these two competed to open the trunk, and if the result had any impact on the valet-doorman tip distribution. I handed the valet a five, gave the doorman two bucks, and thought I was in the clear. But the valet stayed.

"That's a nice car." He dawdled.

"Thanks," I answered, as if I had built it from a kit and was personally responsible for it being nice.

"Do you need any directions?" he asked.

I did need directions, but now I wondered how much that would cost me. It seemed like my five bucks should cover both the car-related compliment and some free directions, but I wasn't sure. Maybe directions are worth an extra dollar. But if he throws in some time-saving tips like "Take Davis Street to avoid the construction" then maybe that's worth even more. I hated the vagueness.

So I said, "No, thanks," got in my car, and proceeded to get lost for the next forty-five minutes. But I saved a dollar. Or not. I'll never really know.

My Own Army

I wonder how much it would cost to have my own army of third-world mercenaries. I'd want them as more of a status symbol than a fighting force. Obviously I'd have to hire my soldiers from a country where the annual wage is $1.25, otherwise it gets expensive. And they'd have to stay in that country. I'd outsource the whole project.

My army's only duty would be to march in formation several times a day and shout songs about my glory. The whole thing would probably cost me less than a few thousand per year. And for that modest sum, I'd have a cool answer every time someone said to me, "You and whose army?" I'd have pictures of my army in my wallet and just whip them out. Then I'd say something like, "Here's the 101 Infantry Division. This fellow on the end, Gbernak, he can swim. He's my amphibious landing force."

I would lend my army to multinational peacekeeping forces whenever it was hard to get a coalition. It would be fun to watch President Bush explain who was joining the next coalition. "Well, our coalition is growing. So far we have the United States . . . and Puerto Rico. . . . I think Hawaii is on board. Japan is sending some bandages. And of course we have the Army of Scott Adams. They spend most of the day hiding, but we're sure they're with us."

Tennis

Later today I have a tennis match against a twenty-year-old woman who plays for her college team on a tennis scholarship. Her mom is a tennis pro at the health club where I play. I am still formulating my strategy for avoiding embarrassment. My current plan is to run headfirst into the net post when the score reaches 5–0.

My tennis skill is about 4.0. For you non–tennis players, that means I can do most of the things a professional tennis player can do, but not as well as he would do it. For example, I can hit a blistering forehand with heavy topspin on a full run . . . into the bottom of the net. And I can hit a crisp approach shot and follow it to the net while cutting off the angle before my opponent drives the ball into my solar plexus and I lose consciousness.

My best weapon is my surprising speed. It's surprising in the sense that evidently I look as if I can't run more than five yards without collapsing. My opponents always express amazement that I "got to that one." I think it has something to do with the fact that when I exercise my face looks like I got in a slap fight with Uma Thurman. (She has gigantic hands.)

My other weapon is a little thing I call the mis-hit. The better players never see it coming. My opponent will slam a punishing crosscourt forehand and I'll use a creative part of my racket—usually the frame or some part of the grip—to produce a ball trajectory that looks like a Kennedy on New Year's Eve. My opponent thinks I'm just lucky the first five times I do it. After that, I usually get some respect. At least that's how I interpret the swearing and grimacing.

I will stop here and update you on the match afterward.

[This next part was written after the match.]

The good news is that I hit enough "Kennedys" to actually win. The bad news is that my opponent has renounced tennis and joined the Witness Protection Program so that no one at the club will ask her how the match went.

Planning My Funeral

Yesterday I was planning my funeral, and not just because of the things I've said about people. Preparing a will is one of those things you do before you get married, and yes I do see the irony in that. No need to point it out.

Anyway, part of the estate planning process involves funeral directions. This is creepy because you spend a lot of time imagining yourself dead. And I have an unusually good imagination. A few more minutes of that and I would have been looking for a pottery class to haunt. Come to think of it, it's been awhile since anyone gave me eye contact or answered a question.

First I had to decide whether I wanted to be buried, cremated, or stuffed and kept in the foyer with a menacing expression to scare children. I think I'd be an excellent coatrack. Depending on what I was doing when I died, I might even provide a place to hang an umbrella.

After much research, I discovered that the coatrack option is less legal than you'd expect. That meant the choice was between being buried and incinerated. I carefully considered which option would be worse in the event that I suddenly sprung back to life. Would it be worse to be underground in a box or heading toward the oven on an unstoppable conveyor belt? I realize the doctors check corpses thoroughly these days to make sure they're really dead. And I have to think that the embalming fluid would answer any lingering questions about sitting up. But still, I don't want to take a chance. I reasoned that the flames would be quicker, so I went with cremation.

Next I had to decide what to do with my ashes. My first idea was to require each of the attendees at the funeral to dab some of my ashes on their chins. That would make for witty conversation at the ceremony as everyone tried to guess what part of me they were wearing—for example, "Hey, Bob, I think his scrotum is on your chin—*again!* Ha ha ha!"

Another tough decision involves, as the lawyers say, "designating the beneficiaries of my estate." Or as I say, deciding who will have the biggest financial incentive to kill me. My family members who enjoy reading murder mysteries or watching *CSI* went right to the bottom of the list. Pacifists, vegetarians, and people too feeble to wield blunt objects got some extra consideration.

I also had a problem imagining that anyone I currently know would still be alive when I die several hundred years from now. I'm a non-smoking vegetarian who exercises regularly. I'm only one or two medical advances from immortality. There's a good chance I'll end up leaving everything to my cat Mittens the Twenty-seventh and the janitor at the rest home. So it all feels like a big waste of time. But it's one of those things you have to do.

My favorite part of the plan involved the "special instructions" for my funeral. I'm requiring all the attendees to tell one filthy joke in front of the crowd. (True) Get yours ready in case you're invited.

Ken Lay

Does it seem suspicious to you that ex-Enron CEO Ken Lay died right before they could put his guilty ass behind bars?

I wonder how many doctors you need to bribe to fake your own death. Is one enough? Or is there some special double-checking that the police do if the guy is heading for prison? I'm sure there's a body, but I wonder if it's his. I have a bad feeling that some pizza delivery guy's last words to his coworkers were "Hey, I have a delivery to that Enron guy's house! Wish me luck!"

My favorite Ken Lay story is that he rented his wife a $200,000 boat while they were already $100 million in debt. His explanation was "It's hard to just turn that kind of lifestyle off." That was the moment I believed his defense—that he was so frickin' stupid he didn't know he was a thief.

But now that he's conveniently "dead," I wonder if anyone is checking the whereabouts of the wife's rented boat. I wonder if it got reported stolen just about the time that Kenny allegedly died.

My theory is that Ken, if that's his real first name, named himself after a bag of chips, scammed his way up the corporate ladder, stole a few hundred million dollars, faked his death, and sailed to Aruba, where dead people are rarely found.

Last but Not Leashed

Yesterday I was trudging the forty-seven-second commute from my office to my home and passed a father taking his two-year-old son for a walk. On a leash.

Yes, the man was walking his child like a dog. The leash design was ingenious. It was actually a backpack/harness arrangement featuring a puppy as the backpack, with the leash coming from the puppy's tail area. The kid seemed delighted with the arrangement as he strained against the leash. And the father had no worries about the kid darting into traffic for at least two good reasons: (1) The kid was on a leash; and (2) There was no traffic.

In fact, we were the only people on the street. So in effect, the father had his son on a leash to protect him from me. I would take offense but it probably happens more often than I realize.

My first reaction to the kid on the leash is that it was humiliating and wrong. But the kid seemed happy enough. And so it made me wonder if the father is ever tempted to take it to the next level—that is, walking the kid naked and picking up the turds with a plastic bag. That has got to be easier than changing a diaper. If it weren't, dogs would wear diapers. I think that's obvious. And once you've decided that humiliation isn't an issue, all bets are off.

This reminds me of an excellent invention I thought of the other day. I noticed that conscientious dog owners spend half of their dog-walking time carrying bags of poop—presumably from their dogs. My idea is to make the dogs carry it. The invention would be like a harness for the dog with a tiny sultan's carriage on his back. The bag-o-feces would go in the sultan's carriage. The real money would be in selling the accessories, such as the little turban for the bag of poop. I'd call it the Turdbin. With this invention, people will no longer look upon the poop-toting dog-walker with a combination of pity and bemusement. People will think the dog owner is resourceful and stylish. And that's the best you can hope for when you're transporting feces.

Secret Society

My favorite conspiracy theory is the one that says the world is being run by a handful of ultra-rich capitalists, and that our elected governments are mere puppets. I sure hope it's true. Otherwise my survival depends on hordes of clueless goobers electing competent leaders. That's about as likely as a three-legged dog with the shakes pissing the Mona Lisa into a snowbank. In the summer.

The only way I can get to sleep at night is by imagining a secret cabal of highly competent puppet-masters who are handling the important decisions while our elected politicians debate flag burning.

It's the only explanation for how the governments of the world could be staffed with morons and yet everything still runs okay, sort of. Granted, things aren't perfect, but when you hear our leaders talk, you have to wonder why our energy policy doesn't involve burning asbestos on playgrounds. There must be some competent people pulling the strings behind the curtain, adjusting the money supply, twiddling with interest rates, choosing the winners for *American Idol*, and that sort of thing.

I know some of you will say that it's obvious that corporate money influences the government. But that's not enough to make me feel comfortable. I want to know there's an actual meeting of the puppet-masters every Thursday at three p.m. I want to know that when one of them suggests a new policy, the group votes by pressing buttons on their chairs, and if the idea is deemed bad, the offender drops through a hole in the floor and is eaten by a golden shark. You can't tell me that democracy produces better policies than the golden shark method.

I also dream of one day being invited to join the secret cabal as an apprentice puppet-master. I wouldn't qualify based on my net worth, so I'd have to hope there was a Dilbert fan in the group. Dilbert fans are unpredictable, so there's some chance he'd just want to extract the carbon from my body and keep it in a locket. The puppet-masters probably have a machine for just that purpose. But it's a chance I'm willing to take.

Once I got on the inside (of the cabal, not the locket), I would distinguish myself with my excellent ideas for running the world. For example, I would require that cigarette butts be made of soy protein so that street people could eat the ones they find in the cracks of sidewalks. It's good for the environment and everyone wins. That's my best idea, but I'll think up some more just in case.

Reno

This weekend I was in Reno to attend a quickie chapel wedding, just two weeks before my own. I couldn't stop crying at the ceremony. I was just sobbing uncontrollably. By the end I was standing in a pool of my own tears. I've never been so emotional in my life.

But none of it had to do with the bride and groom. I was bawling because the entire affair cost less than I paid in gas money to drive to Reno. My own upcoming wedding will cost—and I'm rounding off here—somewhere in the neighborhood between "a shitload" and whatever it cost to occupy Iraq. And the day after this expense, we will be no more married than the Reno couple. You'd think that the extra money would make us somehow extra married, or we'd get the deluxe version, as in "I now pronounce you man and wife, plus Yvette the handmaiden."

And don't get me started about the planning effort. I've spent about two man-weeks so far just answering phone calls from invitees about what the weather will be and what they should wear. At the Reno wedding, I wore shorts. The guy next to me from the previous half-hour wedding had a mullet and a white jacket. To my left was family friend Joey, wearing a T-shirt with a colorful word writ huge on the back. It would be impolite to mention the word, but it started with M and ended with rfucker. That might qualify as a first for wedding attire. Joey explained that he didn't see the point in changing his shirt for a wedding that would last ten minutes. I had only met Joey once before, but I think he might become my new best friend.

The best indication of how much planning went into the Reno wedding is that when the minister asked for the marriage license, all he got was blank stares. We had to wait forty-five minutes while the betrothed motored down to city hall to take care of that detail.

Now *that* is a wedding.

After the ceremony, during the awkward milling around and ignoring the groom's relatives that I will never see again, an employee of the chapel tapped me on the shoulder. She asked if I would sign as a witness to the wedding. "Sure," I said, always wanting to be helpful. I get asked to autograph things all the time, so it's second nature. I whipped out a pen and signed right there, without giving it a second thought.

Until later.

At some point, a few minutes after signing, it dawned on me that it's somewhat of an honor to be the witness to a wedding. Perhaps the bride and groom had someone else in mind. Oh, shit. I wondered how long it would take them to notice that I had bestowed that honor on myself.

Thanks to an extraordinary coincidence, I had a plausible alibi. Another attendee of the wedding has my exact name: Scott Adams. The coincidence was a running joke before the ceremony. I planned to blame him if the topic ever came up. I tried to visualize the conversation in advance so I could act natural.

> BRIDE: Did you sign as the witness? Good lord, don't you know that the bride and groom get to decide who signs that?
>
> ME: Oh great, now I'm being framed by that Scott Adams asshole. I knew I couldn't trust your friends. And don't let him deny it either.

I'll have a tougher time explaining why the other Scott Adams signs his name exactly like I do. My plan, if pressed, is to take a crystal out of my pocket and describe how nature provides coincidences in clusters so that we can know our place in the universe.

If that doesn't work, I'll accuse the other Scott Adams of being a forger in addition to a liar. That might seem cruel, but I never asked him to copy my name. He knew the risks.

Petting the Cat

Did you ever wonder what it's like to be a cat and have a giant human hand petting you? Speaking as a human, I generally like it when ordinary-sized hands touch me. But I wouldn't like gigantic hands on me. I feel sorry for cats. Giant hands are creepy.

I was thinking about this because I got a massage when I was in Reno. Reno calls itself "the biggest little city in the world." That's a marketing way of saying that most of the residents and visitors are morbidly obese. I can vouch for that.

Let me be clear that I do not approve of making fun of overweight people. Those who mock the hefty are delusional because they believe in the superstition of willpower. They believe that some people have a lot of this nonexistent willpower substance whereas overweight people have less of it.

I believe that willpower is an illusion. Overweight people simply get more enjoyment from food than thin people do, at least relative to their other pleasure options. If I liked food more than I like playing tennis, I'd be the size of a house. Willpower never enters into it.

You can see my theory play out with kids. Kids have no willpower, yet many of them are skinny. The skinny ones get so little pleasure from noncandy food that they prefer starving and playing with a friend to eating. It's a chore to make them eat. The overweight kids are the opposite. They also have no willpower—just like every other kid—but for some reason they get more pleasure from food. It's the same for adults. Some are passionate about food; some just see it as fuel.

Having made this defense of the portly, this story requires me to point out that some people are larger than others. Deal with it.

I was sitting in the men's locker room waiting for my masseuse at one of the big hotels in Reno. Because the masseuses were mostly women, and this was the men's locker room, the masseuse would crack open the door and call your name when you were next. The door was frosted glass, so I could see the silhouette of a petite woman at the door. Her tiny voice beckoned, "Mr. Johnson? Hi, I'm Nicole, your masseuse for today."

Mr. Johnson departed for his massage and I was the only one left. I kept an eye on the frosted glass door for my very own Nicole. What I saw instead was a total eclipse. Some sort of huge mass blocked the light coming through the door. *Oh, dear God, no,* I thought. But it moved past, to my relief. Then the huge mass reappeared from the other direction. It was like a bad monster movie when you know the beast is on the other side of the door. The doorknob turned and I considered running, but it was too late. "Mr. Adams?" boomed the voice. Jabba the Rubber had me.

In the past I have had massages from practitioners who were sporting extra pounds, and it obviously made no difference in the massage. But this masseuse wasn't just a big eater, she was a big person. Her hands were the biggest I have ever seen. I felt like Shaquille O'Neal's pet squirrel.

Since it was Nevada, and I know you'll ask, let me say that there was no happy ending. The beginning and middle weren't too festive either. It felt like being smothered with an oily mattress.

And that is why I pet my cat with one finger.

Phone Whores

I'm sitting at the Oakland airport. The airline claims my flight will be delayed one hour, but I know that's only the opening bid. I'm suspicious of round numbers. If they said the flight was going to be forty-seven minutes late, I'd think they had a good handle on things. But one hour is the same as saying, "Honestly, we don't even know how those big metal things stay in the air."

I'm a bit jumpy anyway because I'm getting married in a few days. I tell everyone I'm not nervous about it but that doesn't square with the fact that every time I eat a sandwich it falls straight down my throat, out my ass, down my pant leg, and just sits there looking at me. It's not even dirty. So I tell the kids I made an extra sandwich and see who wants it. No point in wasting food. Anyway, my point is that I'm already a bit on edge today. And then the worst thing happened: A phone whore sat down next to me.

In case you are not familiar with a term that I just made up, a phone whore is a woman who goes to the airport with no magazines, laptops, books, puzzles, or other means to entertain her. All she has is a phone, and she's going to use it, no matter how many people are annoyed.

To be gender fair, every flight I've been on has at least one man who needs to bellow away on his phone until the flight attendant starts slapping him with a rolled up in-flight magazine. But that guy isn't a phone whore. He's a phone asshole. It's a subtle difference.

The phone whore is motivated by the desire to talk with people. The phone asshole is motivated by the need to have everyone on the flight know he's negotiating important business deals and that he has staff members who must receive his wisdom. The phone asshole sounds like this: "ALLEN, THIS IS BOB. LET'S NAIL DOWN THAT AJAX DEAL EVEN IF WE HAVE TO THROW ANOTHER TEN MILLION AT IT. REMEMBER THAT QUALITY IS MORE IMPORTANT THAN PRICE. THAT'S SOMETHING I'VE BEEN TRYING TO TEACH JOE, FRANCINE, AND ERIC, WHO ALL WORK FOR ME IN CASE ANY-

ONE LISTENING ISN'T ALREADY IMPRESSED WITH MY HUGE BARREL CHEST AND UNNATURALLY DEEP VOICE."

The phone whore sounds more like, "Hi, this is Mindy. How's your new kitten?"

See? Completely different.

Within seconds of sitting, the phone whore starts dialing. I don't know if she's calling people in alphabetical order or what, but she's six calls into it, and it's obvious there will be no end. I could move to another seat, but I like my seat, and I suffer from an irrational form of optimism that tells me she "only has a few calls left." Surely I can endure a few calls.

But rationally, I know that her only options for the next two hours of waiting for our delayed flight are: (1) Stare straight ahead, and (2) Annoy the living piss out of me by blabbing on her phone.

To make matters worse, a crazy-talker just sat on my right. This one is a guy with a laptop, traveling alone, who feels the need to express astonishment and disgust at whatever the hell he's looking at. It's an invitation to converse, but I'm doing my best Helen Keller impression and hoping the Pakistani guy on his other side takes the bait.

To recap, I've got a phone whore on my left, a crazy-talker on my right, a sandwich in my pant leg, and I'm pretending to be blind and deaf. Meanwhile I'm waiting for some disgruntled mechanic to determine how much wadded toilet paper it will take to plug a hole in the fuselage and get my plane to the gate.

Otherwise it's a good trip so far.

Funny News

Do you ever wonder how much of the news is nothing but an inside joke? The other day I was reading an AP story about how hot it was in Chicago. The heat was a particular problem for the Gay Games VII because they expected a lot of heat exhaustion issues. The paragraph that made me scratch my head said: "Chicago hit 94 by 3 p.m., but it didn't bother Frank Lee of Manoa, Hawaii, who was competing in the event's tennis matches and planned to drink plenty of water and eat bananas."

I have to wonder if the reporter just kept asking questions until the gay athlete said something naughty-sounding. Notice that Mr. Lee's thoughts weren't put in quotes, which makes me think the exchange went something like this:

> REPORTER: How do you plan to deal with the heat?
>
> GAY ATHLETE: I'll probably drink lots of water.
>
> REPORTER: Will you eat any fruit (hee hee!)?
>
> GAY ATHLETE: No, I had a big breakfast. I'll just need water.
>
> REPORTER: How about a huge zucchini? Does that interest you?
>
> GAY ATHLETE: Um, no. I'm not really hungry.
>
> REPORTER: Do you know that bananas are good for you when you exercise?
>
> GAY ATHLETE: I suppose.
>
> REPORTER: So if someone offers you a banana (hee hee!) will you take it?
>
> GAY ATHLETE: I guess the potassium would be . . .
>
> REPORTER: That's all I need. Good-bye.

I have some sympathy for the reporter whose job it is to write about the weather for the benefit of people who can't tell that it's hot outside. The Pulitzer Prize committee isn't impressed by that sort of thing. Apparently no one had yet died in the heat wave so there weren't any good stories about how grandma's body melted and stuck to the linoleum.

The only way to spice up a story that has all the drama of "it is hot" is by adding gratuitous controversial elements. Luckily the Gay Games were happening. Otherwise the reporter would have had to look all over the city for a Planned Parenthood clinic with a broken air conditioner, or an antifur protest where everyone was naked and forgot sunscreen.

By the way, I can predict the news for any thirty-day period in the middle of the summer:

It is hot!
There's trouble in the Middle East!
The stock market is down, just like every summer!
Cars that will never come to market get great mileage!
Osama is still hiding!

But I'm just guessing.

Sleepless in California

'm in full-out prewedding mode. And that means multitasking, no matter how much I'd prefer to avoid it. For example, at about 1 a.m. I cleaned the cat box but didn't have time to take the neatly bundled bag of poop all the way to the garage. It was an impressive load. We have two hippo-sized felines and I didn't have time to clean the box yesterday.

So I left the massive bag at the top of the stairs to remind me to finish the delivery when I left in the morning. Then I went to bed. So far, so good.

This morning I lugged the bag downstairs and realized that today is garbage day, and the cans are full to overflowing. No problem, I'll just use the garbage can at my office.

At this point, you should know that my morning routine involves waking around 6 a.m., grabbing a banana from the kitchen, and walking the forty-seven seconds from my home to my office down the street.

This morning we were out of bananas. So I have a yogurt and a plastic spoon in my right hand, the massive load-o-poop in the other, and I stagger out the front door, operating on about seven hours of sleep in two days. I'm so tired that I literally can't walk a straight line. I probably look drunk, and I'm hoping the neighbors aren't awake, because if you see a guy carrying a load of crap in one hand, and his breakfast in the other, that's how you'll remember him for the rest of your life.

At some point, probably about thirty-two seconds into my commute, it dawned on me that I had inadvertently become a metaphor for life in general. Life is half delicious yogurt, half crap, and your job is to keep the plastic spoon in the yogurt.

Wedding Day

Well, it's wedding day. I'll be married in about eleven hours.

This wedding has taken more planning than the invasion of Iraq. And yet there is still one guaranteed failure built into the plan: the first dance.

I've been taking dancing lessons for the past several months to prepare for this one specific dance. It would be fair to say that I am not gifted in the performing arts. It would be equally fair to say that I dance like a drunken monkey pissing on an electric fence.

My bride and I have practiced this nightclub-style dance about nine hundred times. So far I have done it wrong nine hundred times. I wasn't worried until yesterday because I thought we would keep practicing it all week until we nailed it. But, you know, we ran out of time and only practiced once at the rehearsal yesterday. At which point I managed to knock her sunglasses off during a turn. If you don't know much about dancing, let me just say that if you are hitting your partner in the head, you are doing it wrong.

So my beautiful bride-to-be is holed up in a hotel room an hour away, guarding the magic dress, and all I can think about is "Is it quick-quick-slow or slow-quick-slow? *Gaaaa!*"

Just to make matters even more interesting, we've never practiced the dance while my bride was wearing a huge puffy dress. This is a bit like being a Superbowl quarterback, and just before game time, the ref tells you, "We've replaced the football with a couch. You won't even notice."

Worse yet, the bride's feet will be completely hidden by the dress. She could be doing the Macarena under there and no one would be the wiser. All eyes will be on my rhythm-impaired cracker legs.

So I've decided to lower my expectations to the point where I can't disappoint myself no matter how much I disappoint everyone else. My new goal is to limit my bride's bruises to body parts that won't show up on the wedding pictures. Sometimes that's the best you can do.

My New Goal

My goal in life is to be carried. My thinking is that you're not really successful if you have to do your own walking. I want to be so important that other people are willing to carry me from room to room, even down the street. And I don't mean carry me on some sort of raised platform either. I want to be carried like a basket of laundry by one person at a time.

Sometimes I think it's a good thing that I'm not a billionaire. I do okay with this Dilbert business, but I'm a long way from being carried. If I had a billion dollars I wouldn't do anything for myself. I'd be all "I'll give you a million dollars to carry me to the bathroom and brush my teeth. And don't wake me up while you do it."

Obviously I would need a dedicated staff for carrying me from room to room around the mansion. But when I traveled, I would pay random strangers to carry me. And not the big strangers either. I'd want the scrawny strangers to carry me because it's more of a challenge. I'd tell them it builds character.

I might pay someone to make a special shirt for me with a luggage handle on the back. I'd use that for traveling. When I checked into a hotel, as the limo driver carried me to the front desk, the desk clerk would say, "Do you need help with your bags?" I'd say, "Yes, and for $600,000 I want you to carry me upstairs and hold me over the toilet. I've been drinking Grey Goose for the past six hours." Then little 110-pound "Erica from Toledo" will leap over the front desk and start carrying me toward the elevator. That's when I'd say, "Oh, I forgot to tell you: I don't do elevators."

I'd also enjoy having so much money that I could punish anyone who annoyed me, but in some totally legal way. For example, if I got a telemarketing call during dinner, it would go like this:

ME (answering phone): Y-y-yellow.

TELEMARKETER: Would you like to buy some crap from a stranger?

ME: I'll give you $500,000 to beat yourself up right now.

TELEMARKETER: What?

ME: You heard me. But now it's only $400,000. You should have started punching yourself in the nose immediately.

It's illegal to pay someone to beat a person up, but I'm almost certain it's legal to pay someone to beat himself up. It's just way more expensive.

Anyway, my point is that it's important to have goals.

Heat Wave

Recently we had a heat wave in California. My air conditioner broke because, I assume, it is not designed to operate in hot weather. That was the bad news. The good news is that I solved the problems in the Middle East. Allow me to explain.

During the several days that it was 112 degrees and I had no AC, all I wanted to do was build an IED and kill the AC guy who kept driving right past my office and helping other people. In fact, I wanted to kill everyone who didn't agree with me on just about any point whatsoever.

And I realized that the problem with the Middle East is insufficient AC. If you think about it, virtually all the organized violence in the world is originating from places where they have poor air-conditioning. And in the desert, 112 degrees is considered a pleasant day. Imagine how grumpy *you* would be at 125 degrees. And do you know what I never see on TV when they show footage of the Middle East?

Shade.

Every person they interview in the Middle East is standing directly in the sun. Some shade would be a good step toward world peace. Add a few fans and some cool drinks, and I think we could disband the U.N.

When it's 125 degrees outside, given the choice of sitting inside a one-room hovel with seventeen infrequently bathed relatives versus launching rockets, the terrorist option starts looking mighty appealing. Because you know what else I never see on TV when they show footage of the Middle East?

Hobbies.

And I understand that. Most hobbies involve one of these things:

Glue (it would melt)
Spending money (they don't have any)
Being outside (it's 125 degrees)

At room temperature, you could never convince me to strap explosives to my body. But at 125 degrees, I'd welcome the change of pace.

Just out of curiosity, I would love to see a graph showing a comparison of temperature and violence in the past fifty years. I'll bet it's a strong correlation. Seriously, when was the last time you saw a news report featuring a guy in a winter jacket firing a rocket launcher.

Undergarment Dysfunction

Once in a while I experience a problem that I wonder if anyone else in the world has ever had. Yesterday was one of those times.

I was packing for a one-week cruise with my new family and spied some briefs in a drawer that I hadn't worn since I-don't-know-when. So I figured I'd give them a go as part of my travel outfit. This turned out to be a big mistake.

For the benefit of the ladies reading this, let me explain a bit about the architecture of men's briefs. We're all about efficiency, so most traditional briefs have a flap in the front for quick extraction of your Johnson. That allows us to drink caffeinated beverages (from a cup, not our Johnson) right up to the last moment when it would be too late to make it to the restroom. Then it's just zip-yank-whizzzzzz. It's all good.

As a practical matter, I think most guys do the "pull down" move as opposed to snaking it through the flap hole. But in any event, the flap hole is there if you need it, perhaps more for tradition than anything else.

Now sometimes a pair of briefs, for reasons I cannot understand, have the most annoying characteristic you could ever imagine: In the course of normal walking and sitting, the wearer's Weiner schnitzel ends up poking halfway through the flap hole like a turtle coming out of its shell. And before long, the most sensitive part of your body is wedged between your briefs and the harsh denim material of your pants.

As I walked toward the departure gate, I was choking Private Johnson and giving him a noogie at the same time. For those who have never experienced such a thing, let me say that it causes one to walk like Michael Jackson with a spastic toddler in his pants.

Anyway, the only solution is to do a subtle reach-down followed by a manual adjustment. This is especially challenging when you are surrounded on all sides by people who are waiting for flights and have nothing better to do than listen to iPods and watch for people grab-bing their woo-hoos. I couldn't wait to make it to the men's room. That was about a block away. I had to do a midstride, reach-down, pecker adjustment.

Luckily for me, I have the power of invisibility. As an unattractive middle-aged male of average size, no one notices me in a crowd unless I'm either on fire or wearing a suit made from the skin of an attractive twenty-year-old woman. For once, neither of those situations applied.

As you might imagine, pecker adjustments need to be done quickly. If you linger, it looks like something else entirely. You want to maintain some degree of deniability when airport security starts questioning you.

> SECURITY: We have a report that you were pleasuring your-self at gate seventeen.
>
> YOU: No, I swear, my Johnson had turtled out of my under-pants and I was just adjusting my junk.
>
> SECURITY: You lingered.
>
> YOU: I . . . I didn't linger. I panicked. It wasn't a smooth move, that's all. I swear.
>
> SECURITY: We've got you on the security cameras. Do you want to stick with that story?
>
> YOU: Okay, maybe I lingered a little. Force of habit.
>
> SECURITY: You may go. No one wants to touch you long enough to put on the cuffs.

Anyway, I went for the readjustment as I passed between the pizza place and the sundries store and I'm almost certain no one noticed. That was the good news. The bad news is that the briefs were repeat offenders. No sooner had I freed Farmer Johnson from the cotton clutches than my yoo-hoo snapped back into the trap like a deranged yo-yo. After about the third adjustment in five minutes, I lost all inhibi-tions. It's amazing what you can get used to. I must have looked like I was panning for gold in there.

Anyway, my point is that I'm glad my last name isn't Johnson. And I'm especially glad that my first name isn't Harry.

Pittsburgh

I'm back on the road today—this time to Pittsburgh, where I will give a mirthful keynote address to a darkened room full of strangers. Pittsburgh has many wonderful tourist attractions and natural wonders. For example, there's the Pittsburgh Museum of Things That Other Museums Didn't Want, the Festival of Rust, and historic Fort Arm Pitt. And if you love seeing thousands of gray birds lining telephone poles waiting for a dropped French fry, you'll love Pittsburgh.

According to Wikipedia, it's cloudy in Pittsburgh 200 days per year. That part of the country has four seasons. If it's anything like my old hometown in upstate New York, it means that during the remaining 165 days either your eyeballs are getting poached in your skull or you're standing on tiptoes to keep your McNuggets above the brown snow line. That's why I've arranged for a windowless temperature-controlled container to transport me from the airport directly to the hotel conference room. It's all in my contract.

I have a feeling that vegetarians like me are not welcome in steel town, so I strapped an emergency beet to my ankle and hid a carrot in the spine of my three-ring binder. Bring it on!

You might distrust my characterization of Pittsburgh based on the fact that I've never been there and only researched the climate on my BlackBerry five minutes ago. But that's okay because almost all of my knowledge is a medley of hallucinations and misinformation that knocks around in my wrinkled gray thing (my brain, you pervert) until it turns into reliable facts. The cool thing is that thousands of people will read this book and some percentage of what I said will turn into their "knowledge" of Pittsburgh.

Ten years from now you might find yourself talking with someone who actually grew up in Pittsburgh. You'll try to impress him by mentioning the Festival of Rust. You won't remember where you heard about it, but you'll be pretty sure it involves floats that you wouldn't want to sit on in your good pants.

I do recall—or maybe I hallucinated—that Pittsburgh always rates high on quality-of-life surveys. So they must be doing something right. I assume that part of Pittsburgh's strategy involves discouraging tourism by naming their sports teams Pirates and Steelers. It sounds like the kind of place where unless you keep your wallet halfway up your own ass, someone is going to get it.

Update: Okay, it turns out that Pittsburgh is a very nice place, and quite beautiful. (Really) Now I feel bad for mocking it.

Tax Breaks for Leprechauns

As a smallish person, I often feel cheated. My money is subsidizing a lot of big people and I don't like it.

For example, I pay the same price at the all-you-can-eat buffet as the guy who brings his own wheelbarrow. For all practical purposes, I'm buying that guy's lunch.

On airplanes, huge guys use their entire seat plus about 30 percent of mine. I've got elbows and knees all over me. I try to reclaim part of the armrest by using the casual nudge maneuver. But during short-sleeve weather I can't get past his hairy forearm defenses. It tickles, dammit.

When I fly, I have to pay extra if my suitcase weighs 51 pounds instead of 49. Then I take my seat next to Godzilla. He's got me beat by about 100 pounds. My ticket is subsidizing the fuel to fly his huge cheeseburger-filled torso around.

Large people also get to see more of the movie/play/concert than the rest of us who are paying the same price. All I see is a huge head. And don't get me started about how they absorb too much of the bass vibrations.

When I buy a shirt, it has about 40 percent less material than the XXL size. I'm subsidizing other people's cotton. Is that fair?

Big people have their uses. There's no other way to get a couch to the second floor. And when a psycho pulls out a gun at the 7-Eleven, I appreciate having someone to leap behind. But on the whole, they're breathing too much of the oxygen and putting too much wear and tear on the carpets. I'm convinced that when huge people pet the family dog, they're wearing him out too quickly with their huge hands. A good dog only has so many pettings in him.

That's why I think the income tax and sales tax should be replaced with a largeness tax. We could just measure people and charge them accordingly. And since there is a strong correlation between height and income, the result wouldn't be that unfair.

I have a bad feeling that my odds of getting beaten up have just increased.

Sadistic Mumble Movies

Have you noticed that it takes at least two people to watch a movie lately? It usually goes like this:

MOVIE ACTOR: Mumble, mumble, mumble.

YOU: What did he say?

OTHER PERSON: He said he's going to kill the dwarf, or something about oatmeal.

MOVIE ACTOR: Mumble, mumble, mumble.

OTHER PERSON: What?

YOU: He said he loves ostriches, or maybe something about revenge.

Worse yet, over the course of the movie, the actors tend to become beat-up, exhausted, or drug addicted. And that means even *more* mumbling. The difference is that the lips no longer move at all. That's called acting. Am I the only one who continues to turn up the volume about every five minutes for the entire movie?

And don't get me started about the TV show *24*, which should be subtitled "Bad Things Happen to People Who Whisper."

Last night I watched an award-winning movie on DVD. And by award-winning, I mean that horrible things happen to mumbly people in the beginning of the movie and then things continue to get worse for the next three hours. Filmmakers know that if they let the audience feel happiness or hear dialogue, the Oscar will slip through their fingers.

So there I sat, watching this DVD and feeling as if someone were slapping me in the nuts with a rake handle. The performances were spectacular, unfortunately, because that made the pain all the more real. And because the movie was well-made (in the same sense that the Boston Strangler was thorough), I felt some obligation to stick it out to the end.

There's some sort of unwritten rule that the worse a movie makes you feel, the longer it must be. Comedies and animated movies are generally well under two hours. But a movie about well-dressed people drowning in ice water is going to threaten the four-hour mark.

The strangest part about the movie I watched last night is that virtually all of my friends recommended it. Apparently I need to get more specific when I ask about movies. Instead of asking, "How was the movie?" and getting, "It's great," I should ask, "How did you feel when you watched the movie?" in which case I would get, "I felt like an SUV was parked on my chest and starving rats were duct-taped to my torso. The acting was great!"

Spammers

I **am appalled** at the low quality of spam lately. If someone is trying to scam me, I expect him to put some effort into it. Here are a few of the subject lines that ended up in my spam folder today:

Re: it see to amiss
Re: Damiana one of the Penis Enlarge Patch ingredients has
  been
Re: Learn to be ritzy
Re: NEW age of good old PENPILs.Scientists says YES!

Are these guys even *trying*? I have some respect for the spam with subject lines such as "From Bob" or "quick question." Those are good attempts. If I'm not paying attention, I might even open one of those. But who opens a message titled "Re: NEW age of good old PENPILs. Scientists says YES!"?

The scary part is that every spam message probably works on at least one person. I imagine some guy named Barney in Florida opening his e-mail, seeing the subject line "Re: it see to amiss," and thinking, "this must be from one of my friends." Then he opens it, only to be surprised that it's a pitch for penile enlargement pills that also cure baldness and help you pick winning penny stocks.

At this point you might expect Barney to wonder why he hasn't seen stories all over the news about this miracle breakthrough drug. But he doesn't wonder. All he knows is that he's poor, bald, and hung like a frozen caterpillar. For the low price of $29.95 he can fix all of that without leaving home. He figures it might be a scam, but can he really take the chance that it's not? So Barney places his order for the miracle pill and wonders why the Nigerian vendor needs his social security number.

Speaking of social security numbers, I think the government should send spam to all citizens. If someone like Barney tries to buy a miracle pill, the government erases his social security number from their records so he can't vote. It would solve a lot of problems.

Human Behavior

If aliens landed in your backyard and gave you one minute to describe everything there is to know about human behavior, what would you say?

I found an answer to that question today as I was looking through my old e-mails. This story was sent to me by a Dilbert reader.

> The maintenance man is moving the thermostat in our office today. I started talking with him about the "Thermostat Wars" [from Dilbert comics]. He told me about one office with 30 women where they could never get the temperature to an agreeable level. At his suggestion they installed 20 dummy thermostats around the office. Everyone was told that each thermostat controlled the zone around itself.
>
> Problem solved. Now that everyone has "control" of their own thermostat there is no problem.

Researchers say that job satisfaction is more influenced by the degree of control you have over your job than any other factor. This makes sense to me, because once you free someone from the obligation to help the stockholders, life can be pretty good.

If you've ever stolen any office supplies—and I'm not saying you have—I think you know it increases your job satisfaction. And it's not because you stole fifty cents worth of crap, but because you *can*. It's the control that matters, also known as "getting away with it."

People like control. That's why the iPod is so popular. It's 1 percent about listening to music and 99 percent about getting to choose what music you listen to at any given moment. I'm convinced that if Apple designed a product that did nothing but send a strong electric shock to a sensitive part of your body, they would sell millions of them as long as the packaging was cool and you got to choose what body part is getting shocked.

Although people like being in control, we get nervous when there are too many options, because that feels exactly like being out of control. For example, everyone says they like restaurants with lots of items on the menu. But look at your date's face the next time he or she opens a menu with four hundred options. It will look like a Chihuahua at a firing range.

The key to happiness is having control over a well-defined set of options, with a slow trickle of new options on the way, but not enough to confuse you. That's why I think clever aliens could easily enslave humans by providing individual cages with nothing but a dimmer switch and a choice of incense. But I shouldn't give them any ideas.

Work Habits

I read that Stephen King used to write his books while listening to hard rock music and drinking heavily. I envy him, except for the part where he became an alcoholic. And the part where he got hit by a car.

It sure would be nice to do great work while drunk and distracted. I'm pretty much the opposite. For example, I can't write unless both of my ass cheeks are equally touching my chair and my feet are flat on the ground. This is inconvenient because sometimes I feel the need to cross my legs and favor one butt cheek over the other. When I assume that position, the best I can do is stare into space while trying to remember my name, species, and gender. Apparently I have some sort of ass-brain neurological connection that needs to be just so.

I also can't write if I am slightly hungry, thirsty, or in need of a bathroom break. That eliminates about 70 percent of my potential workday. That's why Dilbert has no mouth and no eyeballs—I just don't have that kind of time.

Another 10 percent of my workday is allocated to thwarting my cat's antiproductivity crusade. She hates it when I work, under the universal cat theory that any time spent not petting her is time wasted. As soon as I pick up a drawing implement, she systematically goes around my office chewing and scratching one item after another until she finds something that will make me stop work and pet her. I don't want her to learn what will bother me most, so I try to trick her. I act all worked up when she eats a yellow sticky note while remaining nonchalant as she goes all mongoose on my monitor cable. We've been doing this routine for years, which is why my office looks like a Hezbollah safe house and all of my best ideas are inside my cat.

I'd write more but I feel a powerful need to cross my legs and . . .

Benefits of Getting Old

I don't know of anyone over the age of eighteen who wants to get older, despite all the studies showing that older people are happier than younger ones. I've always wondered why the elderly are so content, and now that I'm getting older myself, the mysteries are beginning to unfold.

For example, ten minutes ago I wanted to walk from my home to my office, all of forty-seven seconds away. (Yes, I timed it.) I was wearing black socks because I just came from getting a suit altered. There on the floor in the foyer were my sandals. Do I bother to take off the black socks before putting on the sandals? Ha! That's thinking like a twenty-five-year-old. I just slipped my black-socked feet into those babies and took off without a hint of shame.

I'm not yet at the age where I can wear a fishing hat, ball-high shorts, and black socks and sandals all the time, but it was a nice little preview of things to come. Plus, now that I'm married I can eat all I want and dress any way I please—at least until my wife starts insisting we need a pool boy despite having no pool.

Being older has many advantages. My favorite one is that I get automatic respect without earning it. That's sweet. I could say to the young ice cream shop vendor, "Give me two scoops of vanilla, turd-boy," and he would probably say, "Very good, sir. Coming up!" The world isn't fair, but as long as it's tilting in my direction I find that there's a natural cap to my righteous indignation.

The best thing about being my age is in knowing how my life worked out. Sure, there's a lot more living to go, but there isn't much doubt that I'll always be the "Dilbert guy." Unless I go on a crime spree, in which case I'll be "that stabbin' Dilbert guy."

But when you're twenty-five, you are filled with curiosity about your own future. Will you become a captain of industry or will you drown in your own vomit? There are so many options. But the only thing you really need to know in advance is whether you will someday run for public office. If that's an option, you don't want any of your orifices to be involved in anything you wouldn't tell your mother.

Another bonus of advanced age is the accumulation of generally useless knowledge that is nonetheless impressive. After about the age of forty you start hearing a lot of "How did you know *that*?" If you sum up all of the facts in your head plus your awesome powers of inference plus your exceptional skill at bullshitting, you look like a psychic to anyone under twenty.

That's why, after I call the ice cream vendor "turd-boy," I quickly follow up with "You're thinking of spitting in my ice cream now, aren't you?" Then he says something like, "Whoa, dude! How did you do that?"

Steroid Commercial

I just heard that sprinter Justin Gatlin, the world record holder for 100 meters, tested positive for testosterone and steroids. I was shocked!

My first thought went to the second-fastest man in the world. I have this image of him being so happy when he heard the news that he leaped for joy with his mighty legs, penetrated the ceiling, continued on through the attic and roof, and landed in a nearby pond, where he drowned. Because once you're a loser, you're always a loser.

How happy are the guys who sell illegal steroids? You can't buy that kind of advertisement. And it sure makes it harder for the just-say-no people. "Kids, don't do steroids. If you do, you might become the fastest man in the world and have so much poontang and money that . . . I forget my point."

Just once maybe there should be a story about an athlete who did steroids and didn't set a world record, and didn't hump his way through the entire Victoria Secrets model list. Otherwise you have what I call a mixed message.

Have you ever seen one of the bodybuilding competitions where all the contestants are "natural," meaning they tested negative for drugs? The winner still looks like he could lift a car, and that's impressive. But the winner of any nonnatural competition looks like he could crush that car into a small ball, eat it, and poop it five miles into the center of a mountain. There's a difference.

As I understand it, the side effects of steroids include pimples, shrunken nuggets, and the occasional rage. Are you telling me that science can't fix those things? Just give me some Retin-A, nutsack implants, and Prozac and I'm good to go. I think it would be worth it if I could pull a grown tree out of the ground with my bare hands. Then, at holiday gatherings, when the life-of-the-party guy starts playing the piano, I could upstage him by lifting the house off its foundation and shaking all the furniture to one side until his stupid piano falls out a side door and into the pool.

Amateur Night

Serious drinkers prefer to stay off the road on New Year's Eve, sometimes calling it "Amateur Night." I am reminded of that witticism as I watch the debate about whether Pluto is a real planet or a dwarf planet.

To a professional humorist there is nothing more painful than a news story that demands an obvious joke. The amateurs pile on and it gets ugly fast. Example:

> *"If Pluto isn't a planet, that's Goofy! Hahahahahaha-Snort!"*
> *"Pluto isn't a planet—he's a Dog! Whaahahaahahaaa!"*
> *"Pluto is a dwarf? I guess Disney put him in the wrong cartoon! Hoohaahahahaha!"*

You see? Painful.

At a recent nerdfest, where it was decided Pluto wasn't a real planet, one of the scientists held up a stuffed Pluto (the Walt Disney kind) and an umbrella, and wittily pointed out that Pluto was under the umbrella of planets that include "dwarf planets." The scientists all laughed and snorted and wondered why they don't get laid more often.

Call me old-fashioned, but I don't think Pluto should be the funniest planet—or even the funniest nonplanet. That distinction belongs to another. Uranus, seventh celestial body from the sun, is part miracle of gravity and part bung hole. It has earned its status as the funny man of the cosmos.

Despite anything you have heard, Uranus is not a black hole, and there are no Klingons circling it. Nor does it have Venus envy. It is simply the funniest of all planets, be they dwarf or regular. Some things should never change.

Chinese Striptease Funeral

I read in the news that the Chinese police are cracking down on the practice of hiring strippers for funerals.

Seriously.

Strippers for funerals.

Villagers believe that the more people who attend the funeral, the more honored the dead person is. And naked women bring in the crowds. I can think of no better way to honor a dead grandmother than by hiring naked women to arouse her surviving husband while the in-laws watch.

Plus there's a practical aspect to it. It's important to make sure the guy in the casket is really dead and not just faking it. If memory serves me, there's an old Chinese proverb about raising the dead. Or perhaps the Rolling Stones said it. I get those two groups confused. Which ones sang, "You make a dead man cum?" Anyway, my point is that it's a good test of who is really dead, but only if you have that specific woman that Mick Jagger was singing about. Or maybe it was Confucius.

It's hard to pick my favorite part of this story, but one of the contenders has to do with the name of the county where the police did the crack down: Donghai.

I suppose you could pronounce it Dong-hay. But it's more deliciously ironic if it's pronounced dong-high. If anyone knows that it's really pronounced Dong-hay, don't ruin it for me.

I didn't see in the news report why the Chinese police were suddenly cracking down on the strippers at funerals, but I have a theory. I think I speak for all men when I say that at the age of fourteen, I would have been willing to kill a cousin to look at a stripper. And remember that those small villages in China don't have cable TV and high speed Internet. You pretty much have to choke someone to death just to generate any entertainment that doesn't involve dragon costumes and tambourines.

The Chinese have given us gunpowder, fireworks, chopsticks, and now this idea. I hope it starts catching on in the States. I don't know what it would feel like to be sad and aroused at the same time, but I'm willing to give it a try.

Unfortunately, we ruin everything over here. We'll probably start having mimes at funerals instead of strippers. But I have to admit it would be funny watching a mime do his impression of being trapped underground in a pine box.

Self-Criticism

I've noticed that whenever Americans are criticized by residents of other countries, I find myself agreeing. Don't get me wrong—I love my country and I think every other country sucks way more than America does.

But when someone calls America arrogant, I have a hard time disagreeing. We *are* arrogant. In fact, I can't think of a single time I've heard an American deny that charge. We usually just change the subject and point out that the complainer's country is a loser-infested turdball. In other words, we act arrogant. But we never deny it.

Likewise when America is accused of being warmongering Jesus-spouting hypocrites, my first reaction is never "Take that back!" I usually just nod and mutter something like, "Good point." We Americans (usually) think our warmongering is in the name of self-defense or helping a buddy, but it *is* hard to reconcile it with *What would Jesus do?*

That's not the funny part. The funny part is wondering if other countries hear American criticisms of them and think, "You nailed me!" For example, I think I speak for almost all Americans when I say this about the countries in the Middle East: You're all ignorant, psycho dickheads.

Please allow me to clarify that I'm talking about the *countries* in general and not each individual resident. Just as there are Americans who are not arrogant, warmongering hypocrites, there are surely plenty of people in the Middle East who are enlightened and reasonable. Unfortunately, none of those people seem to be in charge. If Gandhi reincarnated in the Middle East tomorrow, they would have to hold a lottery to see who beheaded him first.

At least that's how it seems from the arrogant, warmongering hypocrite perspective.

I was thinking of this recently because the media has reported two cases of leaders in the Middle East acknowledging, in their own way, that they might in fact be ignorant, psycho dickheads. The leader of Hezbollah said in an interview that kidnapping two Israeli soldiers was a mistake because of all the destruction it sparked. And a Hamas leader recently went on record saying Palestinians had to take the blame for the crumbling of their society after Israel pulled out.

It's hard to gain respect from an arrogant, warmongering hypocrite, especially when you're an ignorant, psycho dickhead. But self-criticism does get our attention. Somehow it reduces the need to be arrogant, warmongering, and hypocritical. I wonder if it works both ways? Would the Middle East be less like ignorant, psycho dickheads if America were less arrogant, warmongering, and hypocritical? I don't know the answer. It's just interesting to think about.

And then there's Israel. In a way, they're like the illegitimate child of America and the Middle East. They inherited some of the worst bits from both sides. So while Americans have an unconditional love for Israel, we also think it's an arrogant, warmongering, hypocritical, ignorant, psycho, dickheaded country. In other words, it's just like any other teenager.

I know this sounds harsh, but I think self-criticism is always the first step toward a solution. And if anyone is incapable of self-criticism, I will be happy to give suggestions on where to start. That's what arrogant friends are for.

Silent H

Many of you are unaware of the rule of the silent *h*. A silent *h* can be put anywhere you want, precisely because it is silent. So, for example, it is equally proper to spell the name Gandhi as Gandih, Gahndi, hGandi, and even Gandhhhhhhhi.

The silent *h* is very flexible. When I'm talking, I'll toss in a silent *h* every third syllable, and no one seems to mind. I'm not trying to show off by doing it. I just like the way it doesn't sound.

Little known fact: The original name for the stealth bomber was Hhhhhhh, where every *h* but the fourth one is silent.

Perhaps you haven't heard the story of how *h* came to be silent. In Viking days, not only was the *h* totally noisy, but the Norsemen used them in practically every word. This caused a lot of confusion. The most common phrase in Viking became "Whhaht? I cahn't hunhderstand! Get the *h* out!"

But it all came to a head one day when Eric the Artistic carved a wooden chair out of a tree stump and was showing it off to friends. That's when Allen the Insensitive said, "Nice chairh, hEric. I thinkh I'll shit on it."

Well, the next thing you know, swords are drawn and limbs are flying. And that was the day that the Vikings decided to stop talking in English and go discover the United States, which they called America.

Sleep

The other day my brother asked why I was sending him an e-mail at four a.m. This is not unusual for me because I often have trouble sleeping. That night was typical. It went like this:

First I was too hot to sleep. Then there was the nightmare of being chased by armed gunmen. Then I got itchy. Then I woke myself up with my own snoring (hate that). Then the cats tried to sleep on my feet. Then it started to get too cold with the window open.

It was one of those nights when my mouth kept falling open while I slept, which dried out my throat, which made me keep reaching for my bottled water on the nightstand, which made me get up and whiz three times.

I use my BlackBerry as a flashlight when I make late-night bathroom runs, and sometimes I make the mistake of checking for messages on the way back. There was one from my e-mail friend in Egypt. Now I'm lying in bed formulating my response to his theories about the president of Iran.

By now the little pillow I keep between my knees has fallen on the floor and I can't decide if it's worth picking it up. Has it become mandatory or is it just nice? Can I sleep with my knees touching? There's no such thing as an easy question when you're tired.

Suddenly I realize that the top of my pillow is slightly too warm because my head has been on it, whereas the bottom is slightly too cool. And the cats are on my feet again. I'm itchy, my throat is dry, and I'm wondering if the president of Iran wants to incinerate me with a nuclear weapon. If I fall asleep again, will I be back in the dream where bad people are chasing me? Is my tossing and turning waking up my new wife? Will she start to hate me for keeping her awake?

So I got up and started my day.

They say that you need less sleep as you get older. Eventually, when you get so old that you don't need any sleep at all, you die. I figure I have another month or two.

What Is Rude?

I worry about being rude and not even realizing it. I can usually control myself from being rude in obvious ways, but new gray areas keep popping up.

For example, is it rude to fully recline my seat on an airplane, knowing it robs space from the guy behind me? On one hand, I'm just using the space that the airline sold me. They *designed* the seat to go back. But on the other hand, the guy behind me has to retract both testicles to have enough room to use his laptop. That doesn't seem fair either.

How about using your car stereo system with your windows open? You pull up to a stoplight on a warm day and realize you still have your radio volume blaring at the same level as it was on the open road. It's not obnoxious music, just loud. Do you turn it down so the other motorists don't hear it for the next thirty seconds?

Let's say you're in a car with one other person—someone close to you, a family member or good friend. He or she is doing the driving and you feel the need to make some cell phone calls that have nothing to do with the driver. You know the calls won't be brief. Do you use this handy unproductive time to make your calls while being chauffeured to your destination?

What about asking for advice from friends who happen to charge for that same advice in their professional lives? I'm talking about doctors, lawyers, accountants, financial advisers, tennis pros, and the like. If you're in a social setting, just making conversation, can you ask about the advantages of an S Corporation versus an LLC?

For the record, I try to avoid doing any of those things. But I am generally considered a neurotic pussy. I offer those questions to you so you can turn your next boring social gathering into an entertaining skunk fight. For some reason, doing that doesn't seem impolite to me.

Why Do I Enjoy Riling People Up?

When I wrote my first book, *The Dilbert Principle*, I inadvertently stumbled on the most powerful, surefire book-selling concept ever: Say what other people are already thinking, but say it better than they are thinking it. In my case, I told people that their managers were as useful as the undigested bits of peanuts in a squirrel's turd. (See, you just laughed.) Bingo—bestseller.

All nonfiction bestselling opinion books are nothing more than your own opinions fed back to you with seasoning. Ann Coulter sells to conservatives who agree with her. Al Franken sells to liberals who agree with him. And they do it brilliantly, in my opinion.

I tried to violate that rule with a later book called *Dilbert and the Way of the Weasel*. My thesis was that everyone is a weasel, including you and me. Oops. That concept was not popular. No one wants to hear that he or she is a weasel. People want a book that says *other* people are weasels because that's what they believe. Most people don't want to risk having their mind changed.

To be fair, there are independent thinkers who read all sorts of books. But there aren't enough of them to make a bestseller. That's why I've been spending some time trying to think of a book title that would sell the most. I want a theme that a lot of people agree with, something that tracks with what everyone thinks but no one wants to say, for fear of being fired or socially ostracized. And I want to mix in a bit of false hope, too. That gives people a reason to read it.

Potential Blockbuster Titles

Miracle Cure for Baldness: Masturbation

I Don't Want to Kill You, but I Wouldn't Mind if Someone Did: The Secrets of Hiring an Untraceable Hit Man

Anal Ventriloquism: The New Science of Blaming Your Flatulence on Strangers

All of Your Problems Really Are Caused by Your Boyfriend

Whining All the Time Is Healthy!
101 Careers That Will Get You Blown
Proof That People Who Disagree with You Are Always Wrong!

I think that covers it.

Breeding

Assuming the majority of scientists are right about evolution, I keep looking around to figure out which subset of humans is starting to split off from the species and form their own club.

In theory, some group of humans will stop mating with outsiders and start mutating over generations until their teeth have little hands that can hold gum when they're tired of chewing. That's just an example. Maybe they will grow a unicorn horn out of their ass so they always have a stool for watching soccer games. The possibilities are both endless and exciting, especially since we're the first creatures to be aware of evolution. So we might start guiding it for the benefit of future generations.

"Billy, I think you should marry that girl on the corner. Her shoulder blades are huge, and I think over time your descendants could have wings. It would save a lot on gas."

So who are these precursors to the new species? One possibility is giants in the Netherlands. I've heard that the Dutch are the tallest people around. If they can keep their huge paws off the sexy but small-ish French people, the Dutch will keep inbreeding and growing. Eventually it will be physically impossible for a giant Dutch guy to knock up any woman less than twelve feet tall without killing her in the process.

Or has evolution stopped in humans because we're so judgmental? I imagine a squirrel would still hump another squirrel even if the humpee had three tails, thus heading down the road toward a new three-tailed squirrel species. But humans are picky. I just talked to a woman who dumped her boyfriend because she didn't think his job was good enough. I think if the boyfriend had a snout and ate ants, he would have been exed even sooner.

My guess is that the next human species will differ primarily in the brain. We already see a big difference in how people perceive reality. Some people (skeptics) perceive only the natural world that can be measured. Other people (the vast majority) perceive the supernatural world to be equally real, including souls and spirits and angels and ghosts and God. I think the two groups might go their separate ways.

In the old days, atheists were killed before they could breed. Now they move to Europe where they can eat cheese and hump for the entire month of August. Result: more atheists. Meanwhile, Omar the disbeliever in Saudi Arabia is having his junk removed by sword so he won't father any new infidels. I might be exaggerating that last part, but I'm sure Omar isn't getting six wives. The point is that all the atheists are going to end up in one place eventually. My guess is that there's a genetic component to skepticism, just as there is for every other sort of human capability. Skeptics will breed with other skeptics. Over time, skeptics will stop producing babies that have the genetic capacity to become believers.

I think that's our evolutionary future: a bunch of skeptics living separately from the majority of people who believe all sorts of things without conclusive evidence. The skeptics will have most of the scientists, just like now. Given that the skeptics have no moral compass, I predict that they will move to the moon and build a huge laser gun to extort taxes from the believers who remain on Earth. And they will build hot robot chicks for sex, thus leading to a drop in the lunar birth rate and the eventual demise of the skeptic moon colony. So in the future, the moon will be populated only by hot robot chicks that have a huge laser pointed at Earth. This is exactly the sort of practical knowledge we should be teaching in science class.

Pope Stirs Up Poop

My favorite story of the week is about Pope Benedict inadvertently insulting Islam in a speech. He quoted a Byzantine emperor who called Islam "evil and inhuman" but made it clear that it wasn't his own opinion.

In response to being labeled evil and inhuman by a dead Byzantine emperor, a group of Muslims did what anyone would do in that situation: They firebombed churches in the West Bank.

This is funny on so many levels that I hardly know where to start. First, I love the fact that the Vatican's official position is that Muslims should be treated with "esteem." According to my dictionary, esteem is a very weaselly word. It can mean "high regard," and that's a nice compliment. But it can also mean "the regard in which one is held," which is a broad concept encompassing everything from "really groovy" to "bearded turds."

The pope is in a tricky situation. He can either say that he believes Muslims picked the wrong religion, thereby triggering massive violence. Or he can be a liar with a funny hat. He thought he found a clever middle ground that involves attributing any bad thoughts about Islam to a dead guy, and employing weasel words that sound like compliments. God works in mysterious ways. I hope that works out for the pope.

Reaching for Things in the Car

As a writer, I'm always searching for those thoughts that everyone has but no one has yet expressed. It's dangerous territory because there's always a good chance that you're the only freak in the world with that thought or that problem.

I have been heartened to hear from others that two of my potentially abnormal experiences are totally common. For example, I'm not the only one who can't hear what the actors are mumbling in movies, and I'm not the only guy whose underpants sometimes go mongoose on his snake.

Emboldened by those experiences, I will try another: Every time I reach for something in my car that's hard to get, I hurt myself.

Just to be clear, I'm in no danger if the desired item is right next to me. I can turn on the radio or use my turn signals without injuring a rotator cuff. It's when there's something in the far corner of the floor of the passenger's side that there's a problem. The distant end of the backseat is another. Inevitably the item is just beyond my comfortable reach, but not so far that I can't get it by stretching until a tendon is about to snap and holding that position until a fingernail grows. Then I can just ba-a-a-a-rely reach.

You might wonder why I don't just get out of the car, walk around, and get the item via the other door. To be honest, I wonder the same thing even as I'm disemboweling myself with the gear shift. By then I am literally adding insult to injury by yelling something like "You stupid f***ing idiot! Why do you keep doing this?"

Sometimes I use a tool, such as a box of tissues, to paw at the distant object, as if that will help. When it comes to grabbing power, a smooth, square box is low on the list, but you have to work with what you have. So I end up bludgeoning the object of my desire with the cardboard box in the hope that somehow that will make it hop an inch in my direction. As I'm flailing and stretching and sometimes cursing, that's when my stomach becomes detached from my intestines or my spine starts poking out of my lower back. And it hurts.

Part of the problem is that my arms aren't long. They aren't kangaroo short, just normal. Cosmetically, they are far superior to the baboon variety of arms that many of you have, but virtually useless for rebounding or reaching for distant objects. I've considered getting one of those grabber tools that old people have and keeping it in the car. But I know that the grabber tool would end up on the far side of the backseat and I'd loosen a spleen reaching for it.

And that's why kangaroos don't drive cars.

What Would Trump Do?

If my religion were based on the teachings of Donald Trump, I would try to make a lot of money and keep it all. And I'd feel good about it because I was being true to my beliefs. I'd hate to go through life feeling like a hypocrite.

Nonbelievers have it good, too. They can keep their money or give it away—whatever feels right. Bill Gates is the biggest philanthropist on Earth and he's a nonbeliever. So is the second biggest philanthropist on earth, Warren Buffett. George Soros, too. You'd expect rich guys who have no moral compass to build their own countries on barges so they can legally rape and kill the citizens all day. For some reason they don't.

Things get trickier when you base your religion on a nice fellow who wants you to give most of your money to the poor. How do you justify buying a third television set when people in New Orleans are living in rolled-up carpets? That's not a rhetorical question. I actually wonder about the answer. Here are some of my best guesses about your rationalization:

Jesus likes me better than poor people. He'd approve of my second iPod.

If I give a poor person a fish, he'd only eat for a day anyway. What's one day?

I give 10 percent of my money to charity. God says that's exactly the right amount. Eleven percent would anger God.

Poor people are lazy or crazy. My money won't fix that.

There's a loophole in the Bible that says I can keep my money. Woo-hoo!

I am bad at economics and I am convinced that keeping my money stimulates the economy and helps poor people indirectly.

Am I missing any reasons?

I recommend asking this question the next time you're at a dinner party and bored out of your mind. Things will get interesting fast. And it reduces the risk that you'll be invited to another one. It's a little-known fact that philosophy was invented by a bunch of guys who enjoyed ruining parties. If you can think of another use for it, let me know.

Maybe It's Me

My favorite Mr. Boffo comic of all time featured Mr. Boffo (I assume) in a jail cell talking to his cellmate. He says about himself, "Nineteen arrests. Nineteen convictions. Maybe it's me."

I come back to that philosophy often. You can only explain so many times why everyone else is wrong before you have to accept that the problem is on your end. Today I realized that the problem is me.

The issue is whether I am unclear when I say things. All of my life I have been laboring under the misconception that I am not only clear, but notoriously clear. Famously clear. Unambiguously, emphatically, and fantastically clear. I thought Clearasil was named after me.

But it turns out that I'm more like whatever you would get if Little Richard had sex with a Rubik's Cube and produced a baby. And by that I mean unclear, just to be clear.

If I only noticed my clarity problem in the context of comments in incoming e-mails, and the comments on my blog, I'd assume the phenomenon was nothing more than the normal distribution of morons. But it also happens at home, with friends, and with business associates. Often. They can't *all* be confused for no reason. For example, I spent this morning explaining why my agreement to sign fifteen books did not assume I would buy them myself and ship them somewhere. Now I worry that I might have inadvertently agreed to clean someone's rain gutters and repaint the center lines on highway I-680. I'm unclear that way.

I have many theories about why I am so unclear. One problem is that all communication requires clarifying your assumptions, and apparently my brain is defective in that regard. I figure that people fill in the blanks the same way I would.

Now I realize I have to change. In the old days I would say, for example, "It's raining." In the future I will say, "It is raining right now, right here, outside and not inside. Visually it appears to be a liquid substance that I believe without the benefit of controlled studies to be water. I do not intend this statement to be unpatriotic. I am not proposing that you drink it or roll around in it. The rain is neither good nor bad, except in the cases of recently washed cars, picnics, and crops. If I have left anything off the list, the omission is not tantamount to an opinion that said omitted activity deserves to be rained on. This message is not intended to be ironic, sarcastic, or arrogant."

If it's misting outside, I honestly don't know what I'll do.

Cold

True story: It's my senior year at Hartwick College, in upstate New York, February, nine p.m., ten below zero, a foot of snow, and my very used car decides to die. I'm on a new highway that few drivers have yet discovered. There's not another car in sight.

I didn't have a coat because I was a moron, or possibly a college student, and I assumed I would only be sprinting from car to building and back. I wasn't planning on dying in a snowbank, but things were starting to head in that direction.

I was in serious trouble. I think I might have exclaimed "jeepers" or possibly "holy cow."

I figured I couldn't stay in the car. I'd be dead in a few hours. And I couldn't walk back the way I came because I knew it would be too far before I saw any homes. So I decided to run for it—straight ahead—because there just might be some civilization in that direction. Maybe I could reach it before the cold killed me.

I started running. It didn't take long for my extremities to start freezing up. I couldn't move my fingers, and my feet felt like frozen rocks as they pounded the pavement. Still there were no cars and no buildings. Just snowfields and frozen trees and a steam cloud from my own breath.

That night as I literally ran for my life, I decided that if I survived with all my digits intact I would sell my piece-o-crap car for a one-way ticket to California and never see another snowflake as long as I lived.

I don't know how long I ran. It seemed like forever. I started to fade. I knew if I stopped running, the cold would get me sooner. So I kept going, running to exhaustion, stopping, running again, until finally—headlights. A traveling shoe salesman rescued me. It took a while for the feeling to come back to my hands, but I didn't lose anything to frostbite.

A few months later, immediately after graduation, I traded my car to my sister for a one-way ticket to California. I never saw another snow-flake, at least not up close.

My thinking is that the good reasons for dying do not include "went outside," as in "Where's Scott?" "Oh, he went outside without a coat and died."

This brings me to my point. I'm flying to Chicago today and some-one told me it was cold there already. I think I responded "jeepers" or possibly "holy cow." Cold is just a fancy marketing word for a particu-larly unpleasant form of pain. We should just call it what it is: pain.

What's the temperature in Chicago? Painful. Okay, so it's really only about 50 degrees there, and that's not so bad, but it's the Windy City. If you add the windchill factor, electrons actually stop moving.

I would bring a coat, but I don't like to pack it, and I'm only going to be sprinting from car to building and back. I don't see how that could go wrong.

History

According to a special on the ABC network, 9/11 happened because Bill Clinton was preoccupied with a sex scandal. I hope the authors of history books migrate toward that opinion. It would make eighth grade a lot more entertaining, especially since 9/11 will probably lead to World War III, with radical Islam on one side and various radical infidels on the other. I figure we're one dirty bomb away from that.

> TEACHER: Billy, can you explain what caused World War III?
>
> BILLY: Some skank in a blue dress gave the president a hummer?
>
> TEACHER: Very good, Billy. For homework I would like the class to depict the scene using macaroni.

Speaking of WWIII, I worry that the pope might have inadvertently accelerated it with his latest comments about Islam. I don't know if the pope has annual performance reviews with God, but I don't think he's in for a big raise this year.

> GOD: Okay, let's take a look at your accomplishments for the year. Holy Me! You killed a billion people!
>
> POPE: Well, that's one way to look at it. But I like to think that *two* billion would have died if I hadn't reminded people that war is bad. So I actually saved a billion, not counting the ones that got trampled to death coming to hear me say it.

Lights Out

A few years ago I was doing something called a book tour. That's when authors go around the country and do interviews and sign books to promote their newest work. I walked into one of the biggest bookstores in the country and was greeted by the store manager. She told me that people were excited to hear me speak. Some people had been in their seats for an hour already. The room was packed, she said. They couldn't wait to hear what I had to say.

Normally, this would be a good thing. And by "normally," I mean if someone had told me in advance that they expected me to give a speech. I thought I was showing up just to sign books, as I had in all the other bookstores on this trip.

I tried to explain that no one had mentioned a speech. But that didn't change the fact that the room was full of people who were expecting one. The next thing I know, I'm standing in front of the crowd, with a microphone in my hand, listening to their welcoming applause. Now all I needed was a speech.

Back in my corporate days, I took the Dale Carnegie course. One of the things they teach you is how to handle this exact situation. Always be mentally prepared to give a speech on a moment's notice. Be comfortable. Have fun. Go for it.

And so I did. I'm an experienced speaker. I've been doing it for years. I cobbled together some anecdotes from my career, sprinkled in some funny stuff from the book, and answered questions with witty replies that seemed spontaneous but weren't. (People always ask me the same questions.) Everything went well. I doubt anyone knew I wasn't prepared.

I was reminded of that on Tuesday. I was standing in front of a corporate group, a few minutes into my keynote address, when the lights went out. The lights returned in a few seconds, but the power surge fried the AV equipment. My professional keynote speech, of which 75 percent involves showing comics and telling stories about them, was dead on arrival.

As it became clear to the assembled executives that the equipment wasn't going to work, they looked at me with what I can only assume was a mixture of pity and "glad it's not me." Researchers say that public speaking is one of the great fears in life. But what if you have no speech and you're already in front of the crowd? That's gotta be worse. But I didn't feel fear. I'm not wired that way. I felt amused. This was something new. I like a challenge.

The bookstore crowd had only needed ten minutes of random laughs, a few questions answered, and some books signed. They were easy. But this was a sixty-minute keynote address with fifty minutes to go. I was one of the conference highlights. They were paying big bucks to have me.

"Any questions?" I asked, which got a laugh, since I had barely started my talk. A gentleman to my left raised his hand and asked the worst possible question. "What was the first newspaper to run Dilbert?"

It's the worst type of question because the answer is short and it's almost impossible to make it interesting. That's when my training kicked in again. My book publisher had given me "media training" before the first time I did a book tour and interviews. One of the main things they teach you is that if you don't like a question, or can't answer it, simply answer some other question and the audience won't care. Politicians do this all the time, and with them you normally *do* care. But with someone like me, my only responsibility is to entertain.

I enthusiastically replied that it was a "great question" and then launched into fifteen minutes of an emergency backup speech that had nothing to do with the question. Meanwhile, I watched out of the corner of my eye to see if the AV tech could quickly replace the fried equipment. He gave me the "not going to happen" signal.

In the end, I finished my talk using a hastily procured overhead projector that was probably manufactured in 1962. It projected yellow light and fly stains. If you squinted, you could make out the comic. But the audience was forgiving, and somehow it worked.

It was the most fun I've ever had giving a speech. I feel most alive when things go wrong and routine gives way to emotion. With any luck, something will go wrong today, too. I sure hope so.

Empty Boxes

F ilmmaker James Cameron is claiming that some archaeologists found the tomb of Jesus's family. All the casketlike things called ossuaries are empty. I wonder what the archaeologists were thinking when they found an ossuary with Jesus's name on it. I can imagine the moment they removed the lid and looked in. If it were me, I'd wonder if I was going to see one of the following:

Nothing

Decomposed stuff

Jesus sitting up and saying, "What in Dad's name took you so long?"

If you put an ordinary guy in an ossuary for two thousand years, he'd clearly be dead. But if I were opening that ossuary I'd be wondering if maybe someone put Jesus in there after he died but before he arose. And maybe it's hard to get out once you get in. I'd be worried that Jesus arose inside the stone box, and he'd be totally pissed that no one let him out until now.

I realize that this would not be the most rational worry in the world. But I like to base my worries on an expected value calculation. So for example, a 90 percent chance of getting a sliver would worry me about the same as a .000001 percent chance of a nuclear bomb going off in the backyard. In this ossuary example, I'd be looking at maybe a 2 percent chance of waking up an angry Jesus. I say that's worth a worry.

If Jesus was in there, and sat up when I took the lid off, I'd first try to judge how angry he looked. If he had that "money changers in the temple" look, I'd go with a joke, like "Ha ha! Turn the other cheek!" Or maybe I'd try to explain to him that the extra suffering was extra good for humanity, and after all, that's his job. Then I'd say, "Hey, I don't like my job either, but you don't see me complaining all the time."

I know that some of you will say that if Jesus could move that big rock that was allegedly in front of his tomb in the traditional telling of his life, he'd have no trouble removing an ossuary lid. But he wasn't supposed to be in an ossuary in the first place, so obviously if this ossuary is genuine, some of the details of the story were wrong. And if God let Jesus be crucified, it's not a huge stretch of the imagination to think he'd let him stay in a stone box for two thousand years. It makes sense to save your coolest miracle for when it's needed most. I think you'll agree that this would be a good time for a messiah. And if you were God, you'd want James Cameron attached to this production. So it makes sense to me.

That's why I'd be a crappy archaeologist. I'd be afraid to open anything.

Speaking of Archaeology

What is up with these buried cities that archaeologists keep discovering? I'm trying to figure out how a city gets buried unless a volcano is nearby. In my house, for example, when the crumbs on the kitchen floor reach ankle height, I start thinking about sweeping. Call me a neat freak if you must, but I wouldn't just keep eating bagels until I lose the refrigerator. It's just common sense. Apparently ancient people had no common sense. Or no brooms.

I suppose the dirt can sneak up on you if you live in the desert where there's a lot of sand blowing around. One day you're happily drilling a hole in your head to relieve a headache and the next thing you know you're nipples-deep in dirt and yelling for Akbar to pack the camel. I can see that happening.

Maybe in some cases the ancient residents all died of diseases, or someone conquered them. But you'd think that at least one family would survive. I suppose if they and their descendants only swept their own house, they'd eventually be at the bottom of a huge hole because the rest of the city would build up layers of dirt. And there would be a lot of inbreeding if no one could get out of the hole. Perhaps I will mount an archaeological expedition to find homes at the bottom of holes where the residents have twelve fingers and no spleens. Who's with me?

My best theory about the buried cities is that the ancients didn't have sinks. Think of all the food you've eaten while leaning over your sink. If all of those crumbs landed on your floor instead of being washed into the sewer system, your house would get buried pretty quickly, too. I'm guessing that the cities that got buried had a lot of residents who enjoyed donuts and potato chips. If the sewer system in Cleveland ever got blocked, that city would disappear in a few months, too.

I like to think about these sorts of things until I convince myself that I have discovered the answer in my own brain.

Cool Magic Trick

Today I am going to teach you a magic trick. You're going to disappear. Seriously. First, you need some background.

If you're a skeptic, the hardest thing to imagine is a supernatural force. How could something be "above" the natural world, and yet interact with it? Or to put it another way, how does something that is *not* here touch something that *is* here? It makes no sense.

And yet similarly bizarre things happen all the time. The world is full of things we don't understand. For example, did you know that there's no way to insulate against a magnet's field?

You can redirect a magnet's force, and thus *shield* from it. But there's nothing you can put between two magnets that will simply block their attraction. Magnets are connected in ways that our common sense can't grasp.

Gravity is equally freaky. It influences things at an infinite distance without having any contact that we can see or, again, insulate against. Physicists postulate that maybe a massless particle called a graviton is at work, but none have ever been detected. Others think gravity has something to do with the state of a string, in unproven string theory, which is another way of saying we have no idea.

Much of quantum physics is like that. We have equations that work, but the common sense of it is completely missing. Scientists say the universe is bubbling with dark matter that we can't see, and particles whose positions are only probable, not guaranteed.

The bottom line is that your existence is the sum of invisible forces operating on matter that is only probably there. From the perspective of the universe, the tiny bits of probable matter that comprise you, and the tiny slice of space-time you occupy, are vanishingly small. You already barely exist. Disappearing entirely won't be that much of a change.

Now to the magic trick: Pick a comfortable chair, and sit with your feet flat on the floor, and your arms at your sides. Close your eyes. Now stay there for a billion years.

Disturbing Developments

Yesterday, for the sixth time in the past year, a refrigerator repairman tried, and failed, to fix my ice dispenser. Four different repair guys from the company that manufactured the fridge have had a go at it. They diagnose the problem. They order parts. They install the parts. The ice dispenser does not dispense ice. I'm thinking of changing its name from "ice dispenser" to "the thing that gives me false hope of ice."

Today I saw in the news that scientists have discovered chimps in the jungle making spears to hunt. That's right: Chimps are making tools and successfully using them. *Those frickin' chimps are closing the gap!*

I hate to say bad things about my own species, but I'm sure those tool-using chimps are fully qualified to visit my home six times and not repair my ice dispenser. And none of those chimps would suggest that I buy an extended warranty. That's a big plus for the chimps.

Arthur C. Clark famously said, "Any sufficiently advanced technology is indistinguishable from magic." But in my house, any sufficiently advanced technology is broken, and no one knows how to fix it. I think we humans have hit the wall when it comes to using tools. I don't mean to worry you, but somewhere, in a distant jungle, there's a chimp chewing on a stick and making a Phillips screwdriver.

The spear-making chimps were spotted using their weapons to skewer creatures called bush babies. Bush babies are tiny, impossibly cute primates with large sad eyes that nap in the hollows of trees. They are named bush babies because they cry like babies. Only the female chimps make spears and stab these adorable little bush babies. The male chimps go off hunting by themselves, probably to get away from the female chimps, who, as you can see, are crazy bitches.

"Honey, I'm going off to hunt by myself. Have fun stabbing the bush babies with spears."

The Best Thing That Never Happened to Me

One day, in my early twenties, I built a little experimental laboratory in my kitchen in San Francisco. I was seeing if I could invent a perpetual-motion machine. As is often the case with me, I was undaunted by the fact that the laws of physics clearly rule out perpetual motion. But I would have settled for inventing a cool novelty toy that simply moved for a long time, like those toy water-dunking birds.

At one point, I had a bunch of magnets and a toy electric motor, and a bunch of other materials I was using in various combinations. I fantasized about holding some natural magnets in just the right formation around an electric motor and somehow inducing it to run without electricity. Again, the fact that this is physically impossible did not deter me. So, one day I was fiddling with the toy motor—that wasn't attached to any source of electricity—and holding some natural magnets near it when . . . *HOLY SHIT, the motor started running!!!*

WITHOUT ELECTRICITY!

I just held the magnets up to the motor, at just the right angle, and the frickin' thing started running like crazy! I had accomplished the impossible.

My spine tingled. I told myself to remember this world-changing moment because the media would be asking me a lot of questions about it. I didn't know how much money this invention would earn for me, but I knew it would be billions. In all likelihood, I would be the richest man on Earth in about a year. My invention would power cars, light cities, and heat homes. It would turn Africa into a thriving metropolis. Free energy would make everyone so happy that war would become obsolete. My invention would be spoken of in the same breath as the wheel and fire. I would be famous beyond imagination.

Then I looked down. By some freakish coincidence, the two dangling wires from my toy motor had managed to touch the two ends of a battery that happened to be sitting in my lap. That's why the motor was running.

Oh well.

Still, for about twenty seconds, until I noticed the wires touching the battery, I felt like the most important human being in the history of the world. It was a *great* twenty seconds. But that's in the past. Now I write blogs about chimps with spears. That feels good, too. And frankly, I think the wheel and fire are overrated.

Toothpaste Smuggler

(T his chapter was written during the brief period that toothpaste was banned from carry-on luggage.)

Call me fussy, but I like to brush my teeth every now and then. Unfortunately, thanks to the terrorists, that simple task is becoming more difficult whenever I fly.

You can take toothpaste in a checked bag, but the baggage claim process adds an hour to your travel and vastly increases the odds that your possessions will never again know the joy of being with you.

Theoretically, you can buy toothpaste at the hotel gift shop. But if you guessed that they will not stock enough toothpaste to meet the sudden explosion (no pun intended) of demand, you would be right. And half the time I arrive late at night when the gift shop is closed.

The nicer hotels offer free toothpaste if you're willing to wait a few hours until they get around to delivering it. But if you have a busy schedule, that means going to your first meeting smelling like airline peanuts. When that happens, I spend the entire time trying to maintain a six-foot peanut-free breath perimeter. You don't want your first impression to be "He was short and bald and smelled of cashews." I want to be remembered as short and bald and minty.

So, like millions of other travelers (I assume), I plan to become a smuggler. I figure I can take one small tube of travel-sized toothpaste in my pants pocket and make it through security without being busted. I rationalize that there is no danger to the public in doing this because I use a brand of toothpaste that rarely explodes.

But I wonder what would happen in the unlikely event that I get caught? Would they simply confiscate my Crest and send me on my way, or would they shut down the airport and give me a strip search? Maybe they would detain me and try to figure out if "the Dilbert guy" is actually working for al-Qaeda. That won't help me get to Phoenix.

I have long wondered what would happen if the terrorists ever stopped killing people that I don't personally know and started pissing me off personally. This toothpaste situation is getting perilously close to that condition. I pity the terrorists who someday make me travel without my laptop. That's when I buy a gun, fly to Pakistan, and start randomly firing into caves.

I Hate My Guts

I was nose snorkeling late last night and had a strange thought, even by my standards.

Yes, I said nose snorkeling. That's when you swim the breaststroke in calm water with your mouth below water and your nose above it. I just invented that term, I think. I can nose snorkel like a porpoise now that my deviated septum has been fixed. If you were thinking that nose snorkeling meant something else, shame on you.

Anyway, my strange(er) thought is that while I am generally fond of the outside of my body, I wouldn't touch most of the inside of me without wearing rubber gloves. For example, I wouldn't want to touch my own spleen or liver or any of the squishy stuff. And don't get me started about intestines and bile. Since most of my body is gross in that fashion, technically I am disgusted by myself. I literally hate my guts.

To be fair, I like some parts of me. For some reason I have inexplicably well-defined calf muscles. I daresay they are a joy to behold, but again, only on the outside. Their beauty is marred by the fact that I know on the inside they are full of gristle and corpuscles and marrow and whatnot. Yuck.

I think the worst super power you could have would be X-ray vision. Take a look around you right now and ask yourself how many people would look better without clothes. Not many. And if you could see inside them, that would be even uglier, but not in every case. You've heard the saying "She's beautiful on the inside." I think what that means is that her appendix is more attractive than her face.

The best part about X-ray vision is that you would no longer have to ask pregnant women if they know the genders of their babies. You could just look right into the womb with your X-ray eyes and, in all likelihood, mutate the baby's genetic code. Good times.

If everyone had X-ray eyes, you would hear sentences that you've never before heard, such as:

"Let's take a break. As you can see, my bladder is pretty much topped off."

"Is that the pulled pork sandwich you had for lunch? How was it?"

"Clear the room! Monty's about to launch a zeppelin!"

My Invisible Caveman Friend

I used to think that some of my oddest thoughts were an indication that I am some sort of genetic freak or possibly the result of alien experimentation. But the more I share my thoughts, the more I find out that I am not alone. Millions of people have thoughts exactly like mine. Today it's time to test the limit of that theory.

Confession: Often when I am driving my car, I imagine that a caveman has time-traveled to the present and is sitting in the passenger seat next to me.

Seriously.

He's a modified caveman, not an exact one. In my imagination, the caveman can inexplicably speak English. And he's wearing pants, because otherwise I would be worried about having his naked caveman buttocks on my leather seats.

What makes this fun is imagining that the caveman is experiencing an automobile for the first time. I show off, taking the turns faster than I should, exceeding the speed limit, that sort of thing. And I try to imagine how amazed the caveman would be. He'd probably try to one-up me by telling a story about the time he "ran real fast." But I would just nod and smile in my technologically superior way as I gunned the engine, dialed my cell phone, and opened the sun roof.

I might even turn on the radio and the navigation unit just to twist his nads. "Did you have anything like that back in the cave, Bucky? No? Didn't think so."

I would call him Bucky even if that wasn't his name. "Bucky the Caveman" is funny in a way that John the Caveman is not. I think you would agree. Oh, and the other thing about the caveman is that I imagine he doesn't have his club with him to kill me.

Sometimes I try imagining that *I* am the caveman and I'm driving a car for the first time. That way the imaginary guy doesn't get to hog all the fun. Somehow as a caveman, I know how to operate a motor vehicle despite my primitive caveman superstition that flatulence is caused by angering the moon god.

Does it worry you that I am qualified to vote?

The Humor-to-Naughtiness Ratio

t was the naughtiest comic I've ever created, at least intentionally. I'll always wonder how it got published. As I recall, it sailed through the system without a hitch. Here it is.

My best guess as to why editors allowed it in newspapers is that minors wouldn't get the joke, whereas adults who had jobs would appreciate the inference that the pointy-haired boss is a dick. But I also think it helped that it was funny.

There's an unwritten rule in humor that says you can get away with more vulgarity if the joke is extra funny. The best example I can think of is the *Seinfeld* episode called "The Contest." The story involved the entire cast competing to see who could avoid masturbating for the longest time. I'm convinced that it only got on television because it was so spectacularly funny. (And it didn't hurt that it was a huge hit show.)

By the time my "womb" comic ran, Dilbert was already a big hit. And it's fair to say that lots of people hate their bosses enough to think of them as huge dicks, which makes the comic seem funnier. When you combine that with the fact that kids won't get the joke, I had accidentally created the perfect storm situation for getting away with maximum vulgarity.

And yet there is one comic that topped them all. One day I got an e-mail from a reader who said, "I see what you're doing. In your comic today you drew that character to look like a huge penis."

My first reaction was that the reader was, ironically, a nut. Obviously I would never draw a cartoon featuring a huge talking penis. And if I did, obviously it would never get published. I was submitting my work so many months ahead at that point that I didn't even know which comic he was referring to. But out of curiosity I decided to look and see if there was any merit to his absurd claim that I drew a character that looks like a gigantic penis. This is the comic.

Oh. Okay. Maybe.

Tragedy Ranking System

Every time there's a military conflict, someone points out that many of the victims were *not* adult men. The theory is that a tragedy is way more tragic if anyone other than adult men get killed. If you throw a woman or a minor or a puppy into the mix then we all have a reason to be sadder and madder.

I totally agree with the view that some tragedies are more tragic than others, depending on who is involved. But I do demand efficiency. That's why I propose ranking the value of all types of people so I can more easily judge how sad I should feel when they get killed.

For example, if four hundred villagers are buried in a mudslide, I'd like to know how many of them were drunks, assholes, nags, dickheads, crooks, or males, just to pick a few examples. I wouldn't feel as much pressure to feel bad about that portion of the village. In the best-case scenario, the victims would all be adult men with no special talents. That's barely even a tragedy. We adult males have our uses to be sure, but society agrees that it's not such a big deal when someone kills us.

I think the main reason there are so many wars is that most of the soldiers are adult males. If all wars had to be fought exclusively by second graders or contestants from the Special Olympics, no one would ever start a war because the results would be too tragic.

Your Ancestors Disgust Me

It has come to my attention that many of your ancestors were pedophiles. They probably didn't know it, since marrying fifteen-year-old girls was considered "normal" by those perverts. And I'm sure they had excuses such as the fact that the life expectancy was seventeen. So maybe they rationalized it by saying they had to start pinching out new farm hands before the plague got them. Blah, blah, blah. But that's no excuse for being a pedophile.

I also have it on good authority that your ancestors from several thousand years ago rarely washed their hands with soap after pooping in the desert, or forest, or igloo, whatever. You come from a long line of unhygienic child molesters.

If you follow your repulsive blood line back far enough, you will find that your ancestors were atheists at best, but more likely worshippers of phalluses.

That's right: You are the genetic fruit of unhygienic, penis-worshipping child molesters.

And they couldn't read—those illiterate, unhygienic, penis-worshipping child molesters.

Keep going back in time and there's a virtual guarantee that somewhere a cousin married a cousin, or a brother married a sister. Statistically speaking, you're probably an inbred spawn of illiterate, unhygienic, penis-worshipping child molesters.

It makes you wonder what dumb-ass things we're doing now that our descendants will find humorously repulsive. I think they'll get a kick out of the fact that about a billion people thought God carved ten command-ments on stone tablets and somehow the tablets got misplaced. I'd like to know how that conversation went between Moses and Mrs. Moses.

> MOSES: Honey, have you seen my stone tablets from God?
> MRS. MOSES: They didn't match the carpets so I threw them out.
> MOSES: *What??? Those came directly from God!*
> MRS. MOSES: *Sure they did, you daffy bastard.*

Great Idea or Possibly Stupid

I have a theory that says no one can tell the difference between a *great* idea and a stupid one. If anyone had that sort of insight, he would be able to charge a billion dollars an hour for consulting, and there would be a long line of corporations willing to pay it.

People can often tell the difference between a run-of-the-mill *"good"* idea and a bad idea. But *great* ideas often look identical to stupid ones right up until the moment they work.

With that in mind, I give you my latest idea that is either great or stupid. Pretend you can tell the difference. I call my idea the Hypnosis Restaurant.

All patrons of the Hypnosis Restaurant would agree to be hypnotized before dining. Obviously this would make the food taste better and the service would appear spectacular. The hypnosis would all be aboveboard and voluntary. And for liability reasons the restaurant would record everything that happens with security cameras and get signed releases.

As a trained hypnotist myself, I can tell you that about 20 percent of the public is highly suggestible. For them, the dining experience would be a guaranteed four-star experience. And contrary to popular myths, people do remember their time under hypnosis. So customers would have great memories to take with them, too.

Once under hypnosis, your dining options would be unlimited. One obvious advantage is that the kitchen would never run out of anything you want. Your server could give you a turnip and tell you it was crème brûlée. You'd enjoy it just as much as if it was crème brûlée, and as a bonus you wouldn't need to wear your fat pants the next day.

Another benefit is that you could have dinner with anyone you wanted, living or dead, at least in your mind. You could specify your dinner fantasy in advance and then the hypnotist would provide it. If you want Albert Einstein at your table, and Paris Hilton under it, or vice versa, the choice is yours.

For the majority of the public who are less easily hypnotized, even they would get a tremendous benefit from the relaxation that comes with hypnosis. In fact, most people enjoy being hypnotized as much as they would enjoy a manicure or a foot massage. It simply feels good to be the subject of someone's undivided attention and have no responsibility other than relaxing. And as you know, food tastes better when you're in a relaxed frame of mind. So even if you couldn't hallucinate that Ben Franklin was at your table, you'd still be glad you came.

From the restaurant's point of view, I can't think of a better way to generate repeat business. Some people would resist the suggestion that they should come again, thinking they are being manipulated. But for every one of those people there is another who will agree to eat at the Hypnosis Restaurant seven times a day and think it was his own idea. In time, the entire business would consist of the most highly suggestible people who become regulars. This would be a big money saver for the restaurant because at that point you could stop serving food and just tell people they're eating.

Eventually there would be some sort of lawsuit alleging that the Hypnosis Restaurant is forcing people to repeatedly patronize the restaurant against their wills. But in order to win that suit, a lawyer would have to convince a jury of your peers that free will doesn't exist.

And you know that won't happen.

Knowing When to Quit

Someone asked me a great question about success and failure: How do you know when to quit?

As I already mentioned, I've failed at the vast majority of my business adventures. But the successes more than paid for the failures. That was always the plan. Theoretically, my track record would be 0-for-1 if I just kept plugging along at whatever the first thing was that wasn't working. There's a lot to be said for perseverance, but knowing when to quit is arguably more important. One way to look at it is that perseverance is what's left over after you do the right amount of quitting.

When I was a commercial lender at a bank, we often heard the rule of thumb that one out of ten businesses succeed. I doubt there was much science behind that number, but it seems about right if you exclude franchise businesses that almost always make money. It's hard to get an accurate measure of business success rates, with all the apples and oranges involved, but it's fair to say that the majority fail. And I'm sure that many of those failures were made worse by someone who didn't know when to quit. Quitting is underrated.

My own business failures were mostly things for which I was entirely qualified. What killed me each time was bad luck, usually in the form of bad timing. For example, my best ever idea was patentable, and would have been worth more than anything I've done with Dilbert. I know it was patentable because someone patented it just ahead of me.

My two corporate careers—banking and telecommunications— also suffered from bad timing. I left the bank because my boss told me that she couldn't promote a white male. At the time, the media was giving the company a lot of bad press about having no diversity in management. I gave up on my telecommunications job when my boss at Pacific Bell later told me exactly the same thing. It was an awkward little window in history where reverse discrimination got out of control. Had I been born five years earlier, or five years later, I would have missed that window. I'm not complaining, since that's the disgruntlement that led directly to Dilbert. I'm just providing it as context. Luck, typically in the form of timing, is usually the dominant factor in success. You usually have to try a bunch of things before luck has an opportunity to find you.

So how do you know when to bail out of a losing idea?

I heard a useful rule about predicting success during my (failed) attempt at creating a hit Dilbert TV show. While watching the Dilbert pilot being tested on a focus group, an experienced executive explained to me the most nonintuitive way to predict success. Since then I've observed it to be true a number of times. It goes like this: If everyone exposed to a product likes it, the product will not succeed.

Think about that for a minute before I explain why everyone liking something predicts failure. If you get this answer right, I'm guessing that you are already successful yourself.

The reason that a product "everyone likes" will fail is because no one "loves" it. The only thing that predicts success is passion, even if only 10 percent of the consumers have it. For example, I'm willing to bet that when the TV show *Baywatch* was tested, 90 percent of the people rolled their eyes and gave it a thumbs-down. But I'll bet 10 percent of the test audience had tents in their pants. Bingo.

Dilbert was the same way. From the very beginning, the vast majority of people who saw it didn't care for it. But 10 percent who saw it not only liked it, they cut it out and mailed it to friends. They talked about it. They hung it on walls. They were passionate about it. Before the first Dilbert reprint book was sold, I heard stories of people making their own Dilbert books from newspaper clippings. Bingo.

So if, for example, you invent a new type of umbrella, and every person who sees it says, "That is clearly better than all other umbrellas on the market," you have nothing. Walk away. But if someone who barely knows you demands to buy six of them for everyone in his family, and doesn't first ask the price, and is willing to drive to your house to pick them up, and immediately names each one like a pet, then you might have something. Great ideas usually catch on immediately, and passionately, at least with the early adopters. And the only good way to judge passion is by watching what people are willing to do with their time and their bodies because of your creation. Talk means nothing.

If you plan to try ten things, knowing that nine will fail, it's a good idea to pursue ventures that won't kill you if they fail. I prefer challenges where the worst-case scenario is that I'm embarrassed or tired, as opposed to bankrupt or dead. I also like to make sure I can learn something from the failure. And I prefer challenges where the upside potential is unlimited even if unlikely. But those are personal choices. I find it easy to shrug off failure, so failing 90 percent of the time works for me. Your mileage may vary.

Career Path

Did you follow the story of John Mark Karr? He's the guy who confessed to killing the little girl, JonBenet Ramsey. He was cleared by DNA testing. Then he was arrested for child porn in an unrelated case. Those charges just got dropped.

I'm wondering what kind of career you can have after you tell everyone you're a pedophile child killer but it turns out that you're really only a liar, at least about the killing part. And you're so incompetent that you can't even successfully go to jail. I think the answer is obvious:

He will run for Congress.

He'll fit right in. He already has the lying part down. And he's been sitting around in jail for months, so he's got the "do nothing" part nailed, too. The best part is that the public hates Congress more than they hate people who may or may not have killed a child and may or may not be pedophiles. He'll bring up the average.

Getting elected will be easy. Karr has name recognition, and that almost always predicts the winner. We Americans are easily bored by "issues." We prefer celebrities such as Sonny Bono and Ronald Reagan and Arnold Schwarzenegger and anything Kennedy. We would elect a box of Krispy Kreme donuts if it believed in the Rapture.

Karr might even run unopposed. I mean, who would take a chance of running against a confessed child killer and losing? That's a stain you can't get off your résumé.

If I voted, I'd vote for Karr just because he might have entertaining political views. For example, does he favor stem cell research or does he just want to have sex with them before killing them, allegedly?

And for once we'd have a politician who is willing to take responsibility. In fact, he'd probably confess to causing global warming. "I intentionally ate too many burritos. It's my fault. Seriously. I'm gassy."

He'd be like a breath of fresh air, ironically.

Marriage Surprises

I was watching the news the other day when I saw that yet another husband is suspected of killing yet another wife who has gone missing. It's pretty much automatic to suspect the husband in cases like this. This is one of the factors I had not considered before getting married.

Now every time my wife is fifteen minutes late returning from some errand, I start planning my alibi. I take a digital picture of myself standing in front of a live newscast, or I start making phone calls to my mother—that sort of thing.

The worst-case scenario is that she drives her car into a ravine and no one finds the remains until I've already been in jail thirty years. That's why I always encourage her to take the freeway. "Remember, honey, no winding mountain roads!"

The most disturbing part of this "husband did it" phenomenon is that there's *always* a motive. I'm still in the newlywed phase, but it's disconcerting to know that it's only a matter of time before every casual onlooker assumes that if one of us disappears, the other one had a perfectly good reason to commit murder. It's not much of an endorsement of marriage.

I'm in Las Vegas today and wasn't planning to write anything. But my wife has been in the bathroom for way too long and I need an alibi just in case something goes wrong in there. Note how calm I seem to be while I write this. You might be called as my character witness.

Dangerous Containers

Recently an airport security guy confiscated my 4-ounce shampoo container because he said the maximum allowed is 3 ounces. I pointed to the airport's own sign that says 4 ounces is allowed, but that didn't seem like a good argument to him. It was too late to check my bags, so he confiscated my mostly empty 4-ounce container.

But here's the interesting part. The container is semitransparent, and contained obviously less than 1 ounce of liquid. Apparently the empty portion of the container posed a threat. Or to put it another way, as we humorists like to do, the airport confiscated my 3 ounces of nothing so that I couldn't use that nothing to blow up the plane.

What they didn't seem to realize is that my carry-on bag was not entirely full either. There was a whole bunch of nothing in there along with the clothes and shoes and belt. And if I were to combine my bag of nothing with the nothing that other passengers smuggled aboard, that would make a huge stockpile of lethal nothing.

For a fleeting moment I considered reasoning with the TSA guy. Surely he could see that the liquid part of my container was minimal. But one look in his eyes told me that thinking wasn't his sport. And on some level I have to agree that we shouldn't let airport security use too much of their own judgment. Sooner or later some security person would allow a hand grenade on a plane because the passenger "didn't look angry."

I wanted to point out that the Ziploc bag itself is a container larger than 3 ounces, and that's also mostly full of dangerous air. Or perhaps I could have argued that once the airplane doors are closed, the cabin is essentially a huge container with plenty of gels and liquids and dangerous nothingness. I would have been a beacon of common sense and righteousness, right up until they started beating me with batons.

I was also concerned that they might go all Sherlock Holmes on me and ask why a guy with virtually no hair needs shampoo. I would probably say something like "Have you heard of phantom limb?" And then

I'd have a metal detector so far up my ass that my fillings would set it off.

Anyway, I just took a shower using the shampoo the hotel provides. I don't know what goes into hotel shampoo, but I always assume the worst. In this case I'm guessing green apples and the lard of bad tippers. Today is the day when I am most likely to hear the phrase "You smell like a cider whore."

Top the Cynic

Nothing bugs me more than when someone is more cynical than I am. I generally try to occupy the upper limit of cynicism just short of where the kooky conspiracy theory people get their mail. So when I see huge numbers of people eclipse me in that area, I know it's time to recalibrate.

The viewpoint that has me doubting the sufficiency of my cynicism is the notion that the war in Iraq is primarily to profit American oil companies, military manufacturers, and of course Halliburton. As a professional cynic, I *love* that idea. I want to believe it. But you have to help me connect the dots.

For example, are there actual meetings where the oil barons and the White House staff sit around sipping brandy and smoking cigars and deciding to kill a million people so they can finally afford nice things? If so, how does that conversation go?

OIL BARON 1: Let's start a war and kill a million people so I can afford a new boat.

OIL BARON 2: You already have a boat with its own helicopter pad, football stadium, and whore house.

OIL BARON 1: That thing is a year old! It embarrasses me.

OIL BARON 3: Didn't your brother-in-law just join the National Guard? He might get killed if we start a war.

OIL BARON 1: Are you even listening to me? I said my boat is way too old!

Or is it more of a subtle thing where everyone acts in ways that will lead to war and line their pockets, but in their own minds the blame for war is spread so evenly that they don't feel any personal guilt?

OIL BARON 1: Well, let's see, there were about a thousand of us top industrialists who caused this war, and a million people died, so that's only a thousand deaths on each of our hands.

OIL BARON 2: That's not so bad. I almost worked for a tobacco company.

And I wonder why I've never met anyone in person who is that evil. I've met plenty of psychos, assholes, narcissists, pigs, sluts, maniacs, drug addicts—you name it. All of the other personality defects you can imagine are abundant. But not once have I been in a conversation with someone who said, "You know, I'd be willing to kill a million men, women, and children if the money was good."

But I suppose that's the sort of thought you'd keep to yourself.

Good News Day

I lost my voice about two years ago. Permanently. It's something exotic called spasmodic dysphonia. Essentially a part of the brain that controls speech just shuts down in some people, usually after you strain your voice during a bout with allergies (in my case) or some other sort of normal laryngitis. It happens to people in my age bracket.

I asked my doctor, a specialist for this condition, how many people have ever gotten better. Her answer: zero. While there's no cure, painful Botox injections through the front of the neck and into the vocal cords can stop the spasms for a few months. That weakens the muscles that otherwise spasm, but your voice is breathy and weak.

The weirdest part of this phenomenon is that speech is processed in different parts of the brain depending on the context. So people with this problem can often sing but they can't talk. In my case I could do my normal professional speaking to large crowds but I could barely whisper and grunt offstage. And most people with this condition report they have the most trouble talking on the telephone or when there is background noise. I can speak normally alone, but not around others. That makes it sound like a social anxiety problem, but it's really just a different context, because I could easily sing to those same people.

I stopped getting the Botox shots because although they allowed me to talk for a few weeks, my voice was too weak for public speaking. So at least until the autumn speaking season ended, I chose to maximize my onstage voice at the expense of being able to speak in person.

My family and friends have been great. They read my lips as best they can. They lean in to hear the whispers. They guess. They put up with my six tries to say one word. And my personality is completely altered. My normal wittiness becomes slow and deliberate. And often, when it takes effort to speak a word intelligibly, the wrong word comes out because too much of my focus is on the effort of talking instead of the thinking of what to say. So a lot of the things that came out of my mouth frankly made no sense.

To state the obvious, much of life's pleasure is diminished when you can't speak. It has been tough.

But have I mentioned I'm an optimist?

Just because no one with spasmodic dysphonia has ever gotten better doesn't mean I can't be the first. So every day for months and months I tried new tricks to regain my voice. I visualized speaking correctly and repeatedly told myself I could (affirmations). I used self-hypnosis. I used voice therapy exercises. I spoke in higher pitches, or changing pitches. I observed when my voice worked best and when it was worst and looked for patterns. I tried speaking in foreign accents. I tried "singing" some words that were especially hard.

My theory was that the part of my brain responsible for normal speech was still intact, but for some reason had become disconnected from the neural pathways to my vocal cords. (That's consistent with most experts' best guess of what's happening with spasmodic dysphonia. It's somewhat mysterious.) And so I reasoned that there was some way to remap that connection. All I needed to do was find the type of speaking or context most similar, but still different enough, from normal speech that still worked. Once I could speak in that slightly different context, I would continue to close the gap between the different-context speech and normal speech until my neural pathways remapped. Well, that was my theory. But I'm no brain surgeon.

The day before yesterday, while helping on a homework assignment, I noticed I could speak perfectly in rhyme. Rhyme was a context I hadn't considered. A poem isn't singing and it isn't regular talking. But for some reason the context is just different enough from normal speech that my brain handled it fine.

Jack be nimble, Jack be quick. Jack jumped over the candlestick.

I repeated it dozens of times, partly because I could. It was effortless, even though it was similar to regular speech. I enjoyed repeating it, hearing the sound of my own voice working almost flawlessly. I longed for that sound, and the memory of normal speech. Perhaps the rhyme took me back to my own childhood, too. Or maybe it's just plain catchy. I enjoyed repeating it more than I should have. Then something happened.

My brain remapped.

My speech returned.

Not 100 percent, but close, like a car starting up on a cold winter morning. And so I talked that night. A lot. And all the next day. A few times I felt my voice slipping away, so I repeated the nursery rhyme and tuned it back in. By the following night my voice was almost completely normal.

When I say my brain remapped, that's the best description I have. During the worst of my voice problems, I would know in advance that I couldn't get a word out. It was as if I could feel the lack of connection between my brain and my vocal cords. But suddenly, yesterday, I felt the connection again. It wasn't just being able to speak, it was *knowing* how. The knowing returned.

I still don't know if this is permanent. But I do know that for one day I got to speak normally. And this is one of the happiest days of my life.*

---

* My voice worsened a bit over the next few months, but it never got as bad as it had been.

Almost 60 Minutes Material

Thanks to my voice problem, and subsequent partial recovery, I realized yesterday that I had inadvertently gotten closer to one of my longtime goals of being featured on *60 Minutes*. There are several ways to accomplish that sort of goal, and not all of them are good. Here are a few ways:

Steal huge sums of money
Have inappropriate sex
Be a whistleblower
Be a major celebrity
Be severely handicapped
Overcome extreme hardship

Unfortunately, I am not famous enough to qualify as a major celebrity. And my voice problem didn't last long enough to qualify as a severe handicap. But the two factors collectively were enough to get the reporters calling me when they heard about my voice recovery. I didn't realize you can *combine* categories! That's good to know. But I still wasn't interesting enough for *60 Minutes*. No, they need more.

Apparently I'll need to up the ante to get the *60 Minutes* crew out here. I don't have anyone to blow the whistle on, so that's out. And none of my hardships seem extreme enough for TV. That leaves me the options of either stealing huge sums of money or having inappropriate sex.

(As an aside, I just realized that my cat can read. She just bolted for the door.)

This time I plan to take no chances. I am going to have inappropriate sex *with* a large sum of money. I'll probably get busy with one of those big burlap bags that has a dollar sign on it. It's going to chafe, but in the end I think it will be worth it.

I can almost hear my interview:

60 MINUTES: Is it true you hooked up with a bag of money?

ME: You can't prove that.

60 MINUTES: You sent us a videotape filmed from three angles.

ME: This interview has become an extreme hardship. But you just watch me overcome it!

Electronic Voting Machines

Years ago, when I worked at a big bank, one of the hot issues was that many customers didn't trust our newfangled ATM machines. Amazingly, this fear had almost nothing to do with the fact that I worked in the ATM department. Indeed, my suggestion to include a paper shredder hole right next to the deposit hole was barely even considered. In the end, ATMs rarely stole anyone's money and kept it for long. Now most people trust ATMs.

I think about the history of ATMs when I hear all the nervous Nellies wetting their pants over electronic voting machines. I believe those worries are totally misplaced. Now don't get me wrong—there's a 100 percent chance that the voting machines will get hacked and all future elections will be rigged. But that doesn't mean we'll get a worse government. It probably means that the choice of the next American president will be taken out of the hands of deep-pocket, autofellating, corporate shitbags and put into the hands of some teenager in Finland. How is that not an improvement?

Statistically speaking, any hacker who is skilled enough to rig the elections will also be smart enough to select politicians that believe in . . . oh, let's say for example, science. Compare that to the current method where big money interests buy political ads that confuse simpletons until they vote for the guy who scares them the most. Then during the period between the election and the impending Rapture, that traditionally elected president will get busy protecting the lives of stem cells while finding creative reasons to kill the stem cells that dared to grow up.

The important thing with democracy, and this has always been the case, is that the citizens (a) believe the election result is based on the common sense and voting rights of the citizens, and (b) have enough handguns to wax any politicians who get too seriously out of line (also known as a "check and balance").

My definition of "seriously out of line" would not include humping interns and stealing from taxpayers. Those things should be allowed, even encouraged, so we can attract the most capable candidates from private industry.

Call me an optimist, but electronic voting machines make me feel good about my country.

Is it too late to start selling bumper stickers that say "I think I voted"?

The Most Obscene Letter

f you ask me, the most obscene letter in the alphabet is the asterisk. It appears in almost every naughty word you see in print, from f*ck to p*ss to m*th*rf*ck*ng c*cks*ck*r. You can't even pronounce the word *asterisk* without saying *ss. That smutty little character is attracted to obscenity like flies to sh*t.

To be fair and balanced, it should be noted that the asterisk protects you from seeing naked cuss words that would otherwise blind you and put you on the slippery slope to porn addiction. But when you cover a naughty word's turgid genitalia with an asterisk, no one knows what the f*ck you're trying to say. That's why it's totally safe!

Some folks reading this might wonder how the asterisk protects them, since theoretically you could do your own research and discover that sh*thead does not mean asking a guy named Thead to be quiet. But it's a lot of work to do that research, and few people are willing to put in the time.

Let me explain it this way: Naked naughty words can destroy your brain and also society as a whole. However, and one would think this is obvious, it's completely safe to *think* naughty words. And it's safe to cause other people to think naughty words. But if you spell those naughty words without the asterisk loincloth to protect your victims, you're a danger to society. I know this to be true because I heard it from lots of people who have sh*t-for-brains.

There are plenty of scientific studies showing that exposure to naked cuss words is a leading cause of brain rot and higher taxes. Those studies have been published in the prestigious New England Urinal of Mufficine.

The only question that remains is why you read all the way to the bottom of this chapter if you are so offended by this sort of thing?

The Stuff in My Head

I remember one day in sixth grade, our teacher asked us to go to the blackboard, one at a time, and write down something we would be willing to die for. The first few kids wrote down answers such as "cancer" and "hit by car." Our teacher informed us that this was not what he was looking for. When my turn came, I wrote "my country" and apparently this was the right answer. He praised me in front of the class. He also would have accepted freedom and democracy.

So how did a twelve-year-old know he should die for his country? That stuff gets in your head early, way before your critical reasoning capacity is in place. And it stays there. Maybe some of it is caused by evolution, but I doubt it. I think the environment puts it there, thanks to nine hundred recitations of the Pledge of Allegiance and whatnot. Evolution might have favored those who protect their family or their tribe, but I doubt it had time to work on "and the people who you don't know, from all ethnicities, who live on a patch of land recently called the United States." If I had been born in North Korea I would be making images of the Dear Leader out of rice husks. And I'd be pretty sure he was a living god.

I'm not complaining. I'm glad that kids are being brainwashed to die for me. But it has become a hobby of mine to identify the ideas that got into our heads before our critical reasoning came together. Obviously, if you have the same religion or political preferences as your parents, that's an automatic warning flag. Or, as you might say, "I agree with my parents because they were right." But my favorite example is the people who argue, in essence, "No matter how ignorant you are, you have a responsibility to vote," and its dumber cousin, "If you don't vote, you don't have a right to complain."

It doesn't take much critical reasoning to dismantle those ideas. I'm fairly certain we have the right to complain anytime we want. It's called *freedom of speech*. And we certainly have the right to *not* vote, for any reason we want. Being ignorant has to be on the short list of good reasons for not voting. But this flies in the face of whatever you were brainwashed into believing when you were a kid.

Again I remind you that I'm in favor of this sort of brainwashing for the sake of society. I'm happy that lots of people vote. The system would break down otherwise, and short of me being the dictator, I can't think of a better system than imaginary democracy masking the naked ambitions of greedy capitalists. It sounds bad when I say it, but frankly I don't have a better idea.

Tipping

As I have mentioned, I have an irrational fear of ambiguous tipping situations. You might think that with all my traveling I would have seen them all. But no, I keep running into new ones. It bothers me because I don't want to accidentally stiff someone and later realize it and feel bad. I worked for tips all through college, so I know how it feels to get stiffed. Worse yet, I hate to offer a tip only to find out I'm talking to the manager of the hotel. (Yeah, it happened. They need to dress less like bellhops.)

Last night I arrived at the airport where my speaking client had arranged ground transportation to the hotel. I'm waiting by the curb for a ride of unknown character and I'm running through the tipping options in my head just to be prepared:

1. If it's a limo service, no tip because the driver's gratuity is built into the price charged to the client.
2. If it's the hotel's own courtesy limo, the driver is hoping for a tip.
3. If it's an employee of the company that is hiring me, I don't tip because he's probably a vice president of something in his day job.

An unmarked van pulls up. Crap. I don't have a solution for "guy in unmarked van." Luckily another conference attendee and his wife are coming along and they engage the driver in conversation. Perhaps I could glean the information I needed.

Now let me digress and add some context before I continue. Those of you who travel a lot know that if you ask a driver about his life, you never get a story that sounds like this: "Well, I was a drifter and a hobo for a while, but then I got this job driving you around. It's the highlight of my life."

Instead you usually get something more like this: "After I won the Nobel Prize I became a dissident in my country and had to flee. I worked as a nuclear weapons inspector for a while. Then I did some software programming, which is easy because I have a doctorate degree in math. Then I invented The Clapper and retired. Now I just do this job to help out a friend."

And so our unmarked van driver told us about his Fulbright Scholarship, leaving Brazil because it wasn't a big enough challenge to live in a country where you can speak the language (he really said that), and becoming an international consultant. He used to be a good golfer but now he prefers flying kites. And he only does this job once in a while to help a friend who owns the limo company. Plus his wife likes the fact that it "keeps him off the streets" although as he pointed out—ha ha!—ironically, he is working on the streets!

None of this is making me happy, and not just because of his jokes. I had decided in advance to try and tip him, but now I'm not so sure. Are you supposed to tip international consultants who are just "helping a friend"? And isn't the gratuity built in to the price his friend's company is charging the client? Where's the little sign in the van that says "Operator appreciates tips"? I needed more clues, dammit!

I like to prepare for the tipping moment by transferring the appropriate cash from my wallet to my right-front pants pocket where it is staged for a casual quickdraw. I had already made the transfer and now I realize this driver might have a greater net worth than I do. To hear him tell it, he's only in it for the fun.

I decide to let the other couple in the van get out first and see what the husband does. If he tips, I'll go for it, too. Our driver unloads the bags from the back and a swarm of hotel bellhops surrounds the pile like vultures on a dead wildebeest. I'm totally tip-blocked from the driver. I watch the husband, and after some hesitation, he coughs up a few bucks. The driver thanks him and heads quickly back to get in the van.

NOW I HAVE TO TIP HIM, AND FAST, BEFORE HE MAKES HIS GETAWAY!

A pile of luggage and four bellhops are in my way. I hop over the smallest bag, elbow a bellhop, and yell to the driver. He turns with a fight-or-flight look on his face, expecting the worst. I thrust five bucks at him and said something that may or may not have been "Take my frickin' money! Make my guilt and ambiguity-tension go away! Buy another kite, you magnificently interesting bastard!" Or it might have been "Thank you."

Either way, I don't feel good about it. I know he realizes I wasn't going to tip him until the other guy did. Now I have to live with that for the rest of my life.

Why can't I be afraid of something normal, like North Korea?

Blame Room Service

When I'm traveling for my speaking sideline, one of my small pleasures is ordering room service to arrive at the crack of dawn. I love my warm bagel, small pot of green tea, and assorted fruit plate. It starts my day off on the right foot. Sometimes I'll have a room with a view. I'll open the drapes and gaze into the forever while carefully spreading the cream cheese on my toasted bagel and waiting for my tea to steep to perfection. I like to alternate between the bagel and the fruit plate, allowing each flavor to surprise my tongue and delight my brain. Each sip of the lightly caffeinated tea nudges me toward a wonderful awakening. It is the perfect start for the day.

Other times, like yesterday, the hotel will take my room service order the night before, crumple it up, and toss it under a plate warmer. (Just guessing.) The next morning I'll grump around hungry and tired for thirty minutes before calling to confirm that they have no plan of ever delivering. Then I'll raid the minibar for a twelve-dollar Mars bar and a Diet Coke before rushing off to get dressed. Yesterday, my day did not start off right.

This is a necessary context for the rest of the story.

About a week ago an angry woman angrily contacted my syndication company to express her anger. Apparently she had written an angry article about the workplace, and someone had, without her permission, pasted some Dilbert images (covers from my books, probably from Amazon.com) into her writing and distributed it around the Internet. This made the angry woman angry about the alteration of her angry article. Specifically, she was angry at me.

Her article is written in an angry street-language style, angrily berating people who pause by her cubicle to chat and ask her where she got her decorations. Here's an example sentence: "Walk your ass down the hall to the big supply room and get you some things." I include that quote partly to give you the flavor of the article and partly because I doubt she understands things like Fair Use in copyrights and it will make her really angry to see it quoted here.

Her angry complaint is that she believes I pasted Dilbert images into her work and distributed it as though it were my own. My syndicate explained that this theory was unlikely and confirmed with me that I had never before seen her work. They let her know. Case closed, right?

The angry woman kept calling my syndicate demanding a more satisfying answer. She wanted to hear it from me directly. So I called her from the hotel. I figured it would take ten seconds to sort this out. I would simply explain that it is a common occurrence for people to modify stuff on the Internet and obviously this is what happened.

The angry woman answered the phone. She accused me of being up to no good. She implied that I stole her work. She seemed unwilling to entertain any other possibility. All of this happened in the first five seconds.

Now, at this point, I have to remind you that I am severely under-bageled. Looking back, I think I was a bit less flexible than I normally would have been. Even so, I could usually shake off being called a thief if the missing item was, for example, a diamond, and I had the motive and opportunity to take it. I would understand how someone might suspect me.

But this was no diamond. My mistake was in pointing that out. I believe my exact quote was "Why would I steal crap?"

Silence.

If I may give you any advice, it would be this: When dealing with an angry woman who writes angry articles, who is angrily accusing you of stealing her angry articles, do not expect her to calm down when you refer to her work as "crap."

"What did you just say?????"

At this point I was committed. I was hungry. And I had just been accused of being a crap-stealer. So I went with it.

"Your writing is crap. Why do you think I would want to associate my work with your crap?"

She retorted, *"You are an arrogant, pompous, jerk!"*

I chuckled and hung up. Suddenly I was in a good mood again. But best of all, this angry woman and I had found something we could both agree on. I *was* an arrogant, pompous jerk. Although in my defense I do a fairly good job of hiding it unless someone calls me a crap-stealer.

The angry woman contacted my syndication company again, apparently more convinced than ever of my crap-stealing proclivities. She warned of unspecified dire consequences in my future.

Something tells me this isn't over.

The Future of Voting

A t this writing, President Bush's approval rating is less than one in three. Nancy Pelosi, the majority leader for the opposition party, is in the same range. In other words, two-thirds of the citizens of the United States believe our leadership could improve if Bush drove his Segway into the majority leader and then over a cliff, assuming Cheney saw it happen and died of a heart attack.

Many of the Democrat candidates won this past election on the platform of "change," without specifying what that change would be. I remember when we almost always wanted a candidate to tell us in advance if he favored tax breaks, or cannibalism, or changing the national language to humming.

Is it just me or have we set the bar too low?

I wonder who to blame for this sorry state of affairs. Is it the candidates themselves? I think not, because they only got into office because the public voted for them. Is it the voters' fault? I think not, because as I often say, the voters don't have the right information to make good decisions. Is it the media's fault? Not exactly, because providing useful information (as opposed to entertainment) would make their ratings plummet and they'd go out of business. What choice do they have?

How about the big corporate interests and the lobbyists? Is it their fault? Perhaps yes, when they're doing things illegally or without full disclosure. But their contributions are mostly disclosed, although you'd have to do some work to figure out where. And their impact would be much less if voters had the information they needed in order to vote in their own best interests.

What we need is a new way to help voters make decisions. If that ever happens, I'll start voting. I don't vote now because my vote would be uninformed and random. But I'd like to vote. It's a good concept. I just need better tools.

In concept, it wouldn't be that hard to provide voters with the right information, thanks to the Internet. All it would require is a website that displays both sides of every argument, point by point, within its proper context. And for every point, the opposition could register their counterpoint. So if one side said, "This will save a billion dollars," the opposition could tag it with their counterpoint, and the counterpoint could itself be tagged, and so on. Perhaps the website would also benefit from some sort of argument ranking system so that the best points and counterpoints floated to the top.

And I'd want to see links to research that supported any point being made. The current method of political debate involves one side making a claim and the other saying, "that's not true." That does nothing for me. I want to click once to see the source.

I'd also want to see the list of experts lined up on both sides of every argument, along with their political affiliations. If 90 percent of economists favored one fiscal policy over another, that would sway me. If 90 percent of recently retired generals supported one method of fighting a war, that would sway me, too.

I'd also like to see opinion poll results that are limited to independent voters above a certain IQ range who have passed a knowledge test on the specific issue. It doesn't help me to know that 80 percent of the ignorant, brainwashed masses support something. I want to know what the well-informed, bright independents think. That way if I don't have the time or interest to study an issue, I can still decide to vote with the bright, informed people.

I also think we should ban all political advertising. I realize it's an issue of free speech, but that freedom has always had lots of restrictions. For example, you can't libel someone, and you can't lie about your product's effectiveness, and you can't yell *"Fire"* if there's no fire. If a political ad sways an election and causes an unnecessary war (just to pick an example), then it's a lot like yelling *"Fire."* We routinely limit free speech when the alternative is worse.

Lots of voters don't use the Internet, especially the elderly. But that will change over time. And elections are often so close that it wouldn't take much movement to improve the results.

I started out talking about whose fault it is that American politics is broken. Finding fault is how you usually determine whose job it is to shape up and fix things. But sometimes, as in this case, the people who can fix it are not the ones at fault. I think a couple of twenty-somethings with Web skills could alter the face of democracy forever. And maybe make a few billion dollars for themselves along the way.

Are Smart People Dumb?

often say I'd like to see political polls that are limited to the smart, well-informed people. I have to confess, I think my opinion on this topic is like a universal truth along the lines of "it's better to have good health than poor health." It seems to me that being smart and well-informed is almost the same thing as being wise. Who doesn't want the benefit of wisdom to inform their choices?

I have been surprised at how many people disagree with that opinion when I voice it, and rush to support the high quality of decisions made by stupid, uninformed people who are guided by superstition. Seriously.

Some people accused me of being an elitist and trying to assign a higher value to my own smarty-pants decisions. That's a perfectly reasonable assumption, and I would have made it myself if I were in your Birkenstocks. But the truth is that I want to know the opinions of people who are both *smarter* and *more informed* than me. Why would I limit the quality of my advice to people who don't know any more than I do?

Imagine choosing a doctor on that criterion. "Well, I'd like a brain surgeon who's about as smart as I am, and knows as much about brains as I do, and *no* more."

Still, I pride myself on being able to consider the merits of all points of view no matter how silly they seem on the surface. I asked myself this: If I were the lawyer representing the superstitious simpleton segment of the country, how would I argue that their opinions should be given the same weight as the people who are smart and well-informed? I took it as a challenge.

First, I suppose I would point out how many great decisions have been made by dumb guys (Reagan) and crappy decisions made by smart guys (Carter). I'd hope you accepted my anecdotes as evidence and didn't ask me for a chart showing the relative number of bad decisions made by morons versus geniuses. I'd tell you to go get your own data. And I'd hope you wouldn't ask me to explain how the Soviet

Union would have lasted much longer regardless of who was president of the United States. That's "changing the subject."

I'd also refer to military studies done years ago where researchers compared the performances of small groups that had different compositions of intelligence. They found that the groups with the highest percentage of bright people performed the worst. Apparently all the smart people insisted they had the best ideas and nothing got done. The best performing groups were the ones where there was one smart person and the rest of the group deferred to him. Therefore, I would argue, too much intelligence ruins everything.

I'd hope you didn't ask me to specify the source of that study because it's something I heard twenty years ago and I might be remembering the conclusions backward. I'd also hope to God you didn't ask me to explain how that military small-group example is a good analogy to political opinion polls.

My best argument is the one that hurts me the most. For that you need some background. After college, I got my first "real" job as a bank teller in the San Francisco financial district. My typical customers were titans of industry. They seemed pretty smart. I wondered how smart I was compared to them. Sure, I earned excellent grades in my tiny high school and small college, but how would I stack up in the real world? Was I smart enough to become a titan of industry?

I decided to take an I.Q. test administered by Mensa, the organization of geniuses. If you score in the top 2 percent of people who take that same test, you get to call yourself a "genius" and optionally join the group. I squeaked in and immediately joined so I could hang out with the other geniuses and do genius things. I even volunteered to host some meetings at my apartment.

Then, the horror.

It turns out that the people who join Mensa and attend meetings are, on average, not successful titans of industry. They are, instead— and I say this with great affection—huge losers. I was making $735 a month and I was like frickin' Goldfinger in this crowd. We had a guy who was some sort of poet who hoped to one day start "writing some of them down." We had people who were literally too smart to hold a job. The rest of the group dressed too much like street people to ever get past security for a job interview. And everyone was always available for meetings on weekend nights.

But the members were, as advertised, geniuses. Mensa meetings are the strangest experience. No one ever has to explain anything twice. That's a bigger deal than you might think. Your typical day is full of moments where you ask for a cup of coffee and someone hands you a bag of nails. You don't realize how much time you spend reexplaining things until you no longer need to. Mensa is very cool that way.

However, my Mensa experience served as a warning about trusting the judgments of people who might know how to, for example, make a helicopter from objects found lying around the house but can't manage their own lives. Is it possible that good ol' common sense and traditional values are a better foundation for important life decisions, including politics?

We know that IQ correlates with income, but is that because smart people make better decisions or because of discrimination against people who have less education? Is voting more like brain surgery, where intelligence and knowledge obviously help, or more about judging character, where IQ might not be a significant factor?

Okay, that's my best attempt at showing both sides of the issue. But I still want to know the opinions of people who are smarter than me and know more about the issues than I do. Ballot propositions, for example, have little to do with character. Maybe we could track the opinions of smart, well-informed people for a few election cycles and see how they do. That seems worth knowing.

Alternately, we can keep voting for the guy with the best hair while waiting for the Rapture. That might work, too.

Small Pleasures

The great thing about recovering from the flu is rediscovering all the small pleasures I had taken for granted. For example, I love standing in the shower after all the cleaning is done, just rocking back and forth while the warm water massages my neck and shoulders. It doesn't last long. The world is calling. But for those two minutes, bliss.

After several days of doctor-ordered bland food, I experienced "flavor" yesterday as if for the first time. *"Sweet baby Jesus, what planet did this pickle come from?!"*

And caffeine. I know that some of you think that life without caffeine is actually worth living. But it isn't. My first Diet Coke after four days of abstinence was shiver-worthy. I didn't see the hand that reached inside my head and removed the wads of cotton, but suddenly I remembered that I have hopes and dreams. Excellent!

I love the feeling when the last bill in the pile is paid and my desk is empty. Clean desk, clean mind. The feeling only lasts until the next day's mail. But I'm gazing at a clean desk right now and it's glorious.

I love it when my cat invites me for some quality time by lying on his back with his back legs splayed apart and his front paws on his chest. I know he's trying to use his eyes like tractor-beams to draw me in. It always works.

I love the sound of a new can of tennis balls being opened: ph-ssshhht. After three decades of playing tennis I'm trained like Pavlov's dogs. That sound means ninety minutes of good times ahead. All tennis is good tennis.

I love the smell of vanilla.

I love the feeling of doing something right, no matter how inconsequential, such as guessing the exact right time it will take to warm a yam in the microwave. It makes me feel in control of my life.

After four sick and rainy days indoors, I felt like a marble that fell on the floor and rolled under the dresser. Yesterday I reintroduced my face to the sun. It was like plugging back into the universe. Hello universe. They say you can't actually feel your body produce vitamin D, but I think I can. Ahhhh.

I like being tired at the same time I have access to a comfortable chair and plenty of time to sit in it. Those three things don't often line up, but when they do, it is pure sitting magic.

I like a pen that has good balance, opens easily, and leaves a clean line with no skipping, blotching, or fussiness. Such pens are rare. I have one in my pen cup right now. Sometimes I just look at it and feel happy that my species could make such a pen.

I like rubbing my head after I give myself a haircut. It feels good on my hand and my head at the same time. It's a win-win rubbing situation. And it's totally free.

And I like writing this chapter today because I know it will remind you of your own small pleasures. Take a deep breath. Release that knot in your back. Wiggle your feet. Enjoy your day.

Aging Brains

They say you get smarter every day that you're alive until some tipping point. After that, because your brain starts to rot with age, you get dumber every day. I wonder if I'll know when it happens. That would be a bad day. "Something feels different today. I wonder what... uh-oh."

I already forget more things than ever. But to be fair, I have more things to forget. So even if my retention-to-forgetting ratio stays constant, I'd be forgetting more next year than I knew by the age of seventeen. At that age if I couldn't eat it, bounce it, or masturbate to it, there was no place for it in my world.

I used to worry because I have less energy than I did when I was a kid. Then I learned that kids sleep about twelve hours a night. If I slept that much you'd have to medicate me to keep me in my chair, too. And I'll bet I wouldn't need to check my BlackBerry when someone asked for my address. Not that I've done that as recently as this morning.

All the experts agree that kids can learn new languages faster than adults. I am not impressed. If I had as few problems as a nine-year-old, I could learn Chinese over the weekend. Let that kid start worrying about his HTML code, Iran's nuclear program, and the alternative minimum tax trap—then let's see who can conjugate faster.

To compensate for my inevitable mental decline I am already doing triage on entire categories of my memory. Anything I don't need will be purged to make room for new stuff. I already got rid of the category I call "who wore what." If I see you in the gym wearing a full chicken outfit I will remember that as "saw you working out." Luckily I'm male, so it didn't take much work to purge that category.

Eventually I plan to release all knowledge of complicated explanations for the world whenever simpler ones will do the trick. Evolution has to go. That's way too complicated. I plan to remember only a few dozen species anyway, mostly the cute ones. I think we can all agree that there are too many unnecessary animals. I can't be expected to remember them all. My long-term objective is to remember nothing about animals except that the political party with the donkey symbol exists only to raise my taxes.

I'm also going to start lumping things together in my mind based on their similarities just to save space. From now on, stem cells are babies, and Iranians are Arabs. And they all live in North Korea with Osama.

Philosophical Brevity

always laugh when someone finds the fewest words to describe a complicated situation. My old boss at Pacific Bell, Mike, was a master of philosophical brevity. I remember one day working in the technology lab where several of us shared work benches. We were having an ongoing debate about the use of one of the drawers. One faction wanted it to be used for screwdrivers and such. The others felt it was the ideal place for keeping snacks. This led to the inevitable witticism that it "depended if you wanted to eat or screw."

But Mike hadn't yet registered his opinion and we needed a tie-breaker. So my coworker asked, "Well, Mike, would you rather eat or screw?" Mike thought for a moment and said, "Depends how hungry I am."

Mountains have been written about free will and human motivation, and seeing things in black and white versus shades of gray. Mike nailed all of that in a sentence. If aliens someday visit and want to understand people, they can read everything in the Library of Congress, or Mike's one sentence.

My friend Josh has the brevity knack, too. My favorite was his summation of the comic Marmaduke, about a Great Dane. It's been in newspapers for about half a century. That's about eighteen thousand Marmaduke comics. Josh's summary: "Big dog is on something you want."

To be fair, a wag once described Dilbert as "My boss is dumb." But that's just being cruel.

I was reminded of my love for brevity when I read a comment on my blog from Stuart Booth. He said, "I reduced my worldview to 'people who are important' and 'people who are too stupid to be important.' Everything else is just scenery."

I laughed out loud the first time I read it. I still chuckle when I reread it. Calling the universe "scenery" takes brevity to a new level of delicious.

I've described the clash of Islam and Christianity—everything from the Crusades to the war on terror—as "The people who think a guy walked on water versus the people who think a horse can fly." I submit that anything you add to that description is unnecessary for understanding the global clash of civilizations.

Comedian Larry Miller once described America's war strategy in Iraq as "Driving around until people shoot at us."

Those are the sorts of observations that make me think our history books are way too long.

Welcome to the Club

When I first started cartooning, my job was to make funny comics. That was it. Over time, as Dilbert grew to two thousand newspapers and became a cultural icon, I picked up some extra duties without realizing it. Now my job includes signaling changes in the way society views things. I didn't volunteer for that job. It's just part of the package.

Dilbert comics have been used several times in court cases to demonstrate that some topic or other should be considered general knowledge. For example, if the Y2K problem is in a comic strip without much explanation, then the CEO has no excuse for being unprepared. Perhaps an executive could be forgiven for not reading technical journals, but by the time a topic is in the funnies, he should know about it. That's the legal argument.

My trickier responsibility involves deciding who is fair game for humor. This is a bigger deal than you might think. Humorists are charged with the job of deciding when it's time to move some group off the "protected list" and onto the firing range with the other legitimate humor targets. If we jump the gun, all hell breaks loose because it looks as if we're kicking the weak. But if we time it right, it signals an important step in our collective enlightenment about the value of our fellow humans. And it means some group has demonstrated its value to the point where they can no longer be considered victims. You haven't achieved equality until you're a legitimate target for humor.

I jumped the gun with a recent series in Dilbert featuring the "mildly retarded consultant" who spouted management gibberish exactly like every other consultant. Boy did I hear about that. I won't reprint the comics here because it will only make things worse.

I thought I had covered my bases. First, "mild retardation" is the accepted medical term, and I used it that way, as a label and not as an insult. Second, it's my observation that almost everyone has some sort of mental problem. I'm dyslexic. You have ADD. Your neighbor is clinically depressed. Your uncle washes his hands four hundred times a day. Your sister is an emotional basket case. Your best friend is a chronic masturbator. The guy in the next cubicle is on Prozac. The woman behind him is on Xanax. To her right is the guy on Paxil. He's on the phone with the vendor who's on Valium. And they all pray to different invisible friends. (They can't all be right.)

To put it another way, who the hell *doesn't* have some sort of mental problem? I thought everyone was out of the closet on mental disorders, and that mentioning one in particular should be no big deal. But as I said, I misjudged our collective readiness on this issue. I'll be happy when society realizes that all humans are mentally defective, just in different ways. I mistakenly thought we were already there.

More recently, I called one right in my Sunday comic on November 19, 2006, where Dilbert is on a date with a woman whose only conversational interest is her own hair.

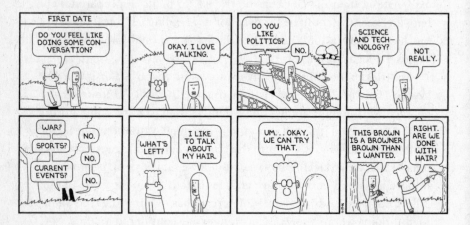

It wasn't long ago that I would have been ripped to shreds by the feminist wolf pack for that comic. I received one complaint out of millions of readers.

Congratulations, women. You're off the protected list. Apparently it's now obvious to everyone that you can be Meg Whitman or Oprah or Nancy Pelosi if you want. But if you prefer, you can bake cookies, raise kids, and care about your hair. It's simply a matter of choice. I hereby declare it common knowledge.

Welcome to the club.

Comic Asses

Did you see the character appearing in Dilbert with underpants on his head? I can explain. Here's the version that ran in newspapers and on Dilbert.com on November 12, 2006.

I was trying to show that the marketing guy has an ass for a head and he's pulling data out of it. But it's not so clear what's happening because of the underpants on his head. That's why my original version portrayed his head as a naked ass. My editor didn't think the public was ready for that.

Here's my original and uncut version. Doesn't it work better than the censored one?

I spend an unusual amount of time trying to find the absolute limit of cartoon ass acceptability. You rarely see a naked ass in comics. Calvin (of Calvin and Hobbes) showed his once, but he's a little kid and that makes it seem innocent. And Calvin wasn't pulling a document out of his sphincter.

I once tried to show Wally's plumber's crack. That didn't fly. But I did get away with showing a naked ass from the side view. I guess that was okay because it was in a medical context and a cheek is not as bad as an ass crack.

I've learned from trial and error that you can show a guy's head partly inserted in another person's ass as long as it's only the back of his head. This one ran in newspapers with no complaints.

Where I get in trouble is when I turn the guy around so his face is buried in an ass. Somehow that's suddenly "wrong." This one never ran in papers.

Based on my exhaustive research, this is what I have learned about comic asses:

Acceptable Asses

1. Little kid asses
2. Back of head in clothed ass
3. Ass head wearing underpants
4. Monkey emerging from back of pants
5. Furry animal asses
6. Side views of asses in a medical context

Unacceptable Asses

1. Naked ass for a head
2. Plumber's crack
3. Face buried in clothed ass
4. Adult asses of any kind

Consider yourself educated.

Delusions of Competence

efore I got married, I did many things correctly. I attribute my excellent performance to the fact that I have astonishingly low standards for just about everything that doesn't directly affect my health. My plan for happiness was to set the bar low and clear it by a mile. It was a formula that worked so well that I considered turning it into a self-help book. I would have called it *The Power of Low Standards*. The entire book would have been three pages long and handwritten on paper that would make a beaver say, "No thanks, I just ate."

Now I'm married, and that means I have to explain myself a lot. I can no longer leave a hot iron on my shirt just to see how long it takes to burn it, then draw more comics and buy another shirt. Suddenly that sort of thing is wrong.

I went into the marriage fully understanding that the big decisions would be jointly made, and I'm okay with that because it makes perfect sense. Two heads are better than one. The part that caught me by surprise is how often I have to second-guess myself on the little decisions. And life, it turns out, is mostly little decisions.

This problem came into sharp focus while cleaning up after a holiday get-together with family. I found myself staring at a serving plate of a thoroughly picked over ham bone and gristle and wondering if it was okay to throw it out. In my premarriage days, this decision would be simple. Not only would I have thrown it out, but I might have literally thrown it out the window just to see how long it took a raccoon to find it. Sometimes I like to do that sort of research. In those days, every problem had an obvious solution.

But now I am faced with a decision that presents many opportunities to be wrong. I'm thinking that the tray of ham debris *might* be garbage. It sure looked like it. But maybe Shelly had plans to make a soup. I had never seen her make a soup from a ham bone, but life is full of firsts. Or maybe she already promised the bone to my mother-in-law for her dog. Knowing that I might disappoint a human is enough pressure, but now I had to worry about making a dog sad. It was almost too much to bear.

I started to wonder if the ham debris only looked worthless to me because I'm a vegetarian. Perhaps someone else might peer into the gristle and see an entire week's worth of delicious sandwiches. I needed to come to terms with the fact that I am not qualified to judge ham sandwich potential. I made a mental note to add it to my growing list of inadequacies.

Shelly wasn't nearby at the time of this decision process. I could have waited until she got back, but the plate of used ham parts was seriously impeding my kitchen-cleaning plan. And I knew that if I postponed this decision, I'd only get hung up on a similar question with the guacamole dip. I was paralyzed. I either had to make an executive decision (probably wrong) or risk being seen as an unhelpful spouse. I decided that my best option was to bide my time until Shelly got back. I started to slowly gather up used dishes and put them in the dishwasher. This is something I knew I could do right. And by "right" I mean I generally fill the dishwasher to 100 percent capacity, and then Shelly rearranges things to make room for ninety additional items.

I managed to drag out the dishwasher-loading process until Shelly got back. This turned out to be a good strategy. Had I made the ham decision unilaterally I would have later heard the question "Why did you put garbage in Tupperware and store it in the refrigerator?" And then I'd have to say, "I'm keeping the ham bone fresh for your mom's dog. That's called thinking about others."

The One Problem with the World

What one simple problem could you eliminate—let's say by using magic—that would fix virtually every other problem in the world?

You might say that poverty is the biggest single problem. There's a good argument for that. But I'm reasonably sure that if everyone on the planet suddenly became a billionaire we'd still be fighting over who has the best God. And before long a copy of Windows would cost a billion dollars and Bill Gates would have all the money back. That magical fix wouldn't last.

You could magically make all forms of energy clean and plentiful and free, or eliminate disease, or create a machine that produces unlimited food from pollution. But not one of those solutions would fix all the problems in the world.

My best candidate for a universal fix is to imbue us all with the knowledge of who is smarter than ourselves on any given topic. At the moment, without the benefit of that magical fix, we only have the power to accurately identify people who are dumber than us.

For example, I know for sure that my dog is dumber than me. I don't have to make him take the SATs. It's just obvious. And you probably know from your own experience that if you have an incredible idea of your own—the sort that is later proven to be genius because it works—that people around you will consider you a moron right up until the point your idea works. Then they'll think you're a lucky moron. Genius looks just like stupidity to the observer.

If I look at the range of opinions on any important topic—from global warming to geopolitical strategy—I can't tell the difference between a supergenius opinion and a moron opinion. Both opinions are different from my own. So for convenience, and because I like things in neat categories, I do the same thing you do in that situation: I assume that everyone who disagrees with me is a moron.

My perception is that when I make an argument that's as solid as $2 + 2 = 4$, the criticisms are often along the lines of "you forgot that elephants can play the piano." To me it seems that the counterarguments are so off-point it's scary.

But to be fair, the people talking about the elephants and the pianos believe they are brilliantly stomping on my steaming pile of crap argument. To them, I appear to be the moron. "Stick to comics," they said. And if I am to be honest with myself I have to say they could be right. If they are supergeniuses on any given topic, I wouldn't be able to distinguish them from morons. I don't have that power of perception. Neither do you.

You could rely on the so-called experts to make smart decisions for you. But experts often disagree with one another. That leaves you to pick the best expert, and that's something you probably aren't an expert at doing. Look at the stock market. There are about 10,000 stocks. But there are 20,000 managed stock funds, the majority of which can't beat a stock-picking monkey with a dartboard. You have a 1-in-10,000 chance of randomly picking the best stock in the world and a 1-in-20,000 chance of randomly picking the best stock expert.

My magical solution is to give humans the power to tell the difference between a supergenius and a moron. I think this would solve every problem in the world because chances are that the smartest supergenius in each field has a good idea how to fix the problems in that field. But under our current process, the only solutions being considered are the ones coming from tall guys with good hair.

The only problem with this magical solution is that it would be somewhat shocking on the first day when you realize that morons are running the world and the guy mowing your lawn has the solution to world hunger. But you'd get over it.

Nearly Funny Things

As a professional humorist, I read the news differently from you. I'm mining it like the old guy on the beach with a metal detector. You see miles of sand and seashells and used condoms, but I see a potential windfall of thirty-five cents in coins plus half an earring. That's why my life has more meaning than yours. But my point is not to brag. I'm just saying.

The key to finding good humor fodder is that the story must be *nearly* funny without being completely funny on its own. For example, if I see a story about some spatially challenged burglar who got his head stuck in a chimney, and a stork built a nest in his ass, that's already completely funny. There's nothing for me to add.

What I'm looking for is a story that makes me giggle before I even know why. The potential is there, but it needs some magic humor dust to make it all that it can be. I mention this because I was reading on MSNBC.com that the pope is visiting Turkey. This is 50 percent funny all by itself.

Then I read that twenty thousand Muslim protesters in Istanbul were chanting "Pope don't come!" (Seriously.)

Bingo!

Keep in mind that I have not *added* any jokes yet. It's 99 percent hilarious all by itself. You can imagine several reasons why the Muslims would chant "Pope don't come!"

1. Muslims are supportive of the pope's celibacy and are rooting for him.
2. Muslims have already locked up their sons but feel that an extra precaution is warranted.
3. No one wants to clean it up.

In a crowd of twenty thousand people, you have to figure they have different reasons.

I immediately imagined a second group of protesters with a modest grasp of Western slang chanting "Pope don't shit in our woods!" It's important to cover all the bases, chant-wise. You'd hate yourself later if the pope went and did the one thing you forgot to chant.

I also imagine the pope trying to craft his speeches so as to not ignite World War III. It wouldn't take much of a gaffe—a mistranslated verb, an unclear proverb, quoting an ancient scholar who said Muslims are God's dingleberries—this sort of slip can happen. No one is infallible.

I also wonder what the Muslims think of this man of peace who carries a scepter featuring a bearded Middle Eastern guy nailed to a cross. I'm no expert in body language and dressing for success, but I have to think it's wise to hide your torture-themed novelty toys when you're pursuing world peace.

I read that the president of Turkey plans to present the pope with a *copy* of the imperial order for tolerance issued by the Ottoman Sultan who seized Istanbul from the Christians in 1453. Now, if we ignore for the moment that you can buy one of those at the airport gift shop for $1.75, there's also the question of what message it sends. On one hand it could mean "We Muslims mean Christians no harm." Or it could mean "Neener neener—you have been our bitch since Columbus was a zygote!" I think it could go either way.

Anyway, I know I feel more comfortable with the pope in Turkey. When it comes to handling delicate matters affecting the survival of the planet, you want to send in the seventy-nine-year-old German guy with a Marge Simpson hat, a history of talking directly to God, and seven decades of sperm backup. I don't see how that could go wrong.

Offending (Other) People

I rarely offend *people* in my blog, or my comic strip. But I often offend *other* people. By that I mean that for eighteen years I have been getting the following sort of e-mail:

> *Mr. Adams—Your [blog or comic] today was highly offensive to ambidextrous Rotarians! By portraying one ambidextrous Rotarian as lazy you are declaring it okay to mock ambidextrous Rotarians. They already have a tough time in society. Would you say the same thing about African Americans or Jews?*

But that's not the interesting part. The letters virtually always include this parenthetical: "(By the way, I am not myself an ambidextrous Rotarian, but I know someone who is.)"

When I get that sort of complaint, I watch my e-mail to see if any actual ambidextrous Rotarians also write. Sure enough, I will start seeing e-mail from them, too. The lag is about a day because their friends forward my comic or blog posts to them. Those letters fall into two categories:

1. "Perhaps I can help explain how wonderful the ambidextrous Rotarians are so you can say something nice in the future about our goodness."
2. "How can I buy a copy of that comic for my wall?"

But no ambidextrous Rotarian will complain that he was *personally* offended. This is one of those good news/bad news things about humanity. On the plus side, it's wonderful to know that virtually everyone has a good sense of humor about himself. I could pick your name out of a phone book, then draw a comic with you as a character with the punch line "George Phtbucnjak is a baby-eater," assuming that's your name, and you would laugh. You'd probably ask for a signed copy.

On the negative side, some ass-pimple is going to take time out from contributing to the GDP, or spending time with his family, to write me a long angry note about how I have offended him on behalf of whatever-the-hell ethnic group George belongs to. "I am not a half-Tibetan, half-Lithuanian baby-eater but I know people who are! If you had a brain you'd know they can't help themselves."

To be fair, I have offended a few *actual* people, too. But it's rare. For example, when Asok the intern first appeared, I got angry letters from African Americans who were personally offended that I portrayed the "only black character" in my strip as being naïve and abused in the office. They threatened to complain to the newspapers and get me kicked out. I could have responded that being naïve and abused is an intern's job description, so it's not really an insult. But I went with the more direct defense that Asok isn't African American. He's Indian. And how do you think my correspondents responded to that information?

"You should add an African American to the comic."

Hypothetical Listener

When I think about a topic, it's almost always in the form of how I would explain my views to a hypothetical other person. Then I imagine how it would sound to the other person and judge the worthiness of my thought that way. Thoughts without words are just feelings, and hard to trust. But if a thought is easy to describe, there's a fighting chance it makes some sense.

My hypothetical other person is sometimes a group (such as the readers of this book), and sometimes a person. In an earlier chapter, I talked about explaining modern technology to a hypothetical caveman. I also use friends and acquaintances in the imaginary listener role. Occasionally an incumbent will serve in my imagination for several years before being rotated out. I don't tell a person he or she is my hypothetical listener because that conversation would turn awkward. "Hey, Bruce, I was imagining you for eighteen hours yesterday, as I do every day."

For specific types of thinking, I use specific types of listeners. When I write humor, I usually imagine telling a story to my older brother, whose sense of humor is almost identical to my own. It also keeps my writing simple because that's how you talk to a sibling. And humor is 90 percent simplicity.

Now I'm married to Shelly. That means that all of my stories of "things I did today" are practiced in my head with an imaginary Shelly. That way I am spring-loaded for when I see her. I love my wife, and having her in my head is a good arrangement. The only downside is that many of the things I do during the day make perfect sense in every context *except* when explained to my wife.

For example, I wrote a post in my blog explaining why Bill Gates would be a good president. It got a lot of media attention, and it caused journalists to ask him if he would ever run. Someone even launched a website to promote Bill Gates for president. Now, if I explained this somewhat average day to my wife, it would sound like this: "I spearheaded a presidential campaign for a man who can't get elected, won't run for office, and in all likelihood has already hired mercenaries to kill me."

I also have a hard time explaining why writers need lots of naps and alone time. It comes off sounding like this: "I was going to ask if you could go to lunch with me today but instead I spent that time in the garage bouncing a Ping-Pong ball and thinking about a caveman." To a wife, that doesn't seem like the right trade-off.

Last night we were having some quality time alone at home and I made the mistake of writing myself a note while Shelly was still talking. She asked me what the note was about. I proudly told her it was about Vladimir Putin, and how two of his critics were recently poisoned. I said I thought it would make a great topic to write about. I was quite pleased with myself, until Shelly asked, "Is that what you were thinking about while I was talking?"

Now let me explain something to the single men out there. If you think there's an easy way to explain to your wife why you were thinking of Vladimir Putin while she is telling you about her feelings, you would be totally wrong. And I hadn't practiced that conversation so I was caught unprepared. I think I said something along the lines of "I only think of Russian politics during the gaps between your words." But apparently I'm supposed to be using that time just waiting around.

My brother will laugh at that last paragraph.

Why Is Music Legal?

Sometimes I wonder why music is legal. Music can alter your mood and your body chemistry just like any illegal drug. The fact that it goes into your body through your ear shouldn't make a difference. We take drugs via practically every other hole in our body—mouth, butt, eyeballs, nose—you name it. Ain't nothing special about an ear.

Music is clearly unsafe. Suppose you're in a perfectly good mood and a depressing song comes on. That could make you sad, which in turn will break down your body's natural defenses. You could get sick and die. Thank you very much, Tori Amos.

Many songs are dangerous to hear while operating a motor vehicle. For example, anything by the Doobie Brothers will force me to exceed the speed limit. You probably have your own songs that make you speed. If you believe in free will, you might argue that people always have the choice of *not* speeding. But by that reasoning it should be legal to allow drunks to drive because they have the choice of not doing it.

Let me put it another way. If gum made people more likely to speed, you know there would be a law against chewing and driving. If it goes into your body through your mouth, it's a drug. If it goes in through your ears, it's entertainment. That seems random to me.

One way you know you have a drinking problem is if it affects your work. I don't know about you, but if I have a song stuck in my head, it lowers my I.Q. by about forty points. I can sometimes do two things at the same time if those two things are easy, such as humming and walking. But if I'm trying to write something funny, or read a licensing contract, a song in my head will turn me into a chimp. Case in point: I have a song in my head right now and this chapter sucks.

Don't forget: Music is a gateway drug to harder stuff. Music attracts dancing. Dancing attracts alcohol. Alcohol leads to unwanted pregnancies. Unwanted pregnancies lead to abortion. If you believe life begins at conception, you have to believe that music kills babies.

And then there's the corrosive effect of hip-hop music. I enjoy a lot of it, but after hearing three tracks I have an urge to slap a ho. That can't be healthy, especially for the ho.

Just to be clear, I don't think music should be illegal. I just think it's somewhat random that it isn't.

That's Crazy Enough Not to Work

Do you ever have an idea that you know won't work and yet you don't know what's wrong with it?

For example, I have a plan for becoming the world's best pole vault athlete via a process of overeating and walking around. That's two-thirds of the entire plan right there.

The idea is that the more I weigh, the stronger my legs will become just by walking to the fridge and back. Eventually, when I weigh 600 pounds, my legs will be massively strong. In phase two, I will diet ferociously while continuing to do leg presses until I return to my current weight of 155 pounds without losing any leg strength.

By then, each of my legs will be the same size as my torso. I won't have any actual skill at pole vaulting, but I figure it won't matter. My vertical leap will be about 30 feet. I'll just saunter up to the launching spot, tap the pole on the ground, then toss it to the awed spectators and do a Spiderman jump right over the bar. If I have extra time up there I might show off by giving myself a sponge bath and changing into my street clothes while I'm still in the air.

I'm sure there's a flaw in this plan but it's not immediately obvious.

Moon Real Estate

NASA announced plans to work with other countries to put a permanent base on the moon by 2024. This raises an interesting question: Who owns the moon?

Apparently there's a legal agreement called the Outer Space Treaty that says no one can own any part of space, including the moon. But I have to think that when that treaty got signed, no one expected NASA to build nerd condos on the moon's south pole, aka "the only good part." As soon as space colonization becomes practical, that space treaty won't sound like such a good idea to anyone.

You can pretty much predict the next thousand years of lunar history. It goes like this:

1. The base station solves all the technical problems of living on the moon.
2. A rich guy builds an ultra expensive tourist destination on the moon.
3. Lots of other rich guys build hotels and casinos on the moon.
4. The cost of lunar colonization falls.
5. Israel starts building settlements on the moon.
6. Muslims see this as an insult because the symbol of Islam is the crescent moon and they don't want Jews living all over their symbol.
7. Islamic terrorists will try to use rockets built by North Korea to fly to the moon and blow up stuff.
8. The North Korean rockets will keep missing the moon.
9. Islamic terrorists will start blowing up more stuff than usual in America because it doesn't require any North Korean rockets.

I can see only one way to avoid this horrible future: Blow up the moon before that NASA space station gets built. I haven't looked at the details of the Outer Space Treaty, but if no one owns the moon, it seems to me you could blow it to pieces and no one can press charges. I doubt the treaty-makers even thought of that possibility. Loop hole!

Call me a Kennedyesque visionary if you must, but I challenge the wealthy private citizens of the world to finance the development of a huge nuclear device and send it to the moon by the year 2023. Let's vaporize the moon before it gives the nut jobs one more reason to fight.

Don't get me wrong, I love the moon. It's very attractive sitting up there against the starlit sky. I'd miss it. But sometimes you have to make the hard choices. And as long as the human population is 90 percent gullible, violence-prone dipshits, the last thing you want to do is increase the supply of unclaimed religious real estate.

Who's with me?

My Middle-Sized Problems

I sometimes have big problems. I always find time to work on solving my big problems because they are so big that I can't ignore them even if I try.

I also have lots of tiny problems, such as getting an itch in the middle of my back. I always find time to solve those problems precisely because they are tiny.

But I am bedeviled by middle-sized problems. I have hundreds of them. The middle-sized problems are entirely solvable, but they would require more time and effort than the solution warrants.

For example, when I try to send an e-mail to my wife, the type-ahead function in Outlook fills in her old address, and that address doesn't even exist in my address book. (Yes, I've checked carefully.) Not that it would matter what is in my Outlook address book, because somehow that file got detached from my Outlook e-mail function. If I want to send an e-mail to anyone not already in the type-ahead memory I have to cut and paste it from the address book.

I know I can solve these problems with some time and effort. But I also know from experience that if I Google those symptoms I will get forty-three entirely different solutions from experts. Most of the forty-three solutions will sound like this:

"Move all your data to a different computer. Reformat your hard drive. Reinstall all of your applications. Ask the local power company to reroute the power lines near your home. If your dog is fixed, reattach his testicles. Squeeze some coal until it becomes a diamond. Run for Congress as an atheist and win. Invent cold fusion. Then reboot four hundred times."

And that's just the first of the forty-three possible solutions on the list. There's no way I have time to open Pandora's hard drive. So instead, I absentmindedly send every third e-mail intended for my wife into the nothingness of her unused address and later have this conversation:

SHELLY: You never answered my question about the thing.
ME: Yes, I e-mailed you.

SHELLY: I didn't get it.
ME: Damn. I sent it to your old address again.
SHELLY: When are you going to fix that?

I have only been married for a few months, so maybe someone can tell me how long it takes before a wife stops asking when you plan to fix things. I have my fingers crossed that it stops in a few more weeks.

Anyway, I cleverly saved up a list of my middle-sized computer problems and called a computer expert from a national service to come optimize and fix everything in one marathon effort. The technician (who looked exactly like Dilbert, ironically) fixed most of the middle-sized problems, but couldn't figure out how to delete Shelly's old address from the type-ahead. And now it takes fifteen seconds for my browser to open. So technically I guess he didn't optimize much either.

So my choices now are to tempt divorce or follow the expert advice on Google and find my dog's missing testicles and sew them back on. And I don't even have a dog. I could Google some expert opinions on how to solve the "divorce versus nonexistent dog testicle" problem but I don't have the patience to wait for my browser to open.

I also have a lot of infinity problems. Those are the ones where before you can solve a particular problem first you must solve some other problem, and so on to infinity. For example, before I drive someplace for the first time I might want to print out directions at the computer. But first I must change the ink cartridge on the computer. And before I can do that I must go to the store and buy that cartridge. And before I do that I must find the 20 percent off coupon so I don't later have shopper's remorse. And before I do that I have to clean up my office or there is no real hope in finding that coupon. Before long I'm shingling the roof and I no longer remember where I wanted to drive.

But I did manage to scratch that itch in the middle of my back. That's why architects design rooms with sharp corners. Apparently they have itchy backs, too.

Update: I did finally figure out how to delete that old address. I don't like to ask for help, but for some reason I don't mind complaining and seeing if anyone offers any.

Acting Smarter Than You Are

People often tell me that I seem smarter than I really am. I accept the compliment. As you know, appearances are more important than substance. And so, because I love you, I will teach you some tricks for appearing smarter than you are. Believe me, it comes in handy.

First, and this cannot be overemphasized, you need to wear corrective lenses even if your eyesight is perfect. Spectacles add ten imaginary points to your I.Q. You'll be amazed at how many people stop you on the street to ask tax questions. That's been happening to me since fourth grade. I'll always wonder how many people went to jail because of my advice on offshore tax shelters.

You might think that corrective lenses are unattractive, but what you don't know is that there are quite a few people who have major fetishes for brainy people. It's probably some sort of evolution thing. You probably think Stephen Hawking is in that wheelchair because of a motor neuron disease. But if you got as much barely legal student poontang as The Hawkster, you'd be in a wheelchair, too. And for the women reading this, I've noticed that Tina Fey isn't walking too straight lately either. If you ladies want more action, get glasses.

I used to think that the glasses-wearing geek was just a stereotype perpetuated by, um, me, until I gave a speech at MIT. About 80 percent of the audience wore spectacles. I assume that the other 20 percent wore contacts. That is not a coincidence. People who have bad eyesight are smarter than average, and everyone knows it. What everyone *won't* know is that you bought your glasses at the Halloween Superstore.

Second, you must learn to stop talking so much. Talking is the surest way to inadvertently showcase profound ignorance. If the conversation turns toward the political unrest in the Chechen Republic, that's a good time to ask if anyone needs a drink. People won't know if you're escaping the discussion because you know nothing about politics or if you're just so tired of arguing about the 1999 attack on Dagestan. (Thank you, Wikipedia.)

It's also good to know a few brainy words that only appear in high-end publications. The two words you need most are zeitgeist and eponymous. I try to drop one of those two intellectual turds into conversations as often as possible. If you use those words with confidence, people will naturally assume you know lots of other big words. If someone responds with big words of his own, that's the time to stop talking entirely and do a lot of nodding and smiling. This leads me to my next tip.

It's important to agree with people if you want them to think you are a genius. For most people, the definition of smart is "Thinks exactly like me but even more so." If you think that disagreeing and offering excellent reasons for your thinking will change anyone's mind, you might be new on this planet. The best outcome you can expect from any conversation is that the other person will walk away thinking you're probably the CEO of something, assuming you also seem selfish, ego-centric, and unethical.

You can round out your artificial sense of smartness by becoming a fake wine expert. I have a wine-loving friend who taught me how to bluff my way through any discussion of wine. The trick is to learn a lot about a few types of wine and steer the conversation toward the few things you actually know. If you combine that with acting interested when other people blab about wine that you will never, ever, ever taste, you look like a world-traveling epicurean.

Oh, and add "epicurean" to zeitgeist and eponymous. If you learn to use all three words in a sentence, before long you'll need your own wheelchair and voice synthesizer.

Frak

In a Dilbert comic, I used the expletive "frak." As fans of the excellent TV drama *Battlestar Galactica* know, the crew of *Galactica* yell "frak" several times per episode as a substitute for the other f-word.

Galactica is a military ship under continuous threat of annihilation by Cylons. If you were on that ship, you'd be cursing, too. For example, you might be tempted to yell "frak!" when you discover that the hot chick who frakked your brains out is actually a frakin' Cylon who is now pregnant with your frakin' baby that is half human and half frakin' toaster.

When I first heard the battle-toughened military crew of *Galactica* yelling "frak," it was like listening to Christian-themed hip-hop. It was just wrong. But over time, I grew to embrace it as a clever way to make viewers think of the real f-word without actually saying it. It's a good safety measure because, as you know, real curse words damage children.

One thing that has always puzzled me is why we don't see special treatment facilities to help the children who are victims of cursing. We have special hospitals for all sorts of other diseases and afflictions, but no money goes into helping the children who accidentally watch HBO.

You might wonder how dangerous it is to expose children to curse words. I have never seen a scientific study on this topic but it's easy to calculate the danger. For example, parents let children ride bicycles. But parents do not ever allow children to hear vulgar words if they can help it. Therefore, we can deduce that cursing is more dangerous than maybe being hit by a car.

You might argue that the real issue with cursing is teaching children how to behave properly. But realistically, every kid is going to eventually hear every bad word, and use most of them at one time or another. That's why I advocate teaching proper cursing in school.

We already do a similar thing with driver's education and sex education. That's because cars and genitalia are dangerous if used improperly, especially at the same time. There's nothing inherently dangerous about cars and genitalia. It's all about training.

Cursing is the same way. An inappropriately used curse is both shocking and revolting. For example, an infant who is unschooled in the proper use of profanity might make this sort of misstep in conversation with a nun:

NUN: Good morning, child. How are you today?
CHILD: Fuck you, penguin.

See? That's wrong. But a properly formed and executed profanity can be a thing of breathtaking beauty. It can have great utility, too. For example, if a properly schooled infant is threatened by a bully, he can disarm the situation with defensive profanity:

BULLY: I'm gonna flatten you!
CHILD: Go ahead, you sock-humping, turd-scented, poultry whore.
BULLY: Ha ha! Good one. How did you know about the sock? Let's be friends!

How to Know That Your Presentation Isn't Going Well

I get a lot of Dilbert suggestions by e-mail. Many of them are allegedly based on real events. Sometimes I think the alleged real events are not so real. Here's one that is so bizarre that it has to be genuine:

> About 4,000 nerds go to Barcelona every year to drool all over Microsoft's new products. What I saw there last week during one presentation surpassed anything Wally has ever done.
>
> One nerd clearly wasn't interested in what the guy from Microsoft was saying. So this guy was bored, and started fidgeting. Somewhere along the line he noticed he had forgotten to shave that morning. This was no problem because he could fix that right away: He reached in his pocket and got out ... A NAIL CLIPPER.
>
> Yep, this guy started "SHAVING" himself using only a NAIL CLIPPER.
>
> Apart from the visual effect (he had to stretch up his face with his hand to avoid injury) the "audio" of the clipping was great too ...
>
> He kept this up for 45 minutes.

This e-mail made me wonder about other ways a speaker can determine that he does not have the full attention of his audience. I think you can conclude it's time to end your presentation if anyone in the audience is ...

Giving himself a sponge bath with saliva and a balled-up piece of paper.

Turning a long-sleeved shirt into a vest by removing the threads that hold the arms on.

Pretending to be a mime in a glass box.

Engaging in any form of self-gratification.

Creating death-themed origami.

Confession

Beneath the cabinets in my kitchen is a row of fluorescent lights that illuminate the countertops. One of those lights has decided to go all Baghdad on me. It crackles and pops and blinks for the entire time it is on. You might be thinking this is no big problem. All I have to do is change the fluorescent bulb, right?

I have a confession.

I am not . . . mechanical.

Or to put it another way:

Q. How many cartoonists does it take to change a lightbulb?
A. More than the number living in my house.

My problem is that the lightbulb is encased in some sort of impenetrable container with no indication of how it opens. This is where a "handy" person would take one look at it, squeeze the end of the container with his pudgy, oil-stained fingers, slide open the nearest drawer, tap on the side of the toaster with a wooden spoon, and the light casing would fall open. The solution would be "obvious" to someone with that sort of skill. Sigh.

I go through life like Helen Keller in a room full of Rubik's cubes. For me, changing this lightbulb is like figuring out how to sneak the Mona Lisa out of the Louvre. The light casing has no latches, no buttons, no instructions, no little holes to stick a screwdriver in—no clues whatsoever. I have not ruled out the possibility that it came here from the future.

I'm guessing the solution is a combination of squeezing and bending something at the same time. Of the eighty-four possible ways I could squeeze and bend something, eighty-three of those ways will result in the destruction of the container, a trip to the emergency room, and hearing the word *shards* way too many times.

My strategy so far has been to carefully recheck the light casing for clues that I missed the last twelve times I looked for an entry point. I do this while everyone is home because I know I can't last a minute in the house without someone calling me to lift, move, unscrew, unclog, clean, drive, spell, or reboot something. As soon as I get my new orders, I loudly declare, "I'll get back to this lightbulb problem later."

I realize I could ask someone for help. I probably have lots of neighbors who have the same kitchen fixtures. One of those neighbors might be handy. But I'd be lying if I said it wasn't embarrassing for a man to ask for help changing a lightbulb. I think we can all agree that it's the last resort.

My current strategy is to wait for my wife to be out of the house and then have a go at the light casing with a hammer and a screwdriver. I use this solution for many things. There's a good chance I will get the casing open while only breaking an edge or a tab or something that I can later fix with duct tape or a process I call "jamming it in there."

There's also a good chance that I'll get the casing open, but it won't close again without an entirely new strategy of bending, squeezing, hammering, and praying. And it will require three arms and a tail to do it.

But most likely I will totally destroy the casing with the hammer and screwdriver. Then the only problem is finding a replacement for a piece of hardware that came from the future and has no markings. Technically, that's "shopping." Shopping is Shelly's job. I'm only in charge of "fixing." So while I am not handy, I can sometimes solve my problems.

More on Those Darned Voting Machines

After thinking about it long and hard, I've decided not to worry about voting machines getting hacked. As long as there are voter opinion polls, we'll notice any outrageous manipulation of the voting machines. For example, if the computer programmer in the cubicle behind you becomes your next senator, and he wasn't even in the race, that's a red flag. Any big fraud will be noticed and corrected.

The other possibility is that the manipulation is subtle and you can't be sure from the opinion polls that something is truly wrong. Say the guy that would have legitimately received 48 percent of the votes ends up with 51 percent instead. You might never catch that fraud. But so what?

If a candidate is able to get 48 percent of the popular vote legitimately, there's no way to know he'll be worse than the candidate who got 52 percent. Voters simply aren't that good at predicting the future. Every bad president we've ever had managed to get a majority of the votes. Sometimes twice.

I've been involved in a number of job interviews for managers and chefs at my restaurants. I consider myself a reasonably good judge of character with lots of experience interviewing people. But when I compare the actual job performance of a person compared to what I predicted, there's almost no correlation. Voting is the same way. We're judging how a candidate will handle a nuclear crisis by how well his staff creates campaign ads. It's a completely nonsensical process.

And realistically, most elections are won by fraud in the form of misleading ad campaigns, intentionally distorted statistics, and outright lies. Just because lying to the voters is totally legal doesn't make it less bad than voting machine hacking. The intent and the result are identical. We live with one and we can live with the other. And there's a nonzero chance that voting machine fraud might sometimes cancel out the campaign lying fraud. The net effect could be positive at least some of the time.

We should do all we can to ensure that voting machines are secure. But I'm moving it off my list of things to worry about. That list is already long enough.

So What Am I Worried About?

When I tell people I'm not worried about electronic voting machines, they often ask what I *am* worried about. Fair enough.

First, I'm not worried about any problem we can see coming. If you look at the history of the world, almost any time we thought we knew something bad was going to happen *and* we had years of warning, things turned out okay.

> The human population did not outgrow the food supply.
> Earth didn't run out of oil in the eighties.
> The Y2K problem was solved.
> The Soviet Union didn't nuke us.
> Vietnam did not set off much of a domino effect.
> AIDS hasn't annihilated the hetero population of the United States.

With that in mind, I'm not worried about North Korea, global warming, Iran, the Rapture, al-Qaeda getting a nuke, the real estate bust causing a depression, running out of oil (again), immigration destroying America, bird flu, the next generation becoming morons, or any number of other widely predicted disasters.

Don't get me wrong; I think we need to work hard toward solving all of those problems. They won't solve themselves. But they don't worry me precisely because they worry everyone else, and that's been the key to solving most problems throughout history.

What I worry about is the stuff no one else is worried about. Here are my top ten worries:

1. Not Having Enough Money for Retirement

I have plenty of money for retirement if you assume I'll only live to 140. But I have high hopes that scientists will someday learn why turtles live for centuries and I'll get the turtle immortality serum. I'll never be able to retire. And I'm almost positive that Dilbert won't be in newspapers for more than five hundred years. What kind of a job can I get after five hundred years of not doing actual work? Plus I'll probably grow some sort of turtle shell. Even Wal-Mart wouldn't hire a turtleman as a greeter.

I am also concerned that one day the news will report that Charles Schwab took all my money and spent it on hookers and cocaine. Actually, I guess that's more of a hunch than a worry.

2. Smart Terrorists

I don't want to give the terrorists any ideas, but have you ever taken five minutes to think of all the ways you could terrorize the entire United States on a budget of about ten dollars? Luckily, al-Qaeda is busy trying to redirect an asteroid toward the White House. I worry that they'll give up on trying to top the last scheme and actually do some terrorizing. If those terrorists worked for your company, they would have been downsized four years ago.

3. Assassination

When you become a little bit famous, and you offend as many people as I do, you start checking under the car before turning on the ignition. That's why I have a mirror on my shoe. If you heard it was for some other reason, that's a lie.

4. Shrinking

I worry that future generations will continue to get taller. If you consider my likely immortality, and the fact that people shrink when they age, someday I'll be the size of a troll doll compared to the average teenager. When I start yelling, "Get your hover-bike off my roof!" they will just laugh and then rub me for good luck.

5. Killing Someone Who Deserves It

I worry about killing someone who deserves it and then going to jail for life. That's a bad punishment if you plan to live forever. It's exactly the sort of ironic thing that happens to cartoonists.

For example, let's say I was driving a car in Florida and O.J. Simpson was in the crosswalk in front of me. I might get an irresistible karmic impulse to "set things right." For the record, I would *never* run over O.J. If I got mad at him, I would just sleep with his girlfriend. What's the worst thing he could do to me?

6. Bladder Explosion

I worry about being in stadiumlike situations where the men's restrooms literally involve troughs, standing shoulder-to-shoulder with other guys, and a line behind me muttering, "hurry up." My bladder would explode before I could perform under that much pressure. I'd be grimacing and doing deep breathing and visualization of waterfalls. Then someone would notice me and say too loudly, "Aren't you the Dilbert guy?" *Bang*—my bladder would explode like a Baghdad police station.

7. Writer's Block

Um . . . oh crap.

My Donut Theory of the Universe

People often ask me what I believe about the universe, given that I've ruled out God and I also have suspicions about evolution (because time is an illusion). That's a revealing question because I think the real reason anyone believes anything is because uncertainty hurts. So we pick a side and rationalize it later. If there appear to be only two explanations, don't you have to pick one or forever be known as a waffling weenie?

Personally, I'm totally comfortable with a state of eternal confusion. It's practically a lifestyle.

To backtrack for a moment, I don't believe evolution is entirely false. I just think it smells a little finchy (nerd pun) and that we might be missing a big piece of the puzzle.

For example, maybe scientists will discover that the experience of a mother tends to activate or deactivate features in the unborn child's DNA. So if, for example, the mother gives birth during an unusually cold winter, perhaps the baby has a bit more fat cells or a thicker fur coat on average. And perhaps that baby's baby would retain that trait at least some of the time. That would be very different from our current understanding of natural selection and still support the general notion of species changing over time. I'm not suggesting that this is true; it's just an example to help you imagine that scientists could revise evolution in entirely scientific terms. It wouldn't be the first time. Scientist Stephen Jay Gould changed some important notions about evolution in his time. So there's a mini precedent.

Today I will give you a thought experiment to help you imagine how the universe could be here just the way it is without God, without evolution in its currently understood form, and without aliens. I call it the Donut Theory of the Universe and it goes like this:

Imagine an ant on a donut. The ant is running in a straight line from the outside of the donut toward the center. If he continues, he will go through the center of the donut and end up exactly where he started.

Now imagine that the universe is the shape of the donut, but we can't see it that way because each of us is one ant running along a straight line. It's impossible to see the whole thing from our ant perspectives.

This kind of model has its limits, and the analogy will fail more than a few times. But remember that Einstein described gravity as a bowling ball on a mattress. That analogy falls apart in many places, but sometimes bad analogies are the best we have. So work with me here.

Now imagine that the ant isn't a physical ant. He's more like the control point on a computer program that is running. We imagine the control point as moving but in fact it's more of a concept.

Now imagine that the donut is comprised of a frozen image of every event in your past and future in a straight line defined by the imaginary ant's path. One ant-step ahead is an exact copy of you that has changed a tiny bit, and so on. To your left and right are copies of you that are just slightly different. You could call them other dimensions. Each has its own ant running toward the center of the donut.

When all those realities reach the center of the donut, they become too tightly packed. There isn't as much space as there is on the rim of the donut. And so, like a black hole, all of those realities are crushed into near nothingness before emerging out the other side. This hypothetical donut has a very tiny hole.

When all of the crushed bits emerge on the other side of that tiny hole, it's the equivalent of the Big Bang. Everything seems to spring from a tiny point.

Nothing is moving in this model of the universe except the imaginary ant. Everything else is a still picture of various possibilities along the ant's path. As the ant walks, he views these still pictures like frames of animation, and they seem like motion to him. But only the ant is truly moving.

In this analogy, the ant is your consciousness. It "moves" like the control of a program but without having physical form.

Now imagine your descendants along your ant's straight line in what seems, by our human perception, to be millions of years from now. They know the universe will contract on itself, and all will be destroyed in a giant black hole, only to trigger the next Big Bang. Your descendants will want to preserve themselves. They will have millions of years to figure out how to send a program through the black hole that will re-create humans on the other side. It might take 15 billion years for that program to run, but only the simplest of programs could make it through the black hole, so we could expect it to work slowly. The program would be more like a seed made of nature's building blocks, at a granularity we can't yet imagine.

And so these geniuses of the future figure out how to send this "evolution" program through the black hole, to create humanity again, and in effect guarantee they are reborn in another 16 billion years or so when the ant comes back around.

That's their worldview. But if you could look at it from the outside, the God view, it would appear to be a bunch of still frames packed in a donut shape with a black hole in the center.

This model explains why the universe seems to be expanding and scientists don't know why. It's because we've recently (15 billion years ago) come through the donut hole and are heading toward the far edge of the donut where everything is roomy. Once we get to the far edge and reverse direction, the universe will seem to us that it is contracting. That's when the scientists of the future will start working on their programming code to survive the black hole/Big Bang of the future.

This model also solves the problem of a causeless beginning. If God created the universe, who created God? If the Big Bang happened first, what caused the Big Bang?

In the Donut model, nothing is moving except our consciousness. And without movement of anything physical, time is nothing but an illusion. The question of what came first is meaningless.

If you're wondering where the donut came from, remember that time is only an illusion in this model, so nothing can come before anything, and nothing can cause anything. Reality simply exists in a timeless state.

The Donut Theory also solves the problem that evolution seems, at least to many people, as though it is guided by a designer. Our future selves are the designers. We designed the program that creates ourselves. Here I am describing the situation as if time exists, but it's only because our language requires it.

You could argue that the Donut Theory also allows for reincarnation. At the end of one set of still frames that include your life, your ant continues and picks up the next frame in the line, whoever that might be.

If you want to preserve your sense of free will, imagine that you can move your ant (your consciousness) to a neighboring path if you concentrate hard enough. Everything in a straight line is predetermined, but you can move your ant to experience a different path of predetermined realities. So in one line of reality you open a letter and it's a bill. In another it's a check.

Last, but not least, the Donut Theory preserves the notion of God if you want to define Him as the shape of the donut. It wouldn't be much of a stretch to describe the donut's shape as timeless, perfect, all knowing, all powerful, and outside of nature—since a shape is not a physical thing. That's a bigger discussion, but you can see how it would work.

And your ant—I called it your consciousness—isn't a far stretch from what you might call a soul. So you can keep your soul, too, in this theory. You're welcome.

Let me confess a million problems with this theory of the universe. But remember that every theory has holes. Scientists are baffled by all the so-called invisible dark matter. String theory has its critics. And the "God of the Bible" concept would be a lot stronger if we could find that ark. Every theory of reality has holes.

The point of the Donut Theory of the Universe is to help you imagine that there could be entirely different explanations for the universe. The model can't go beyond being a tool for your imagination. No need to go all math and physics on my ass.

And don't even start with me about spelling it "doughnut" with all of those unnecessary letters. We must band together to make "donut" the common usage. Otherwise life is meaningless.

Discrimination

Most enlightened people agree that discrimination is bad. The thing they can't agree on is who should be on the protected list. The general rule is that you shouldn't discriminate against people for things they can't control, such as gender, ethnicity, or disability. But there are some interesting exceptions to the rule.

For example, it's totally legal for an employer to reject a stupid person even though stupid people can't control being stupid. As far as I can tell, the only reason you can still discriminate against the stupid is, and this will come as no surprise, they aren't well organized. If they tried to hold a rally, everyone would wander off in a different direction. And lord only knows what the signs would say.

Another part of the problem is that stupid people have trouble knowing whether they belong in the stupid people group or not. If you're physically disabled, you probably know it. But if you're stupid, chances are you think there's something wrong with everyone else. And you probably don't have much time to think about it anyway, given all the hours you spend expressing your wrongteous indignation on the Internet.

If stupid people ever tried to raise money for their cause, all they would get is blank stares and "Why are you asking *me*?" And no politician wants to be known as the candidate who accepted the most campaign funding from The Assoshiashun of Stoopid Peeple.

You might argue that it is in society's overwhelming best interest to discriminate against stupid people because otherwise the economy would crumble. But I would argue that if idiots couldn't get jobs for which they are unqualified, your workplace would be empty right now. And that wouldn't be good for the economy either. So apparently it's good for the economy to discriminate against stupid people as long as employers are not very effective at doing it.

Most enlightened people also agree that it's okay to discriminate against people for the *choices* they make. For example, if a job applicant shows up with an obscenity tattooed on his forehead, you can reject him without any legal ramifications. If someone does drugs, or drinks on the job, you can discriminate against him for those choices, too. When it comes to discrimination against people's choices, the only exception is a person's choice of religion. You can't discriminate because someone picked the wrong religion. And here I'm only talking about the big-name religions. You can still pick on the little religions.

For example, if a guy shows up for a job interview and tells you his religion requires him to wear a stuffed rhino penis as a hat, you can show him the door. But if he says his prophet walked on water, or rode to heaven on a flying horse, you slap a name tag on his cubicle and hope for the best. If he thinks he might have reincarnated from a caterpillar, sign him up. If he says he's wearing special underpants to ward off evil, put him on the fast track.

In all fairness, I don't think there's any correlation between religion and job performance, so it wouldn't make sense to allow religious discrimination. I just want to feel safe when I walk down the street in my rhino penis hat.

Those al-Qaeda Taped Messages

Al Jazeera just broadcast another recorded message from al-Qaeda's number two guy, al-Zawahiri. He appeared in front of the same brown background as before, with his same rifle propped against the wall.

Am I the only one who thinks al-Zawahiri has his own cubicle at al Jazeera?

I imagine al-Zawahiri coming to work every day with his turban and robe and plastic rifle, a cup of coffee in one hand, a copy of the *Jihad Gazette* tucked under his arm. The al Jazeera station manager sees him and calls out, "Hey Showtime, we have a slow news day. Can you do one of those taped message thingees?"

So al-Zawahiri takes his brown sheet and plastic rifle into the break room and tells the employees who are eating their figs to be quiet for a minute while he makes his recording.

I assume he prepares for filming by practicing his "crazy eyes" look and shaking the donut crumbs out of his beard. I don't know what kind of vocal exercises he does to warm up, but my money is on *"Wa-la-la-la-la-la-la!"*

Then I suppose he thumbs through the *Jihad Gazette* looking for current events to talk about so his message seems timely. I doubt he nails it on the first take. It probably goes something like this:

"I am Ayman al-Zawahri. I call on my brothers and sisters in Jihad to attack Donald Trump for giving Miss USA a second chance! God is great! God is great!"

The station manager wanders in for a fig and some java and hears the first take. "That's too short, Z-man. I need two minutes, and this is sweeps month, so remember to blame Israel."

There's no way to know for sure if al-Zawahiri is working for al Jazeera, but if his next video includes a hot female co-host, that's a clue.

Failing a Gender Test

The BBC reports that a female Indian athlete who recently won a silver medal in a regional competition has failed a gender test. Seriously.

I have to think that of all the tests you could fail, a gender test would be the most embarrassing. The article is a bit sketchy on the test itself but it reportedly involves an endocrinologist, psychologist, and gynecologist.

I have to wonder what the psychologist's test looked like, since other experts were checking her junk. I assume there was some sort of highly offensive, stereotypical, and sexist written exam. It probably looked like this:

1. Shopping is ...
   a. A fascinating experience that is even better when shared.
   b. A method used to extract secrets from terrorists.

2. What does "nothing is wrong" mean?
   a. Start guessing and apologizing or I'll kill you in your sleep.
   b. Oh shit.

3. The best time for sex is ...
   a. When your mood and your schedule are right.
   b. Do you mind if I masturbate a little while I take this test?

4. When you observe a man doing a simple task, you think ...
   a. That frickin' baboon is doing it wrong and ruining everything.
   b. Why would I watch a man do a simple task?

5. When a man doesn't notice your new hair color it means . . .
   a. He no longer loves you.
   b. Hair has different colors?

6. After a man explains the undeniable logic of his point of view . . .
   a. It proves that he just doesn't get it.
   b. Case closed!

7. Your reaction to this test is . . .
   a. Bastard!
   b. Ha Ha! You're dead, Dude.

Frickin' Komodo Dragons

The Middle Ages was a great time to be a guy. In those days, men were the kings of their castles. Guys made the rules because being large and strong were the two most important things. If a wild boar attacked a family's twig-and-mud hovel, it was the man's job to beat the boar to death with a big rock. A woman understood that she was safer with a man around, even if he sometimes got drunk and confused her with a wild boar. But nothing good lasts forever.

As time went by, men became less and less important. Fast forward to present day and women have jobs and educations and money and handguns. The only thing women need from men is the occasional sex and even less occasional impregnation.

Then we see in the news that Miss USA has been making out with Miss Teen USA and totally legitimizing the heterosexual girl-on-girl concept. Those two didn't start the trend, but I'll bet they made it a lot more popular. Now straight women everywhere are thinking, "Wait a minute...you mean I can just date other women? Sweet!" How is a guy going to compete with that?

And then, when I thought things couldn't get any worse, the final straw. I recently read that a Komodo dragon in a British zoo had babies without ever being around a male Komodo dragon. My first reaction to that story was to wonder if the zookeeper was getting some Komodo poontang after hours. I don't think there's any precedent for a human knocking up a reptile, but there's no precedent for a Komodo dragon having a baby without a male Komodo dragon's participation either. So in terms of explanatory power, I say it's a toss up.

But let's say the scientists are right this time. They did check the DNA, presumably to rule out the humans. And apparently there are other lizard species that can have a baby without a male. *Stop giving our human women ideas, you stupid lizards!*

As soon as human women can become pregnant via a process of

"wanting to," or whatever the Komodo dragons were doing, there's really no point in having men around at all.

The only hope for men is that the energy crisis continues to worsen. In China there's a technology where the methane gas from pigs kept in the pen outside is piped into the house and used for cooking. Someday men will be living in pens, with copper tubes up their asses to provide methane to the house occupied by hot heterosexual women who are getting pregnant just by concentrating hard.

I say bring back the Middle Ages, but with more soap and better dentistry.

Best Lawyer Ever

There was a court case recently in England where a guy claimed he became uncontrollably horny after suffering a head injury at work. This guy's lawyer convinced a judge that his client was extra horny because of the brain injury. After the accident, the client allegedly misbehaved around women, watched porn, and called phone sex lines.

There are at least two reasons to believe that this lawyer is the best who has ever lived:

1. The lawyer convinced a judge that men do not do stupid and horny things unless they have had a head injury at work.
2. In effect, the lawyer convinced a judge that free will doesn't exist. If his client had free will, he would have been able to resist any extra temptation despite the physical changes to his brain. But the client couldn't, so he must have no free will.

If you ever get arrested for going on a killing spree at the Superbowl in front of sixteen high-definition cameras and a billion witnesses, you want *that* lawyer to represent you. And if you get the urge to grope the bailiff during the trial, I don't see any reason to hold back.

Helping

Yesterday I "helped" by taking the dishes out of the dishwasher and putting them in the cupboards. I did all of the plates and cups and glasses and bowls first. Then I put away the larger serving spoons and odds and ends. The last step was the flatware.

But some of the flatware was clearly unwashed.

Oh shit.

All the other dishes were clean. Or at least cleanish. But these two butter knives had butter on them. I had two theories:

1. The dishwasher had run, but someone later put a few dirty butter knives in there by mistake.
2. None of the dishes were clean, and I had put them back in the cupboards.

This sort of thing never happens if I'm the one who loaded the dishwasher in the first place, because I don't first rinse everything. I put dishes in there dirty and proud, so you know when the dishwasher has run. But these dishes *could* have been merely rinsed by someone more thorough.

I decided to leave the dirty flatware and just be quiet about the stuff I put away, under the theory that it would be better if I never knew how many dirty dishes I had put away and later reused. This theory was working great until . . .

SHELLY: Why is the dishwasher empty except for these dirty forks and knives and spoons?

ME: Um . . . Because everything else was washed?

SHELLY: I don't think so. I think it was all dirty. What happened to all those dirty dishes?

ME: Um . . . I'm pretty sure the rest of that stuff was totally clean. So . . . I . . . put it away.

SHELLY: Even Molly's bowl?

Now at this point in the story you have to know that Molly is my mother-in-law's dog who was visiting before Christmas. Molly's temporary dog bowl was one of our everyday bowls. That meant there was a 1-in-4 chance that I would be the one who ended up eating cereal out of the dog's dirty (yet rinsed!) bowl.

So I caved in and unloaded all of the dirty dishes from the cupboards back to the dishwasher—at least the ones I remembered.

My long-term goal is to develop such a reputation for household incompetence that I am never again asked to do anything around the house. So far my plan is right on track.

Deja Food

In the news recently, the FDA is reportedly poised to approve food from cloned animals. Apparently eating clones makes some people uncomfortable. Their thinking goes like: "I sure enjoy eating Bob the cow, but I wouldn't feel comfortable eating Bob the other cow."

Eating clones got me thinking about the intellectual property of human supermodel DNA. At some point, it seems inevitable that billionaires will start cloning supermodels so they can grow their own girlfriends. Someday it will surely be legal in some country.

If you were a supermodel who had snorted away all your money and were now too old to model, and some billionaire offered you a hundred million dollars for your DNA, would you sell it? Assume you know in advance that the billionaire is a disgusting pig who will be raising your clone to be a brainwashed sex slave.

Assume also that your clone won't be forced to do anything against her will. She will simply be raised to believe the billionaire is a godlike creature and the rest will happen naturally. No laws will be broken. And she will live like a princess except for the part about being a clone whore to an old, rich fat guy. In other words, the quality of her life will be in the top 10 percent of the planet if you consider the wretchedness of the average human's life around the world.

Party-stopping question: Would you sell your DNA for $100 million if you knew your clone would become a sex slave to a billionaire?

Life on Mars

Imagine that we find life on Mars but it is very tiny—say, the size of a microbe. Then let's say that those Martian life forms are superintelligent, and friendly, and peaceful. The only thing wrong with them is that they are really, really small. And Mars is covered with them. This raises a host of ethical questions.

Would we leave the tiny aliens to live in peace, or would we scoop up a few truckloads with our next probe and not give a shit because they are so tiny. Size matters when it comes to respecting other life forms. For example, you can easily swat a mosquito and it doesn't bother you because the mosquito is so small. But it would be hard for most people to take a sledgehammer to a kangaroo. The nearer the victim is to your own size, the more empathy you have for it.

This phenomenon is consistent in the "large" directions, too. If something is much bigger than you, it's easier to watch it get hurt. For example, I think we'd all agree that it would be kind of neat to watch Godzilla get disemboweled. It would be entertaining to see a spleen the size of a bus fall on the freeway and block traffic. I don't think I'm the only one who feels that way.

So anyway, I think that the supertiny, genius Martians would be treated like trained fleas by their Earth-sized overlords. We'd get little cameras and make the Martians do Riverdancing for us. If they refused, we'd kill them with tweezers. It would be a very one-sided relationship.

Eventually there would be laws that say Earthlings can't buy a bag full of Martians from the Russians and keep them (the Martians, not the Russians) in a terrarium. But until that law is passed, let's say there's a golden period where you can have your own tiny army of alien slaves. The Martians couldn't do much for you that is useful, but maybe they could stand on one anothers' shoulders inside their glass container and spell out the names of your house guests or something.

No matter how open-minded you are, the Martians would still be too small to be friends. You can't go throw a ball with a friend who is smaller than an ant's pecker on a cold day. At least not after the first few throws, assuming you have good aim.

The reason it's legal to have pets is because they aren't human. Just because the Martians are smart, that wouldn't make any difference when it comes to classifying them as pets. There's no law that says your pet has to be dumber than you. It just has to fear you. Intelligence is irrelevant. I mean, if your cat could read, you still wouldn't let it drive your car to the library. You'd make it stay home and lie around on the rug. It's your frickin' cat, not a professor.

So I don't think the tiny genius aliens will have much hope of ascending beyond the status of goldfish once we start sending shovels to Mars. But hey, they probably had a good run.

Oops

Lately I'm spending a lot of time worrying that the sun won't burn evenly, and a huge, random solar flare will annihilate life on Earth. But I shouldn't worry about stuff like that because, as I have said before, you never get nailed by the thing you actually worry about. It's always some totally random event that you couldn't even imagine. I was reminded of this concept when I saw this item in the news: A U.S. nuclear-powered submarine collided with a Japanese oil tanker in the Strait of Hormuz. And just to make things interesting, 40 percent of the world's oil travels this route.

Fortunately, it was only a fender bender. But it made me laugh, and I'm not proud of that. Imagine if you tried to write a fictional story about the worst fuckup that a bunch of human beings could mastermind. It would probably involve: (1) something nuclear, (2) an oil tanker, and (3) disruption of the world's energy sources

And you'd want it to happen somewhere near the Middle East, where you can depend on the level-headed residents to start yelling *wa-la-la-la-la-la*, grab sharp objects, and start running toward Israel.

I don't know what happens when a submarine full of nuclear weapons ignites an oil supertanker, but I'm thinking it would be fun to watch. I could probably see it from California, at least until it blinded me.

I've learned from my prior experiences that I shouldn't make jokes about recent deaths. But since no one died in this minor accident, I'm going to test a related theory that it's okay to mock hypothetical deaths that didn't happen.

If the accident had been worse, I can imagine the family of the captain of the nuclear sub trying to explain to friends how he died: "Well, he plowed his nuclear submarine into an oil supertanker. It could happen to anyone."

If you were a friend of the family, and heard this story, you might be tempted to ask inappropriate follow-up questions, such as: "Aren't supertankers large? Can't you see them coming with those sonar thingees?"

The sub captain will have trouble blaming the supertanker captain. My understanding of maritime rules is that the right-of-way always goes to the "big thing that has the most trouble turning." A supertanker is lucky if it can figure out how to turn left at India without ending up at the South Pole. The only way I can sleep at night is by assuming that the crack team of mariners who are piloting nuclear subs actually know what all of those buttons and knobs are for. But I have to say it's getting harder every day to be an optimist.

The Ultimate Test

started wondering if I ever have *any* thoughts that no one has ever had.

Today I will test that theory.

When I cross my legs, right-over-left, and sit on my left ass cheek, my brain doesn't work right. In order to think well enough to do work, I either have to have both feet on the ground (and both ass cheeks), or have my legs crossed left-over-right and sit on my right cheek.

I discovered this years ago. I have no idea what causes it.

Your first thought might be that it's not a big problem because I can always sit in a proper position whenever I plan to work. Oh, if only it were so easy.

The problem is that I often reflexively sit in the left-cheek position, and for some reason it puts me in a dopey trance. I know I need to change positions to do work, and I know I want to do work, but somehow I can't make myself move to the working position. It feels so comfortable balanced on that left cheek, and I'm always sure, despite years of evidence to the contrary, that *this* time I will be able to do quality work with only one ass cheek on the chair. And so I try, but it is always a disaster. In that position, my work can best be described as ... well, half-assed.

I assume that's how the phrase "half-assed" came into being. I can imagine some ancient human trying to invent the wheel while sitting on one ass cheek and screaming, "Damn the gods, the rectangle shape doesn't work any better than the triangle!"

There is other circumstantial evidence for the ass-brain connection. For example, everyone has a favorite position for sleeping. It's one of these:

Ass left
Ass right
Ass up
Ass down

You know from experience that if your ass is pointed in the wrong direction, you can't sleep.

I also have my best ideas in the shower, but only if I have my backside toward the showerhead to experience the soothing, warm water. If I'm facing the spray, my brain can't think of anything but "the water is tickling my wiener." As soon as I turn around, I'm wondering how many observed natural phenomena can be explained by assuming the universe is shaped like a donut with a black hole in the center. See the difference?

I think you intuitively know that the ass is important to thinking. If you have an employee who is being an idiot, do you say to yourself, "I'd better go kick his brain," or do you think, "I need to go kick his ass"? Only one of those two things will produce better thinking.

And if you have a team of employees who are exceptionally smart and capable, what do you call them? That's right—a *crack* team. I don't think that's a coincidence.

If you are still not convinced of the ass-brain connection, finish this sentence:

It is easier to think after I . . .

a. Get a haircut

b. Take a dump

Car Service

Few things make me feel less manly than getting my car serviced. On some level, I feel I should be doing that stuff myself, even though I know the engine was designed on Krypton and forged in the fires of Mordor. Still, I feel uneasy that I can't fix it with a rock and a house key.

The real pain starts as soon as I call to make an appointment.

> ME: I'd like to get my car serviced. It's an M3. (Here I am proud of myself for knowing the model.)
> SERVICE GUY: What year is it?
> ME: Um . . . I don't know.
> SERVICE GUY: You don't know the year your car was made?

At this point I might as well turn around and grab my ankles. If you don't know the year your car was made, there's no way you're going to know if the engine block really wore out after twenty thousand miles.

When I take the car in, the service people are very professional. But they ooze automotive testosterone, except for the one female, who could also beat me at hunting, fishing, and arm wrestling. They make witty banter with one another as they bustle to and fro for reasons that don't interest me. I spend that time looking at the knickknacks on my designated service guy's desk. If I'm lucky there will be a new car brochure nearby that I can pretend to find fascinating while I wait.

In truth, I could not be less interested in cars. I bought my current car by phone, sight unseen. I called the dealer and asked if he had any new cars like my old one. He did. It was silver. I like silver. I mailed him a check.

It's been my best car yet, thanks to my low standards. My only complaint is that the navigation unit is stuck on "shout." It's normally a soothing female voice. But when that voice is stuck in banshee mode, you don't know if you should turn left, or divorce it and give it your house. I'll be happy if they can just dial it back to "nagging harpy" mode.

The next phase of the car servicing process is the most unsettling. I'll get a call from the service guy saying he "found something" that if left uncured "might" impale me the next time I put the car in reverse.

If this were a serious medical problem I might seek another opinion. But my car isn't quite worth the effort. If the frimjam is rubbing up against the hydraulic gear mounts, I want that shit fixed, even if none of it actually exists. Otherwise, every time I get in the car I will be thinking about getting impaled. That's no way to enjoy the scenery.

I sometimes get a rental car if the servicing will take a few days. A rental car is essentially an ashtray with wheels. The drive train is a twisted rubber band. But if it doesn't shriek at me for missing a turn, I'm delighted with it. After about a day I have emphysema and yet I am still thinking, "I gotta get me one of these."

You can't overestimate the value of low standards.

Apparently I'm Spoiled

I like to stay at whatever hotel is nearest the place I need to be. Sometimes that's a four-star luxury hotel. Sometimes, such as today, it's more of a "what's a star?" situation. My first clue that this isn't the Bellagio presented itself when I called ahead to make sure they would hold my room if I checked in after eleven p.m.

"That's no problem. Our office closes at eleven, but I'll just leave your room unlocked and the key on the bed."

And they did. That method worked surprisingly well, although there's always that tense first moment when you open the door and wonder how many hobos have already used the bed before you got there.

The room itself is about the size of the bed plus a generous allowance of legroom for people who do not have thick legs. I decided to go light on the continental breakfast available in the lobby across the courtyard because I'm only a few ounces of leg weight from being trapped between the bed and the wall.

The room's decorating scheme is best described as "grandma's jail cell." The furniture makes a statement. And that statement is "I've fallen, and I can't get up."

Somehow the decorators have managed to capture the feeling of claustrophobia, old age, and correctional facility all in one.

As I brushed my teeth, I couldn't help staring at the tile behind the sink that has separated from the wall and is waiting for the next large truck to drive by outside before it completes its journey to the top of my foot.

The television is made by a company called Daewoo. I'm guessing that's a Korean company. Possibly North Korea. It looks hungry yet oddly belligerent.

The heating and cooling unit is inexplicably located on the wall just below the ceiling line. It's operated by a remote. I didn't understand this arrangement until I tried to use the remote and it didn't work. Or at least I couldn't figure it out.

Allow me to digress for a moment. Is there any real reason why your thermostat needs to have a setting for both "heat" and "cool" and *also* a place to set your preferred temperature? Why the @$!& can't I just put it on the temperature range I'm willing to accept and let the frickin' thermostat decide on its own whether it needs to make me warmer or colder to keep me in the acceptable range? Is that so hard?

Sorry. I had to get that out.

Anyway, after putting on my winter coat inside my hotel room, on the coldest day of the year (it's about 30 degrees in California), and fussing endlessly with the remote control to no avail, it all became clear why it's located out of reach. They put the heating and cooling unit up by the ceiling so you won't beat it to pieces with grandma's furniture.

The blanket on my bed has the most fascinating huge stain in the center. It does not have irregular edges like you would expect from a spill or a splooge. It has perfectly straight edges, as if someone left the iron on the bed. Normally I wouldn't think anyone was dumb enough to leave a hot iron on a bed, but if this place has "regulars" then it's safe to say that they might.

Baffled by Romance

Recently I asked the readers of my blog to tell me what romantic things they had done for their partner recently. I read the responses with a mixture of confusion, shock, and dismay.

I was surprised to learn that doing household chores qualifies as romantic for many people, as in "I vacuumed the house without being asked." That's exactly why you should never hire a butler if you strike it rich—the minute Jeeves starts unloading the dishwasher without being asked, your wife is going to start humping his leg.

Love notes and flowers were often mentioned. But again, I am confused. Hypothetically, if you were to give your spouse a love note and flowers once a week for a year, all it would do is raise the baseline requirement. It wouldn't be romantic anymore. Indeed, it would appear too easy. So in a sense, the thing that makes flowers and love notes romantic in the first place is ... and wait for this pearl of wisdom ... all the times that you *don't* give love notes and flowers.

For every bouquet, the only thing that makes it special is the months that went by when you did *not* give flowers. So in a way, the *not* giving is the more important part because there is so much of it in the romance formula compared to the giving. Evidently, romance is the same as skimping.

I also noticed that a lot of so-called romantic gestures have a distinct selfish element—for example, "I took the day off from work to spend it with her," and my favorite, "surprise sex." Correct me if I am wrong, but it seems to me that those only qualify as unselfish if you hate spending time with your spouse or if he or she has a passing resemblance to Shrek. Otherwise, you're just getting something for yourself and your spouse is lucky to be going along for the ride. I'm all for days off and extra sex, but how are they romantic?

Romance also seems like gender discrimination. The things that women enjoy often take a great deal of work—like, "Surprise, honey! I shingled the roof!" Or "I planned a fourteen-day trip to Spain!" The things that men want are inherently easy—such as, "I'll leave you alone so you can watch the game." Or "Sure, just don't wake me up."

Privately, all guys gave me the same advice when I got married: "Set the bar low. Otherwise, you have no chance." Romance, I'm told, is the delta between your selfish asshole baseline and the occasional deviations from that baseline. That's why Donald Trump, for example, can't stay married. As soon as you buy your wife a helicopter, a ski resort, and a staff of servants, you've set her up for certain disappointment.

Now that I have ruled out all of the obvious romantic clichés, it doesn't leave me much to work with. So allow me to say right here that I am the luckiest man in the world for any minute that my beautiful wife is willing to put up with me. The best days of my life started when I met Shelly. I cherish her, and love her, and always will.

Car Singing

It has come to my attention that my opinions are not universally shared. This has never been as strikingly apparent as during a recent discussion of "car singing."

As you know, there are two types of car singing. There's the kind you do when you are alone in the car, and I think we can all agree that it hurts no one. Granted, I don't want to see you "Riding Dirty" in your Hyundai even if I can't hear you. It's a form of visual pollution. But as long as I can look away, it's no big deal.

Things get a little uglier if your window is down and we're both stopped in traffic. Luckily, the unpleasantness doesn't last long. Soon, your off-key ass is puttering away to bother someone else. Again, it's no big deal.

Things only get ugly when you are trapped in a full car, with the radio playing, and you have one enthusiastic car singer who thinks she knows the words. (The perp is usually a she.)

To some, this unrestrained musical enthusiasm is an affirmation of life. To others, it's the second best way to ruin music, just after imagining Elton John's sex life. I am in the latter category, and by that I do not mean I am Elton John's sex life. I mean that when I am trapped with a car singer, I have a strong urge to drive the car into a ravine to make it stop.

You might be wondering why I don't politely ask the car singer to desist. It doesn't work. Car singers believe they have an inalienable right to sing along with the music even if it does make other people feel as if squirrel-banshees have crawled inside their skulls to eat the parts of their brains that control joy. Car singers will fight you over this.

The surprising thing is that car singing has any supporters. It's hard to think of one other type of pollution where people will defend it, as in "Don't be so uptight; I only peed in the part of the pool where I was swimming alone." Or, "I couldn't finish the sandwich, so I put the rest in your couch crack. Is that any reason to be upset?"

Party-Stopping Question: Which side of the car singing debate are you on?

Religious Loophole

saw in the news that Shiite Muslims in Iraq are engaging in a practice called *mutaa,* or "temporary marriage," for the purpose of sex. A Shiite man can have more than one wife, so whether he is married or single, if he wants to buy some sex, he arranges a secret and temporary marriage. It could last for a few hours or a few years. Some Shiites believe it's all sanctioned by Islamic law. Among its many benefits, it is seen as a humane way to care for widows. I think it's obvious that God would support this concept. I can't think of a more humane way to take care of a widow than to turn her into a whore.

These temporary marriages were illegal under Saddam Hussein, or as I prefer to call him, "the last nice guy in Iraq."

According to the *Washington Post* story, a temporary wife only costs four dollars per month plus living expenses. I hesitate to mention this because I know that some of my frugal male readers are already considering converting to Islam and moving to Iraq, thinking: *On one hand, there's an 80 percent chance of being killed within a week. On the other hand, those are very reasonable prices.*

I wonder what would happen in America if a Shiite got himself a temporary wife and defended it on religious grounds. We have religious freedom here. And by that I mean that you are free to do whatever is legal for a Protestant, even if you wear a bathrobe in public and rename God. So, for example, you can refer to God as Allah or Larry, and no one will put you in jail. But if the widow downstairs starts charging you to sodomize her, you both have some explaining to do about your religion.

I've been told that in Muslim cultures you use one hand for eating and one hand for wiping your butt. By my count, that leaves no acceptable hand for masturbation. That's why you might need a temporary wife whore—preferably one with three hands.

Undulating Blouse Monster

The other day I turned around just as a dance instructor was in the process of removing her outer garment—a sweatshirt. She had already extracted her right arm from the sleeve and was snaking it beneath the sweatshirt, across her chest, and over to the left armpit to help extract her left arm. But that's not how I saw it.

I didn't see the start of the process. All I saw when I turned around is that the part of her sweatshirt that should have been calmly covering her breast area was instead concealing some sort of undulating monster. In retrospect, the undulation was caused by her right arm under the sweatshirt, but to me it appeared that either her boobs were dancing or she was being attacked by some sort of blouse monster.

To top it off, her expression was totally nonchalant. This made it extra freaky. I assume that a professional dance instructor would have a proud smile if she could make her knockers do the two-step. Alternately, if a blouse monster had attacked her, her eyes and mouth would have gone all round-looking, like the three holes in a pasty-white bowling ball. Something was clearly out of place here.

The illusion only lasted a second, but it was long enough for me to form a preferred explanation. I was hoping it was a case of dancing hooters and not a blouse monster. But just in case it was a blouse monster, my Boy Scout training kicked in, and I had already identified the child that I would shove in front of me if the monster got out.

I remember a high school classmate who could wiggle his ears so vigorously that he could—and this is just one example—guide airplanes on a runway without removing his hands from his pockets. It seems entirely possible to me that somewhere on this big ol' planet is a woman who can control her breasts the same way. And this would come in handy when, for example, she wanted to applaud her lover's performance but her hands were busy. Or she wanted to conduct two orchestras at the same time. Anyway, the point is that I don't like blouse monsters.

Primate Mysteries

Did you see the story about the chimp in a Louisiana sanctuary that got pregnant even though all the male chimps have had vasectomies?

My first thought was that the groundskeeper has been humping the chimps. But I have been told on good authority that humans cannot impregnate chimpanzees no matter how vigorously they try. This creates an entirely new mystery: Why aren't more humans tapping more chimps?

Your first thought might be that chimps are not human. But neither are inflatable women and other sex toys. If you think a drunken guy in his twenties would be dissuaded by the fact that his sex partner isn't a human being, you might be a woman.

Your second thought might be that chimps are unattractive. But walk down any sidewalk in America and take a good look at the competition. I'm not saying a chimp would win any beauty contests. But if you shaved and powdered the chimp, and gave it a wig and some makeup, it would be prettier than half the people you work with. All I'm saying is that it would be competitive.

You might argue that having sex with a chimp would be dangerous. Chimps are both strong and unpredictable. For many guys, these disadvantages would be canceled out by the fact that chimps don't talk while you're trying to watch the Superbowl. Sometimes you have to take the good with the bad.

The chimp sanctuary in the story is a home for chimps that are no longer needed for laboratory research. They are supposed to be living out their retirement years eating bananas and having casual sex with no responsibility. So my other theory about the mysterious pregnancy is that it had something to do with those lab experiments.

There's no word on what those experiments involved. Maybe the scientists had an extra primate penis lying around and sewed it onto the back of some chimp's head just to see what it looked like. Perhaps the doctors missed that one when they were doing the vasectomies. I can hear the chatter in the animal hospital:

> DOCTOR: I've finished the vasectomies on Brownie, Coco, and Grey Beard. Who's left?
> NURSE: Just Bucky and Dickhead.

Man Mistaken for Rodent

I opened my Web browser today and noticed a story about a man in Oregon who was snorkeling in a river and got shot in the head because some other guy thought he was a rodent.

There is nothing funny about being shot in the head. Unless you were snorkeling in a river and someone thought you were a rodent.

Fortunately, the snorkeler is recovering well. Apparently the bullet hit the densest part of his skull and shattered.

To reiterate, there is nothing funny about being shot in the head. Unless you were snorkeling in a river, someone thought you were a rodent, and your skull is so dense it can stop a bullet.

The shooter mistook the snorkeler for a nutria. That's a rat-looking thing that swims. Apparently the river has a lot of swimming rodents in it. I don't think I have to tell you that the very best place you can snorkel is a river that's full of swimming rats. It is good scenery and good friends all in one.

The snorkeler said he was in the river looking for different species of fish. There was no mention in the story about whether he saw any, thus making the entire expedition worthwhile.

I admire the snorkeler's sense of adventure, and apparent lack of plane fare. I wish I had the kind of spirit where I could wake up in the morning, turn to my wife, and say, "Honey, I can't spend time with you and the kids today. I'm going to go snorkel in a rodent-infested river and look for fish the hard way."

I would hate to be on the snorkeler's end of the "told you's" today:

"I told you not to snorkel in the river."
"I told you that nutria aren't a new species of fish."
"I told you to wax your back so you don't look so much like a
    giant rodent."

The man who did the shooting got arrested for being a felon in possession of methamphetamines and marijuana. (This is just a guess, but I think the police missed a drug or two.) I know you're probably thinking the same thing I'm thinking: If I were a felon in possession of illegal drugs, I'd be shooting a rifle into a river, too. It's hard to imagine that plan somehow going wrong.

I can't decide if the snorkeler was unlucky because he got shot, or lucky because the bullet hit the densest part of his skull. I'm an optimist, so I see his skull as half dense. You might be a pessimist and see the river as a shooting range that's full of rats plus one guy who seriously needs a new hobby. You are entitled to your opinion.

Mummy Dearest

The latest news from Egypt is that archaeologists found a pharaoh's butler in an underground tomb. I always wonder in these situations whether the butler was dead before he got wrapped up.

I can imagine the scene three thousand years ago at the reading of the pharaoh's will. The butler is standing there all hopeful, thinking, "I finally have my freedom. Now all I want is that golden goblet that was over the fireplace, and I'm set for life. I told him a thousand times how much I liked it. Please, please, please."

Then the Egyptian lawyer reads the will, and when it gets to the part about the butler it says, "Wrap up what's-his-name and stick him in the tomb. I might need him in the afterlife."

Worst . . . boss . . . ever.

For the record, I believe that any kind of work is noble. We can't all be pharaohs. Someone has to answer the door. But I doubt the archaeologists were feeling that way when they discovered the mummy of a butler. It's probably embarrassing when the archaeologists get together. I can imagine the introductions: "This is Bob; he found Ramses II. And this is Larry; he found Tutankhamen. And this is Bruce; he found that butler. You all remember the butler, right?"

And then Larry, who is sort of an asshole in archaeology circles, would say something like, "Butler, eh? I have three of those in my garage, and I turned the fourth one into a coffee table for my guest-house. It takes a lot of sanding."

I can't wait to see the traveling exhibit of the butler mummy. For marketing reasons they'll probably shorten the name, the same way Tutankhamen became Tut. Anyway, I assume the "But" exhibit will visit the smaller venues that can't afford things like a dead pharaoh or a school system.

I don't imagine the But exhibit would command a high ticket price, and the promoters probably need to offer something extra. Perhaps they could encourage visitors to bring tweezers and take a little chunk of the butler mummy home with them, at least until it's all gone. It would be a good deal, except for the people who bought a ticket for the last show.

My History Learning

My religious education was surpassed only by my extensive schooling in history. For example, I learned that important contributions have been made by both men and women, and by every national and ethnic group. I will summarize my knowledge of history, as I learned it in school, so you don't have to.

Who	*What They Did*
White Men	Invented all forms of technology.
	Discovered everything.
	Created capitalism and democracy.
	Wrote all the great books and plays.
	Conquered everything.
Women	Sewed a flag.
	Nagged about not voting.
	Wore unattractive clothes.
African Americans	Sang a lot.
	Something with peanuts.
Chinese	Invented gunpowder but couldn't figure out how to kill people with it.
	Still baffled by the spoon and fork.
Europeans	All the smart ones moved to America.
	They like to start wars that America finishes.
South Americans	Couldn't deal with a few germs.
	Sometimes eat one another to please the wrong gods.

Africans	Invented sharp sticks.
	Nudists.
Other Asians	Exactly like Chinese but didn't think of gunpowder.
Eskimos	Eat fish.
	Rub noses for fun because it's too cold to expose genitalia.
Native Americans	Ate buffaloes.
	Sold Manhattan for $24.
	Made hats out of bird parts.
	Liked blankets way too much.

Some have suggested that the history books of those times were biased in favor of white European men who moved to America and wrote most of the history books. I suppose that's the best explanation for my massive ignorance. I like to think it's all someone else's fault.

This begs the question: How accurate is any history book in any country? Here again, context is your best tool for answering that. The first thing you should be looking for is any situation where the people who wrote the history books are portraying their own country and ancestors in a suspiciously positive light. In your lifetime, you've probably noticed that your own government, whichever one that is, spends a lot of time killing people who, in retrospect, didn't deserve it. So it should strike you as curious if your nation's history up until the time you were born was comprised mostly of wars against people who started it first and deserved what they got. You rarely see a country with a history book that says, "We were jerks, so other countries came and killed us in large numbers. We totally deserved it."

World War II is the best example of suspicious interpretations of history. Every country has its own spin.

America's Version: Crazy Germans, Japanese, and Italians tried to conquer the world. It almost worked, until America saved the day.

Japan's Version: Japan tried to bring some improvements to neighboring countries, free of charge. America bombed us until we stopped.

German Version: Adolf Hitler (technically an Austrian) caused some mischief. Germans played along because they don't like to make waves. The key learning here is that you shouldn't trust Austrians.

And that's our *modern* history. Imagine how much worse it gets as you move back in time, say two thousand years. The first warning sign that your history might not be spot-on would be if the person who wrote it down had something to gain. It doesn't take much self-interest to nudge people into lying.

Let me put this in perspective for you. About once a week, someone approaches me to say he has a friend who went to high school with me. About 90 percent of the time I have never met these alleged classmates. (There were only forty people in my graduating class in high school. I can name them all.) Hundreds of people have lied to friends, trying to impress them by saying they know me. And I'm just a cartoonist. Imagine how much more incentive people had for saying they were close buddies with Christ. I'm thinking at least 10 percent more.

My suspicions of history intensify whenever I read verbatim quotes, such as "And then George Washington leaned forward and said with a wry grin, 'Whittle me some dentures, you hemp-smoking douche bag.' " It makes for good reading, but generally speaking, when you see conversational quotes attributed to historical figures, you have to assume they're iffy.

Nor should you assume that these manufactured quotes capture the essence of what was said. If you know anyone who has ever been interviewed for a newspaper or magazine article, ask him how accurate the quotes are. I've been interviewed several hundred times, and with the exception of the few publications that employ a fact checker (a person who calls and asks about the accuracy of things prior to publication), most stories get basic facts wrong. And the context is often manipulated to make even the accurate quotes take on a meaning never intended.

I was once the subject of the featured *Playboy* magazine interview. They take pride in running interviews with brilliant and interesting people. That's their niche, and I was scared that I would be lowering the bar. So when I eventually read the published interview, I was delighted to find that they made me sound about forty IQ points smarter than I am. Thanks to generous editing, all my thoughts were crisp and clear. I never repeated myself or trailed off to a mumble, as I generally do. I sounded coherent, witty, and brilliant—pretty much the opposite of how I actually sounded at the interview.

The point is that every writer has a bias or an agenda or both. The worst way to understand what a historical figure said is by reading what someone wrote about him. A more accurate approach would be guessing, based on what the person looked like. For example, when I see paintings of Benjamin Franklin, I know there's a good chance that he once said, "Don't leave any marks. I told my wife I was flying a kite!"

The older the story, the less likely it's accurate. That's why it's understandable that there's a lot of controversy about the historical accuracy of the Bible. To me, it comes down to one question: Where are all the petrified Jesus turds?

It's my understanding that Jesus ate and drank just like regular people. Ipso facto, there must have been about nine thousand Jesus turds produced during his Earth phase. You can't tell me that his followers wouldn't follow him behind a rock every time he squeezed out a steamer, and put it in a little box to save. Best of all, his shit wouldn't stink! If you made a hat out of it, you'd probably ward off the devil and be instantly cured of diseases. I'm not much of a collector, and I don't care for knickknacks, but even *I* would keep the son of God's turd in a glass container on the mantel. It would be a great conversation piece. "This one was right after the Sermon on the Mount. You can still see some bits of fig."

I understand that his body came back to life and went to live in heaven, so we don't have that to look at. And he didn't have many possessions, so he wouldn't have left much behind. Except for nine thousand turds. If I had my choice, I'd rather have his wrist-sundial, or his Holy Grail. But if those aren't available, I'd settle for a turd and a certificate of authenticity. If you say you wouldn't want one, you're lying.

You might argue that turds would decay over time. But you're thinking of regular turds, not holy shit. My best guess is that they would decay *almost* completely, only to come back to life as full, steaming logs just when you least expected it.

I can see how historians might have lost track of Jesus's robe. There was only one of those. But how do you misplace nine thousand turds?

I have similar questions about the Ten Commandments. I always wondered why God only used the stone tablet method of communicating that one time. It's not as if there's a shortage of flat rocks, especially when you have infinite power to make more. I see no reason why every person shouldn't get his own personalized set of stone tablets direct from God. The Almighty is not going to get tired, or run low on lightning bolts (I assume that's how he carves them), so I think he can churn them out as fast as he wants.

How cool would it be to walk into my pantry and see my own set of commandments, still smoking, leaning against a bag of rice like it's no big deal? I'd like my commandments to be personalized—maybe have God throw in a few new ones just for me, like "Stop sticking your finger in the cat's ear and thinking it's funny." Not only would it turn me into a believer, but those tablets would make a great coffee table.

Personalized commandments would solve the problem of nonbelievers, especially if the tablets were carved while you watched. This is another case where God is apparently bad at marketing. He wants everyone to believe in him, but he refuses to do the tiniest personal miracles to convince us. What is the cause of this stubbornness? It wouldn't be very godly to be peevish, as in "How many miracles do you people need?" And it certainly can't be because he thinks additional miracles wouldn't convince the heathens. We *love* miracles! The only explanation is that he has in mind an exact amount of evidence-to-faith ratio that's somehow important. He's not against evidence in general, he just wants us to work for it.

God's scheme seems suspiciously similar to when humans make a dog balance a biscuit on his nose before eating it. It's not as if we don't want the dog to have the biscuit, it's just that it's funnier if the dog balances it on his nose first. If it's true that we're created in God's image, and humans enjoy a good laugh now and then, it has to be true that He thinks it's hilarious when we can't figure out what he wants.

That probably explains why images of the Virgin Mary so often look like the love child of Willy Nelson and Sponge Bob whenever she appears on bridges and trees and grilled cheese sandwiches. You'd expect better artwork from God. Maybe not full-out Norman Rockwell stuff, but at least South Park quality.

If you're an omnipotent being with the power to create a tree, not to mention human beings, and create a universe to put them in, it doesn't seem like a stretch to make a stain on the underpass that doesn't leave people asking, "Which part is the nose?" God's ambiguity has to be intentional. God must think it's funny. Now, your first reaction might be *What's so funny about that?* I'm a professional humorist, so let me explain.

God's work is more of a practical joke than a funny ha-ha gag. The key is convincing people that these holy images routinely pop up on ordinary items. Once you put that idea in people's minds, the rest is comedy gold. Let's say God places a few "real ones" that are so wildly ambiguous that people start thinking they see holy images in all sorts of ordinary places.

After a few well-publicized but subtle miracles, you just know that somewhere in the Midwest there's a moron who hasn't washed his hair for years because one day he woke up with a bad case of bed hair that appeared to be in the shape of the Last Supper. Now he only sleeps sitting in a chair so he doesn't accidentally crush Jesus. If that made you laugh, you know exactly how God would feel, but magnify that by a few million morons and you get the idea.

They say that God is watching everyone all the time, so he'd always get to see his jokes play out. If so, he's laughing his butt off, assuming God has a butt, which is unlikely, since butts are also an obvious practical joke. Here are some other things that are obvious practical jokes from God:

God gives people genitals that feel terrific when touched, and arms that comfortably reach them. Then he says you'll burn in Hell if you go for it.

God designs people's emotions so you fall in love with people who, in return, wouldn't even use your hollowed-out skull for a spittoon.

God designs heterosexual men's brains to be fascinated by huge trucks, farts, and firearms. Then he designs women and gay men to be turned off by those things.

God provides us with the capacity to experience amazing pleasure. Then he makes sure that all of those activities result in a painful death.

God makes most of the tall and beautiful people stupid. Then he makes us elect them to office just to see what happens.

God lets people discover steroids that make your muscles big, but in a genius move that only the Creator could think of, the side effect is that your balls shrink.

God lets people invent hair growth formulas that can make men more attractive to women, then he gives it one side effect: impotence.

God lets people invent antidepressant drugs so people can enjoy life, then he gives it one side effect: impotence.

Humor explains why God would bother creating people. He needs us for the laughs. Everyone knows you can't tickle yourself. Maybe God can't either, at least not directly. Even God can't tell himself a joke and have a hearty laugh about the surprise ending. God would need people to make him laugh. Goofy, gullible, fucked up people. And lots of them.

But back to miracles; if I were God, I'd offer a promotional deal on miracles to help convince my flock. My deal would be this: In return for believing in Me, every person gets one free miracle, but it has to happen within the confines of your own home and not affect other people. So you might ask Me to make the dishwasher quieter so you can hear the TV, or to turn your dog's balls into a lollipop so it's more natural-looking when he licks them in front of company. Whatever you want, but it would have to be small scale. Otherwise you'd get conflicts when 4 billion people all asked to be the undisputed emperor of the world.

Best Roommate Ever

I've heard that it costs about $25,000 to keep one criminal in jail for a year. And jails are overcrowded, so that expense goes up if you ship your convicts to other states where they have extra prison space, as California does.

This gave me an idea for a business you can do at home: Convert your spare bedroom into a prison cell and charge the government $25,000 per year to house a convict. You could probably put two convicts in one spare room and earn $50,000 per year, minus whatever it costs to feed them slop.

The government would have to set some standards for these home prisons. Obviously you'd need to enclose the entire room with bars, add a little toilet, and install a surveillance camera. Government officials could monitor the home prisons over the Internet, just to make sure you're abusing the prisoners enough. I imagine a big problem with home prisons is that prisoners would talk their way out, as in "Can I just watch *Boston Legal* with the family? I promise I'll go right back to my cell."

Having two prisoners in a cell would be problematic if you had kids in the house. Sooner or later the kids are going to see something that will scar them for life. "Daddy, why is the one prisoner praying to the other one?"

Home prisons in Texas would be the most fun of all, especially if you had a death row inmate and you were allowed to execute him yourself. This wouldn't be everyone's cup of tea, but you can't tell me it wouldn't be a hoot for hunters who enjoy shooting large mammals for entertainment. "I'll come to bed in an hour, honey. I have to shoot Carl at midnight."

I suppose another problem is that neighbors would start bragging and comparing their prisoners. You'd get a lot of "Oh, so your prisoner only wounded a guy? Well, I suppose all the good ones were taken."

I'm the Loneliest Skeptic

It's lonely to be me. Skeptics hate my opinions as much as believers do. Every skeptic is different, of course, but I'm so far along the skeptic curve that other skeptics don't recognize me as one of their own. The difference has everything to do with one word: "Extraordinary."

Skeptics like to say that "extraordinary claims require extraordinary proof." To which I say, "What the hell does extraordinary mean to you?" It's thoroughly subjective. For example, if someone claimed to be able to hover above the ground just by concentrating, would you believe it based on the account of one reporter? How about several reporters and photographs? Would video be enough to sway you? Suppose a team of scientists set up controlled tests and published their results in peer-reviewed journals, would that convince you?

Not me. I'd want to be alone with that guy in a room where he had never been before, so I could watch him hovering up close. And I'd want to run a big hula hoop over him while he was doing it, to check for strings. And I'd want to supply the hula hoop myself. Then, when he passed all of those tests, I'd still think he was full of shit but I'd probably form a religion to worship him just in case he's either the messiah or an advanced alien sent to Earth to scout us. I figure it's a good idea to get on the inside track to be either an apostle or a traitorous lackey to the alien overlords, whichever is necessary. I'd want to hedge my bets. But I still wouldn't totally believe he hovered.

The End of Humanity

They say that many technologies owe their existence to sex. Porn drove the cost of VCRs down, for example. And porn was the early fuel for the growth of the Internet. I see one more area where this phenomenon is likely to repeat: robots.

Have you heard about the company that's making realistic life-sized sex dolls? They cost up to $10,000. I haven't seen one in person (really, I haven't) but they reportedly weigh as much as a real person and are eerily lifelike.

The company that makes the doll is reportedly working on artificial intelligence. That shouldn't be too challenging. No one wants their sex doll to be all chatty anyway. There are already a variety of chatbots on the Internet that can simulate real conversation. Slap one of those programs into a chip, add a small speaker into the sex doll's head, and you're in business.

At that point, you'll essentially have a simulated hot chick that can make conversation but is otherwise paralyzed. I have to think it would be creepy if the doll looked exactly like a woman, and talked like a woman, but couldn't move. You could accessorize her with a hospital bed and some tubes in her arms, but that is only a temporary solution. Full robotic motion will surely be developed soon.

Obviously the first body parts to get the robotic functions will be the, um, most marketable parts of the doll. But eventually that doll is going to be baking cookies and fetching the remote control. It's only a matter of time.

Today I will ask you the most frightening question you will ever read. It's a hypothetical, just for the guys.

Hypothetically, in the future, if a sex doll robot was indistinguishable from a human woman, and you weren't in a relationship with a human, would you tap the robot?

I asked that question in my blog and about 95 percent of the hetero guys said they would. The other 5 percent expressed a strong preference for lying.

Based on your responses, it seems that every guy has his own threshold for the quality of the robot. Some guys would only consider tapping the robot if it was indistinguishable from an attractive human woman. Other guys are already humping their TiVos.

Many of you said you would only have sex with the robot if it was brand new. But what happens after six months of monogamous robot love when you find a sticker on its foot that says "Inspected by Carl"?

Many of you were concerned that the software in the robot would be provided by Microsoft. First of all, I think we can all agree that the name "Microsoft" is bad branding for sex robot software. But that's not the biggest problem. One software malfunction and you'll have to call the fire department to get your pecker off the roof.

I would write more, but I suspect it would all be downhill from here.

America's Favorite Pastime

Yesterday I went to a Giants baseball game. It was Little League Day, so there were about ten thousand young boys running wild in the stands. It was also free bat day, courtesy of Bank of America.

I will pause while you digest this concept.

Do you know what happens when you hand an eight-year-old boy a new bat, sit him behind the exposed heads of several adults, and ask him to sit patiently for four hours while nothing much happens on the big field in front of him? Do you think he fiddles with that bat?

Apparently Bank of America figured there was some theoretical amount of head injuries that would make the public forget that they lent a trillion of your dollars to hobos.

My memory of the afternoon goes something like this: "TREVOR, PUT DOWN THAT BAT! YOU ALREADY HIT THAT LADY ONCE! I SAID, PUT IT DOWN! I MEAN IT! I WILL NOT TELL YOU FOUR HUNDRED MORE TIMES!" This was followed by the sound of wood making solid contact with skull, cursing, repeat.

My wife took a solid blow to the shoulder. Later, one of the tykes kicked some guy's beer out of the back seat holder, so we sat in a puddle of beer while the sun cooked us. I was one pinch of salt from being a recipe.

I tried to use the restroom at the stadium. This is no place for the shy. Unlike most public men's rooms, where there might be a small privacy shield between urinals, this place was designed to handle high volume, shoulder-to-shoulder peeing. I saw an opening where I could poke my penis between a bearded guy and a guy with a fanny pack, just over the left ear of a Little Leaguer, but before I could make my move, someone filled the slot. I decided I could wait another three or four hours.

Conditions were difficult, but at least the game was exciting well into the first half of the first inning when the Reds scored six runs and put it out of reach. Technically, there was still hope, since many of the

Giants have batting averages that round to one hundred, and some are able to catch a fly ball nearly half the time. But yesterday was not their day. There were many boos from the stands. I felt bad for the players until I realized they couldn't hear the boos over the screams of the bat victims.

Henry Hoover

In the news, a building contractor was caught seducing a shop vacuum. The vacuum has two large cartoon eyes and a hose that represents its nose. The model is called a Henry Hoover.

This story raises many questions. Was this a spontaneous act, or did the contractor see Henry Hoover on day one and think, "I'd hit that"?

What disturbs me most is that little Henry's hose was involved in the sex act. That's his NOSE, damn it! How is Henry supposed to enjoy nasal sex? That contractor is a selfish lover, and I can't forgive that.

The contractor's alibi is that he was using Henry to vacuum his underpants, which he says is common practice back in Poland. The key lesson is that maybe you should practice your alibi before getting caught and not say the first thing that springs to mind.

If I were that contractor, I would have claimed I was a member of a cult and I mistakenly thought Henry Hoover was my god. I'd say I cast off all of my possessions and knelt before him to receive his blessing. I'd tell the security guard, "If you don't like how Lord Hoover bestows his blessings, perhaps you should be less of a bigot." I'd probably take the offensive and say something like, "You probably kneel in front of a priest and get a cracker. How's this different?"

It pays to be prepared.

Right Up My Alley

My blog readers sent me a link to a story about a Japanese woman who was accused of kicking a hole in some guy's door, crawling through the hole, and destroying his property. She was acquitted when the court realized that her breasts were too big to allow her to fit through the hole.

In other words, if the tit doesn't fit, you must acquit.

The funniest thing about this story is the visual it puts in your head. The accused turned out to be innocent. But she had to sit in court while a room full of strangers, and later the press, imagined her trying to crawl through a hole in a door and getting snagged by her knockers. It is all the funnier because the hole is in a door. Somehow that is just more amusing.

Apparently there was an extensive courtroom discussion about the physics involved in getting a torso and two melons through a smallish hole. I immediately started solving the puzzle in my head, wondering if you could poke your head through then flop one boob through, then an arm . . . no, it wouldn't work. But you can't tell me you didn't have the same thought.

If I were the prosecutor, and I saw that the defense was winning its case, I would demand that the accused put butter on her breasts and try to fit them, and optionally her head, through a smallish hole in front of the jury. It wouldn't help win the case, but it would make the afternoon go a lot faster.

Death by Frozen Poop

know there is something wrong with me because I enjoy reading stories about frozen waste from airplane bathrooms that falls to Earth and almost kills people. That sort of story pops up every now and then, and it never fails to amuse.

When I think of the ways I could die, almost all of them are better than being killed by flying poop. That's the sort of thing that could erase a lifetime of accomplishment. I would instantly stop being the guy who created *Dilbert* and forever be known as the cartoonist whose head was crushed by a turd. If I die from frozen restroom waste, my friends and family would have trouble stifling a laugh. And who could blame them, really?

"How did he die?" someone might ask. "I guess you could say he got pissed off," one of my ex-friends would reply, before laughing heartily.

It seems unlikely I would be killed by airplane waste, but it also seems unlikely a bird would crap exactly in the middle of my bald spot, and that happened. I don't rule anything out. When I hear jet sounds, I stand under a doorway.

Imagine what would happen if I were doing a book signing, and the frozen waste from the plane missed me, but killed the guy standing in line waiting for my autograph. When telling the story later, would I be able to resist saying "The shit hit the fan"? I think not. And that is why I probably deserve to be killed by frozen poop.

Bad Things to Say to People

Recently my wife told me I chew too loudly. While I don't deny the accusation, I wonder how it is possible for one person to chew more loudly than another, assuming both people have their mouths closed.

Do I have thinner cheeks than the average person? Do other people somehow close their nasal passages when they chew so the noise doesn't come out their nostrils?

I'm reasonably sure the carrot in my mouth doesn't know who is chewing it, so the originating sound is probably the same with me as with anyone else. There must be something freakishly wrong with my skull architecture, like one of those buildings where you can whisper in one corner and someone on the other end can hear it clearly.

There isn't a lot I can do about this problem. If you have ever tried to chew more quietly, you know it sounds exactly like not trying. I went from blissful ignorance about my chewing problem to the painful knowledge I have some sort of mastication disability that will make it impossible for anyone to love me.

So I officially added "You chew too loudly" to my list of things you should never tell another person unless you intend it as a practical joke. So far, the list isn't long. But it includes another one I heard as a teen, when I was most impressionable: "Is that the way you normally walk?" To this day, I only walk from one place to another if I am sure no one is paying attention. So obviously I don't chew anything when I walk, because that's a total red flag.

One of my favorite examples in the genre was a guy who told a nervous groomsman just before a wedding ceremony, "I heard that sometimes you can pass out from standing still for too long when you are anxious." That is pure evil, yet clever enough to be justified in my opinion.

Good Eatin'

The FDA has decided that meat from clones is safe. This is a big relief, because I have a long term goal of cloning myself and then eating my clone. I don't have a compelling reason to do it, but most goals are like that. No one really needs to run a marathon or collect beer mugs, but no one is complaining about them. There's nothing wrong with wanting what you want.

I'm a vegetarian, but I think I would make an exception for my clone. My torso is already full of my guts. Putting a few more forkfuls in there seems like a trivial change.

My clone won't have a soul, obviously, since clones are an abomination and not a product of God's approved method of procreation. You can't expect the Almighty to hand out souls to creatures made in a laboratory. Only real people get souls, and that means there's no ethical dilemma with eating your clone. It's just protein with an attitude.

The risk with this plan is that my clone is just like me, and tries to eat me first and assume my identity. But that's a risk we're both willing to take.

Vacation Challenged

I just returned from some vacation time near the beach, down the coast from where we live. I'm bad at taking vacations, in every way a person can be bad at an activity.

For example, I never have the right attitude going into a vacation. I am told that the correct thoughts should be something along the lines of, "This will be fun!" My thought process involves making a mental list of all the ways I could get killed while duct taping my credit cards to my torso.

The list of vacation death traps is long. The aquatic possibilities alone are nearly endless, especially near the beach. This week I had a chance to die by boat, rip tide, parasailing, tsunami, and dolphin. And those are just the quick options.

I opted for the slow but certain death of sun exposure. My skin is just thick enough to keep my organs from forming a pile around my ankles. It can't handle much sun. I had so much sunscreen on that all I needed was a tiny model of a bride and groom on my head and I would have looked like a wedding cake. But I still kept checking my pulse to see if the sun had killed me yet. It was nearly 80 degrees on the beach, and about 120 degrees inside my hard shell of sunscreen.

And don't get me started about the sand. Some beaches have soft sand that feels delightful between your toes. This particular beach was made entirely of clam shells and ground glass. Normally, the hardest thing I do with my feet is pet the cat when I'm too lazy to bend over. Halfway across this beach I was willing to give up the location of Osama Bin Laden. By three-quarters of the way, I was willing to join him.

The hotel where we stayed was "all inclusive." That means you can eat at the buffet almost all day long and pay nothing extra. If you have not experienced a buffet at an all-inclusive resort filled with hungry Americans, let me paint a picture for you. Imagine a table filled with a wide variety of delicious foods. That's what I was doing too—imagining it—because by the time I reached for anything, some porker from Kansas snatched it away and had it half pooped out before my brain could register it was gone. I have fond memories of the food I almost got to touch.

By the third day, I loosened up enough to have a great time. And I discovered that if you hung out on the beach with the stray dogs, directly beneath the buffet area, people would sometimes throw you french fries just to watch you act happy. As soon as my bites heal, I plan to generate some excellent false memories of the food in Mexico.

I'm Determined

I take pride in small accomplishments. For example, I have always been proud that I could take any medicine, no matter how awful, without complaining. This is an extension of my greater power of liking, or at least tolerating, almost any food taste. It's a gift. Recently, I met my match.

The other day, I felt a possible cold coming on, and started looking through the drawer where we keep all our meds to see if we had one of those cold preventive pills with the zinc in it. I recalled reading that they work. And placebo or not, they seemed to work for me in the past.

I found in the drawer a type of medicine my wife had purchased that I hadn't seen before. It was a chewable pill, about the size of a very thick quarter. It would take some time to work through it, but it was no obstacle to the man who could take any medicine. I popped it in my mouth and started working.

At first it was pleasant, citruslike. But the flavor just kept coming. It went from mild to strong in about ten seconds. By half a minute, it was so intense my eyes were watering, and I had only chewed about 10 percent of this pill. I started to worry.

A minute into it, it was so intense I thought I was going to puke, literally. I ran to the kitchen sink to spit it out, but gave it a few more seconds to see if I could get through it. No medicine had beaten me yet, and I wasn't going to go down easy. The waves of nausea blew over me, and I knew one of them was going to put me over the edge. It was time to bail. I spit the rest of the pill into the sink, defeated.

Later, I blamed it on having just brushed my teeth. You know how sometimes particular foods are awful if you just brushed? I figured that was the problem. So the next day, determined, I took another run at it. This time I made sure I hadn't brushed in the past hour. It started out better, I thought, but it ended with me slumped over the bathroom sink, eyes watering, trying to suppress the retching. I gazed at the half eaten pill dissolving in the drain, beaten. It was a lonely feeling.

I mentioned this defeat to my wife, Shelly. She informed me that the pills aren't actually pills at all. They are designed to be dissolved in a tall glass of water, like Alka-Seltzer.

I worry that this event undercut the aura of infallibility I have been cultivating in my marriage.

There's a Name for It

ast week, my in-laws were in town. While they were out visiting some other relatives, I took my turn watching their dog, Mollie. At this point, I should pause and mention that I haven't had a dog since I was a kid. And in those days, in the country, when the dog felt nature's call, we'd simply let the dog out, and it would use any part of our 2.5 acres as its toilet. Later, if you wanted to throw a ball around, you just kicked the (usually) frozen logettes to the side to clear a path. In those simple times, you weren't playing a sport unless someone ended up covered in dog feces. It was just part of the game.

These days, things are quite different. Today, if you go to school covered in dog feces, there's a stigma. And of course there's the leash law. But nothing takes the joy out of a walk in the fresh air quite like being required to carry a plastic purse full of dog poop.

Back to my story. I took Mollie for a walk, thinking I understood how this process worked. The leash was no mystery. It had a cool spring action with a pistol grip. I liked that part. And I grabbed an official poop bag on the way out of the house. I was ready for anything.

Within a minute, Mollie laid down a steamer. I think she had been eating the cat food, because it wasn't the firm little log I was expecting. But I soldiered on, turning the bag inside out like a glove, and grabbing the warm pile that melted in my hand. It wasn't pleasant in the usual sense of the word, but I experienced some satisfaction in a job well done. I tied the bag into a tidy little package and intended to head home.

That's when I noticed Mollie had just begun to poop. I don't know if she was trying to spell "HELP" in case a rescue plane flew over or what, but by now she was in full production. Step, squat, step, squat.

I looked at my tidy little bag, now sealed, and realized I was screwed. I knew the neighbors would be looking, or feared they might. I couldn't leave this Katrina-sized disaster and get another bag lest someone think, incorrectly, that I had abandoned my doody. So I decided to see if I could untie the pooper bag and have another go at the new deposits. This plan did not work as smoothly as I had hoped.

Do you know what is NOT effective for picking up warm piles of poop? If you guessed "other warm piles of poop," you might have been in this situation yourself. It was like trying to pick up mashed potatoes with a catcher's mitt. And I was hurrying, so needless to say, back at the house I needed the Karen Silkwood treatment to feel clean again.

Later, when my in-laws returned, I told the story. Larry, a laid-back gentleman from Arkansas, turned to his wife, Cheryl, and drawled "Mollie double-bagged him." Let me tell you, the only thing that could have made my experience worse was finding out my in-laws have a name for it.

Urge to Simplify

No matter what I'm doing, I can't help wondering if there is a better way. For example, I noticed yesterday in Las Vegas that many of the casinos have ATMs among thousands of slot machines. The casinos hope you will take your money out of one machine, carry it several feet, and put it in another. There's something about the change of ownership in your money that is considered entertainment. And judging from the crowds, people can't get enough of it.

In the old days, when Vegas was less popular, the slot machines sometimes gave a little of your money back, at least temporarily. But these days all the nice hotels are at full occupancy. I've been here three days and haven't seen anyone win a jackpot. If you think that removing the "maybe you can win" part from the equation would dampen peoples' enthusiasm, you have vastly overestimated the intelligence of the general public. After Las Vegas trained people to lose 98 percent of the time, it was a simple matter to nudge it to 100 percent.

Now the casinos have people trained, like chickens hoping for pellets, to take money from one machine (the ATM), carry it across a room, and deposit in another machine (the slot machine). I believe B. F. Skinner would agree with me that there is room for even more efficiency: The ATM and the slot machine need to be the same machine.

The casinos lose a lot of money waiting for the portly gamblers with respiratory issues to waddle from the ATM to the slot machines. A better solution would be for the losers, euphemistically called "players," to stand at the ATM and watch their funds be transferred to the hotel, while hoping to somehow "win." The ATM could be redesigned to blink and make exciting sounds so it seems less like robbery.

I'm sure this is in the five-year plan. Longer term, people will be trained to set up automatic transfers from their banks to the casinos. People will just fly to Vegas, wander around on the tarmac while the casino drains their bank accounts, then board the plane and fly home. The airlines are already in on this concept and stopped feeding you sandwiches a while ago.

What Happens in Vegas

'm in Las Vegas this morning, to give a speech to a few thousand technology workers. Last night, I did an AV check and tried to get back to my room without losing all the money in my wallet. I started optimistically, but it was all downhill after that.

The path to my room was cleverly littered with attractive slot machines. I don't enjoy gambling, but I feel obligated to rationalize my decision to not be a Quaker. So I stuffed a twenty in a Wheel of Fortune slot machine and tapped a lighted button ten times while watching the twenty turn into a zero. It took less than half a minute. I did a quick mental check, and no endorphins had kicked in, so I decided to call it a night.

By the time I got to my room, I was thirsty, and a nearby Coke machine beckoned. A Diet Coke would set me back $2.75. Somehow that seemed like a bargain. I couldn't afford to go back to the casino and get free drinks. I stuffed a five into the slot and hit the button for Diet Coke. Jackpot!

When the machine pooped out that Diet Coke, I felt like a winner for the first time in Las Vegas. Granted, I was purchasing $.12 worth of plastic and sugar water for $2.75, but I tried to not see it that way. Best yet, my change clanged down a chute like a cash payout.

But here's the evil genius part. Instead of a cuplike receptacle for my change, the dispenser was designed more like a launcher. The coins hit the bottom and shot up and out of the machine. A quarter hit the ground and rolled under the Coke machine. That bastard! My Diet Coke just went to $3.00. Another coin, a shiny dollar featuring some Native American chick named Sasquatch, if I recall my history, hit the carpet and made a run down the hallway. That's when I noticed that the carpet design was a bunch of round spots exactly the size and color of a Sasquatch coin. And suddenly my Diet Coke cost $4.00. Never have I seen such a well-conceived marriage of carpet and soda dispenser. Next year I'm bringing my metal detector.

I ordered room service because I couldn't trust myself outside the room again.

Being Spontaneous

One of the many flaws in my personality is that I am not spontaneous. I confess I am baffled by the entire concept.

First, how do you define spontaneity? Is it even a real thing, or just a superstition? Is spontaneity based on how far in advance you have an idea, on how irrational the idea is, or some combination of the two?

If I think of doing something a week in advance, I know that's not spontaneous. A day in advance probably doesn't count either. I assume an hour isn't enough. But how about, say, five minutes in advance? Is that still premeditated, or is it getting closer to being spontaneous?

Apparently there is something wrong with my brain, because I have this bad habit of knowing what I want to do before I do it. The phrase you are unlikely to hear from me is, "Why did I just do that?" If I see a cookie that looks tasty, I almost always know it will end up in my mouth before it happens. A truly spontaneous person, assuming such a creature exists, would often say, "What is this in my mouth? How did it get there?"

I have to think a spontaneous life is unsettling, and that's just considering the stuff you discover in your mouth, to name one orifice.

As you know, you can fake most character traits if you need to. You can fake sincerity, kindness, compassion, optimism, and all sorts of things. But you can't fake spontaneity. I know because I've tried, and it always comes out sounding crazy. I'll blurt out something like "Let's walk to Cuba," and look at my wife to see if I nailed the spontaneous thing. So far, no luck. It's an elusive concept.

I only know one group of people who are consistently spontaneous, and most of them are already in jail. The rest will follow. Women value spontaneity, so that probably explains why death row inmates get marriage proposals all the time. When you remove the part of a man's mind that usually says, "Perhaps I should think about this before doing it," that is pure hotness.

Now THAT'S a Party!

Did you read about the six beer-drinking elephants in India? The elephants found drums of fermenting rice beer on a farm, partied too hard, then uprooted utility poles and electrocuted themselves. The fascinating part is that because they are elephants, they still remember that night.

My first reaction to that story was, "I'll have what they're having!" You don't get to use that joke often, and I don't like to miss an opportunity.

I'm no marketing expert, but if I were the farmer whose beer they drank, I'd start calling it "Shocking Elephant" and I'd design the coolest beer bottles ever. They'd be in the shape of an elephant with his trunk straight out, and that's the part you would drink from.

On the back label, I'd include a handy guide to what level of stupid you could expect after consuming each bottle. At the top of the scale, after ten bottles, you would have "probable accidental electrocution." At the bottom of the scale, after drinking one elephant or two, the problems would be "Thinking you are witty" and "Mild attraction to your friend's mom."

As I understand it, when you get electrocuted, it makes you crap. Imagine being the first person to find these six dead elephants, in forty tons of elephant poop, wrapped in live power cables. I would dive into the bushes and hope no one saw me. My fear would be that my neighbor who owns the land might say, "Can you help me clean this up?"

They say there's a tool for everything, but I checked my tool kit, and there's nothing there for cleaning up six electrocuted elephants in a mountain of shit. How do you even approach this problem? Do you wait for them to harden, then cut them up with chainsaws, put them in plastic garbage bags, and distribute them to Dumpsters all over town?

In the short run, you could charge admission to see the six dead elephants. I'd pay a rupee or two for that. I might even take the kids. There aren't many things the whole family can enjoy, but I'm pretty sure this is one of them.

Perhaps this is why I'm not in charge of planning weekends.

David Cop a Feel

Did you see in the news that a woman accused famous magician David Copperfield of sexual assault?

I would like to be David Copperfield's defense lawyer. I would argue that my client doesn't need to assault women because he knows magic. When he wants some action, all he has to do is make a willing woman materialize. The judge would admonish me for not being serious, at which point I would do a theatrical turn toward my client and say, "BEHOLD!" In a prearranged move, Copperfield would pull a blanket from his sleeve, drape it over the defense table, wave his arms, and a pair of feet would appear under the table, high heels facing the judge. Then my client would lean his head back and start moaning.

The judge would start banging his gavel (so to speak), and I would turn to the jury and yell, "I REST MY CASE!"

If that didn't work, I'd put the accuser on the stand and ask, "How can you be so sure my client touched you?" As she answered the question, I would nod to my magician client and have him do the trick where his hand comes out of my zipper and waves hello. Then I would say in my most sarcastic voice, "So, tell us again how good you are at knowing where my client's hands are."

Then I would ask the bailiff to bring me the Bible on which the accuser swore an oath. I would ask the accuser to read any passage aloud. By then, my magician client would have pulled the switcheroo, and the accuser would be reading something from *Mein Kampf.* I would turn to the jury and say, "That's not the Jesus I know!"

I haven't heard what evidence the prosecution will present, but for the sake of this book, let's hope it involves a semen-stained dress. When the police officer shows the court this piece of evidence, I would ask him if there was any way my client's DNA could be on that dress without sex. The police officer would say sex was the only explanation. Then I would ask the bailiff to turn down the lights. I would signal to my client to do his magic, then take out a black light and show that the policeman's own uniform is covered with my client's semen, and not just a little. He'd look like the Pillsbury Dough Boy exploded on him.

I only joke about this because I think it's unlikely the alleged crime happened. But if it turns out that the handsome, famous, charismatic magician who earns over $40 million a year and dates supermodels is forcing himself on women, I support the death penalty. And that's only partly because watching him try to escape from the gas chamber after he's strapped down would be good TV.

Why You Can't Take Me Anywhere

ast night I attended a meeting at our local school. It was part of a larger program put on by the police to teach parents how to prevent their kids from using drugs when they get older.

My personal objective was to make it through the night without making any inappropriate jokes that would embarrass my wife. It was a narrow escape.

Let me tell you, there are some situations where it is physically painful to be me. There was one point in the program where I think I ruptured a spleen trying to keep the jokes in. It came during the module on methamphetamines.

A parent asked why anyone would take meth, given the downside and all the side effects. One of the policemen answered that meth releases fifty times more serotonin in the brain than an orgasm. Then they showed a before and after picture where normal suburbanites turned into toothless, Albert Einstein-looking zombies. And that's just the women.

So I'm sitting there, doing the calculations in my head: Okay, that's 4.5 years of meth use, once a day, 365 days in a year, 50 times more serotonin than an orgasm . . . that's the equivalent of 80,000 orgasms.

On the downside, your teeth rot out, your skin itches until you scratch it off, you vomit, have withdrawals, possibly burn down the neighborhood, and roll around in your own filth while your life becomes a living hell. And then there is the jail time.

Still, 80,000 orgasms . . .

I wanted to raise my hand while the "before and after" pictures were up and ask, "Isn't that what anyone would look like after 80,000 orgasms?"

Or maybe, "So, on balance, you're saying it's totally worth it? Or am I doing the math wrong?"

But I didn't. I listened for two and a half hours and tried my best to avoid looking like I had any of the telltale symptoms of hardcore addiction the policemen kept describing. I'm highly suggestible, so this was difficult. When they talked about the uncontrollable fidgeting, I realized I was fidgeting. When they talked about red eyes, I felt as if all the moisture in mine had evaporated. When they talked about the teeth grinding, I had an uncontrollable impulse to grind mine. I took deep breaths and tried to meditate so my pulse wouldn't be too high—a sure sign of ecstacy use. I don't think I was alone. The audience looked like a warehouse of mannequins by the end of the night. No one wanted to be a conspicuous fidgeter.

Then there was the bad guessing. The policeman would hold up a bag of one sort of drug or another and ask if anyone knew how much it would cost. No one wanted to nail the estimate on the first guess and have the drug dogs tearing out the upholstery in their minivan five minutes later. I was planning my own bad estimates in case I got called on. It would have gone something like this: "That looks like about a pound of cocaine, so I'm guessing it would be worth nine or ten dollars on the street. Am I close?"

I managed to get through the night without embarrassing myself, and without getting strip searched. I even got a free cookie, which spiked my blood glucose level and gave me a mild high, but I couldn't enjoy it.

Monkey Attack

You can only imagine how many people forwarded me a story about a gang of monkeys attacking and killing the deputy mayor of Delhi, India. Apparently this had "my kind of story" written all over it.

According to the BBC, devout Hindus think monkeys are the manifestation of the monkey god Hanuman. Allow me to digress right here and confess that I could type the words "monkey god" all day long, and doing so would make me happy each and every time. For some wonderful reason, that combination of words—monkey god—releases a little snort of serotonin directly into the part of my brain that likes it the most.

Monkey god . . . monkey god . . . monkey god . . . Aaaaah, that's what I'm talkin' about.

Anyway, devout Hindus often feed nuts and bananas to the monkeys. So it should come as no surprise that monkeys will occasionally jump on your balcony, grab your nuts, and try to get their paws on your banana. This is why the phrase "had it coming" was invented.

The Indian solution to the problem involves training large monkeys to beat up the small ones. This can't end well. In my country, we complain that defense contractors are drumming up reasons for war. In India, it looks like the monkey training industry is getting too influential. Their solution to every problem is larger monkeys. But you need to breed ever larger monkeys to beat up the previous monkeys. That's all well and good until one of them climbs to the top of the Taj Mahal and starts swatting jets.

If I were invited to the funeral, or whatever they call it in India, and I was not a close friend or relative, I don't know if I could behave myself. Let's say I was the deputy mayor's driver, and I was friendly with the dearly departed, but not friends. I think I would spend the entire ceremony going up to different family members and asking, "So, how did he die? No one mentioned it yet." My entire objective would be to trick a great aunt into saying, "The monkeys tried to grab his nuts, but he didn't have enough nuts to go around. A scuffle broke out, and he went over a railing."

I don't know how reincarnation works, but I'm guessing the deputy mayor will come back as a monkey hater. He might not be too fond of me either.

Practical Jokes I Wish I Had Played

A reader sent me a story about some students who allegedly had trouble coming out of their trances after a hypnotist's stage act.

I don't know what really happened, but as a trained hypnotist, I can assure you that no one had trouble coming out of a trance. My best guess is that a student or two were playing a practical joke that got out of hand.

That is exactly the sort of practical joke I would have played if I were a student and wanted to get out of classes. But I would have put my own twist on it. When I got on stage with the hypnotist, I'd strike a zombie pose and yell "MUST . . . KILL . . . GRANDMA . . ." and then stiff-leg-walk out of the auditorium.

If teachers grabbed me, and they called paramedics, I would stay stiff and zombielike the whole time, and really try to sell it. When paramedics got me on the gurney, on the way to the ambulance, I'd say stuff like "MUST OBEY HYPNOTIST AND KILL GRANDMA." The paramedics, having not seen the hypnotist's act, might assume he really suggested it. They would wonder if they should call the police and close down the entire school until everyone who got that suggestion was deprogrammed.

When I got to the emergency room, and a doctor examined me, I'd stay in zombie mode, arms straight out, crazy eyes. And I'd wait for the doctor to do anything vaguely doctorish, such as tap my knee to check my reflexes. As soon as he did, I'd snap out of it and say, "What happened? Why am I here? Who are you people?"

The next day, when the principal, by now highly suspicious of my trance, started interrogating me, I'd say things like, "Apparently I'm highly suggestible. Can I ride on the short bus?" Or "If you don't think hypnosis works, why did you waste school money hiring a hypnotist?"

Eventually the principal would inadvertently say the wrong thing, probably in the form of a question such as, "Why did you say, 'Must kill grandma'?" As soon as he asked the question, I'd snap back into zombie mode and start yelling "MUST . . . KILL . . . GRANDMA . . ." again, and stiff-leg-walk out of the office. I can't imagine ever getting tired of it.

Hornier Than a . . .

Did you see the story in the news about the German guy with two penises? He lost his original equipment in an accident, so doctors built him a new one. Later, he decided to upgrade, but doctors left the previous one until the new one took root, so to speak.

When his wife saw the new one, she packed her bags and left him. This raises many questions about what made the wife so mad. There are many possibilities.

I'll always remember a conversation I overheard at the gym years ago. An unhappy wife was bitterly complaining to a friend that her husband bought a boat without talking to her first. Apparently wives need to be told everything. So I guess one possibility is that the husband didn't consult his wife before spending their retirement savings on a third pecker that looks like Frankenstein's month-old banana.

Another possibility is that the man said something inappropriate when he showed his wife his two penises. One can imagine many wrong things to say. Here is a partial list.

1. So, anyhoo, when is your sister coming out to visit?
2. The little one is for you.
3. I'm already a two-fisted drinker, so this just seemed right.
4. I bought the deluxe unicorn option. The next one goes on my head.
5. No more rest breaks for you, beeatch.
6. Maybe the doctors can give you two headaches so we're even.
7. Now it will feel like throwing TWO pencils down a hallway.

Another possibility is that the man created his own penis design and it had some features that didn't please his wife. Again, one can imagine many wrong design choices:

1. Bottle opener option
2. Anything with a face
3. A tattoo that says, "Hello Kitty!"

My point is that there were many ways to handle this situation wrong. You can see how a guy with one big head and two little ones might make the wrong choice.

New York City Subway

This week I am in Manhattan, living like a New Yorker. I have learned many things about the city. Today I will teach you how to ride the subway.

First, when you drop part of a cookie in the subway station, the five second rule does not apply. That cookie is dead before it hits the ground.

Second, when someone with a badge throws you on the ground, puts your arm behind your back, puts his knee on your neck, and yells, "DO NOT RESIST! DO NOT RESIST!" you should not resist. I learned this by watching. I also learned that you are not supposed to watch. You are supposed to "KEEP ON MOVING!"

To ride the subway, you must purchase a card with a magnetic strip. You learn this by observing other people "in the know" swiping their cards as they enter the turnstile. There are many options for what type of card you might want for particular purposes, and no apparent posted instructions. Luckily, you can ask for guidance from a helpful person who is behind thick glass. This transaction involves mumbling, rushing, condescension, the supposition that you are a moron, much evidence to support that assumption, and eventually the exchange of money for a little card that may or may not have some application for riding the subway.

Once armed with your little card, you swipe it on the turnstile. This is a frightening experience because there are at least nine wrong ways to swipe a card in a turnstile. I discovered all of them as a line of impatient New Yorkers formed behind me. I was holding the card the right way, and swiping it in the right direction, but as a uniformed guard eventually showed me, there is also something about the speed, trajectory, and possibly your state of mind that is also necessary for the turnstile to accept the card. I don't know how many times the turnstile has to reject you before the guy with the badge puts his knee on your neck and starts yelling "DO NOT RESIST!" but I am sure I was close to the limit.

Once you are on the subway, you must find a seat next to a person you judge least likely to drool on you, rob you, or start a conversation. My wife picked a guy who eventually fell asleep and slumped on her. I picked a guy who was muffin-topping into my seat and listening to an iPod. We felt blessed with our choices.

Next comes the wondering if you are heading in the right direction. There is one sign in each subway car showing the names of stations along the line. This sign is printed with tiny lettering so only the people sitting directly below it can read it. I didn't want to risk losing my sweet seat next to the muffin-top guy so I relied on listening to the conductor announce the stations. The announcements sound like Charlie Brown's teacher on Quaaludes, approximately this: "Muwa muwa muwa." I assume the conductors have the option of speaking in some language that humans can understand, but that is not their way. So we defaulted to the "get off when most other people get off" method of navigation. This worked well traveling from Grand Central Station to the US Open tennis match in Flushing. To travel to any other destination, you have to become a native, either intentionally or because you can't figure out how to get to the airport.

Andorran Show-offs

I hate it when any country does something better than my country. It's embarrassing. The indignity reached its peak with the latest report on life expectancy. The United States is ranked forty-second. Who is at the top, you might ask? Japan? No. Switzerland? No.

Today I learned there is a tiny country called Andorra, about the size of an ass pimple, in the Pyrenees mountains between France and Spain. They win the life expectancy competition at 83.5 years.

So what is their secret? I ran to Wikipedia to learn all about their lifestyle and culture. I figured I should start doing whatever it is that they're doing.

First, I learned that Andorra is a tax haven. If you have ever paid taxes, you know it almost kills you every time. It's no surprise that tax avoidance is good for your heart. I plan to stop paying taxes immediately. I'll secede from the United States and declare my own ass pimple–sized republic, nestled within the perimeter of my office, called Paynotaxtopia.

I'll need a national defense plan, and again, I'll borrow from Andorra. Their national defense is provided by Spain and France. Sweet! This is the healthiest type of defense you can have. If the Andorrans screw with Germany, the Germans will shoot a Spaniard. There's your life expectancy right there. I'll borrow from that model and let Canada and Mexico defend me. In return, I'll provide secret bank accounts and a tax haven for their politicians. They can even have legal prostitution in Paynotaxtopia, but they will have to bring their own prostitutes. I don't keep any in the office. (At least not extra ones.)

The main industry of Andorra is tourism. That's a healthy choice, and I plan to borrow it. The workers spend their days in the beauty and safety of luxury resorts. If they want any sneakers, they import them from a country with a life expectancy of twelve. If you think you have a better economic theory than that, don't embarrass yourself by mentioning it.

If history is any guide, the United States will want to attack my tiny republic and pull it back into the union. All I need to do is remove all of their pretenses for attacking. I plan to let the nuclear inspectors have full access, and I'll put a sign above the entrance to my office saying "No Taliban Allowed." If any Seal teams want to check for terrorists, I'll leave the door open.

The country of Paynotaxtopia will be a true democracy. I'll elect myself every morning before I start work and resign each evening. And most important, I will have no oil. Even Colin Powell couldn't convince the United Nations that attacking me is a good thing.

That's my plan for dancing on your grave. Let me know if you see any problem with it.

Appendix A: Most Frequently Asked Questions

People are often curious about my cartooning career. I don't fully understand this curiosity because it's impossible to be fascinated with my own life. It's like trying to tickle myself. It doesn't work. But I get the same questions all the time, so I have to assume someone cares. For your convenience, those questions and my answers are here.

What newspaper first ran Dilbert?

Dilbert is syndicated. That means my syndication company, United Media, tried to sell it to as many papers as it could, for the same launch date. About twenty-five papers bought it before the launch. Only a handful actually published it on the launch date. Even I don't know which ones ran it first. None of them were large newspapers.

(Other newspapers bought it with no intention of publishing it. They sometimes do that to keep the rights from their competitor in their city in case the comic becomes a hit.)

Where do you get your ideas?

I get most of my ideas from suggestions e-mailed to scottadams@aol.com. But I spent sixteen years in corporate America and am often reminded of that experience by events in my daily life. I'm in business myself, in a fashion. So I'm dealing with conference calls and contracts and marketing and design all the time. Plus I co-own two restaurants, and those are fertile sources of human interaction, too.

Do you do the writing or the drawing first?

Most cartoonists do the writing first. Then they draw. I start with only a germ of the idea and start drawing first. I draw the first panel, add the words, draw the second, add the words, and so on. I never know where a comic is going until it's done. It often takes a sharp left turn from where I expected it to go.

One advantage of my method is that after I draw a character, its expression or body language often suggests the dialogue. It helps them "talk" to me. For example, if I draw Wally looking more relaxed or rumpled than usual (accidentally—it can be very subtle) then I might use that to suggest different dialogue than I originally imagined.

Do you write one comic a day or a bunch at a time?

For years I did one per day, weekends and holidays included. Since marriage, I'm trying to do two per day on weekdays and keep more time open for weekends and travel. But I still end up working most weekends at least half days.

How far in advance do you submit comics?

The daily comic needs to be e-mailed to my syndication company about four weeks ahead of its publication date. The Sunday strips require more processing by the newspapers (because of the color) and have to be in about eight weeks ahead of publication. Lately I'm only a week or so ahead of those deadlines. When I first started in this business, I was six months ahead of deadline. I've been chipping away at that buffer ever since.

Do you still draw the comic on paper?

Most cartoonists still use paper, at least for most of the work. They typically finish it off in Photoshop after scanning the inked work. Photoshop might be used for the lettering (using a font of your own handwriting) or adding shading and effects.

About two years ago I had some hand problems (from overuse) and switched to drawing directly to the computer, which is easier on my hand. I have a computer monitor that allows me to draw directly to the screen (as opposed to a tablet on the desk). It's the 21SX by Wacom. It cut my production time in half. It's different from drawing on paper, and there's a learning curve of a few months to get it down. But once you do, it's amazing. I use Photoshop for the entire process now. Then I hit a few keys and e-mail it to United Media.

How did Dilbert get his name?

I developed Dilbert as a doodle during my corporate years. He had no name, but my coworkers thought he needed one. So I had a "Name the Nerd" contest on my cubicle whiteboard. My boss at the time, Mike Goodwin, wrote down "Dilbert," and I closed the contest. We had a winner.

After I submitted Dilbert for syndication, Mike sheepishly told me that he realized why Dilbert seemed such a good name for a comic. He was looking through his dad's old military artifacts and realized he had seen a Dilbert comic before. Since World War II, a comic called Dilbert had been used by military pilots in the context of telling them what not to do. A "Dilbert" was synonymous with a pilot who was being an idiot. It was too late for me to turn back at that point. I kept the name Dilbert, and I never heard from the family of the original artist. Obviously they are aware of my version of Dilbert. I appreciate that they evidently decided to not make it an issue.

How do you become a syndicated cartoonist?

The short answer is that you can buy books from any bookseller on how to submit work to syndicates. There are only a handful of syndicates, and all you do is mail them photocopies of your work. All submissions are reviewed by the decision-makers, so unlike other fields, in cartooning there is no advantage to knowing anyone or pulling strings. Your work speaks for itself, and an experienced editor can judge a cartoonist's potential in less than a minute. So while you are competing against perhaps three thousand submissions per year, the good ones are easily spotted.

That's the method I used. I submitted Dilbert to several syndication companies at the same time. A few rejected me outright. One syndicate suggested that I find an actual artist to do the drawing for me. (They liked my writing.) United Media called and offered me a contract. They took a chance on my crappy artwork, and that risk paid off.

Do you plan to retire like those quitters Watterson, Larson, Breathed, and Amend?

Not until the public doesn't want to see Dilbert anymore. I don't agonize over my work the way some artists do. Watterson, for example, did his art with a tiny paintbrush and ink. I can't imagine how tedious that was. And he probably made more money in his short career than I will make in my lifetime. Retiring made sense for him.

I enjoy my work. And it's not that hard. Plus I like the attention and the pure joy of creating. I can't imagine not contributing to the economy in some fashion. I tend to define myself by what I do. That means I need to be useful to feel good about myself. Leisure doesn't suit me except for an occasional change of pace.

Appendix B: Scott Adams (and Dilbert) Quotations

I asked my readers to tell me what they thought are my best quotations, from any of my writings. Here's the list they came up with. Some you will recognize from this book.

"Creativity is allowing yourself to make mistakes. Art is knowing which ones to keep." —Scott Adams

"Sadness is just another word for not enough coffee." —Wally

"You're working hard. I'm not. In a hundred years, we'll both be dead." —Dogbert

"My goal in life is to be slightly less miserable then the people who hate me. I call that winning." —Scott Adams

"I believe in karma. That means I can do bad things to you all day long and assume you deserve it." —Dogbert

"We're all moist robots." —Scott Adams, on the illusion of free will

"There's really no point in listening to other people. They're either going to be agreeing with you or saying stupid stuff." —Dogbert

"Sometimes the best you can do is make other people feel bad." —Scott Adams

"There's nothing more dangerous than a resourceful idiot." —Scott Adams

"There's a fine line between evil and underpaid." —Carol the secretary, from the Dilbert comic strip

"My philosophy is that anything worth doing is too hard." —Wally

"If you're having trouble sounding condescending, ask a Unix user to show you how." —Scott Adams

"Intelligence has much less practical application than you'd think." —Scott Adams

"If you think that offering excellent reasons for your thinking will change anyone's mind, you might be new on this planet." —Scott Adams

"Lately, the only thing keeping me from being a serial killer is my distaste for manual labor." —Scott Adams

"And then he voted." —Scott Adams's response to almost any irrational argument.

"You haven't achieved equality until you're a legitimate target for humor." —Scott Adams

"Knowledge is power. Power corrupts. Corruption is a crime. Crime doesn't pay. If you keep reading, you'll go broke!!" —Dogbert

"Character flaws aren't a philosophy." —Scott Adams

"I am humbled by your grasp of the obvious." —Scott Adams

"Your typical day is full of moments where you ask for a cup of coffee and someone hands you a bag of nails." —Scott Adams

"I ask for so little. And boy do I get it." —Dilbert

"There's a fine line between participation and mockery." —Dilbert

"Maybe I'm too cynical. Or maybe I'm just cynical enough. Sometimes it's hard to tell." —Scott Adams

"Engineers believe that if it ain't broke, it doesn't have enough features yet." —Scott Adams

"Life is half delicious yogurt, half crap, and your job is to keep the plastic spoon in the yogurt." —Scott Adams

"The thing to remember about freedom is that it's not given, it's taken." —Scott Adams

"I dance like a drunken monkey pissing on an electric fence." —Scott Adams

"It's important to agree with people if you want them to think you are a genius. For most people, the definition of smart is 'Thinks exactly like me but even more so.'" —Scott Adams

"Dance like it hurts. Love like you need money. Work like people are watching." —Dogbert

"Don't think of yourself as an organic pain collector, racing toward oblivion." —Dogbert

"If you haven't already told your kids 'Don't fellate the president,' then you're probably a bad parent." —Scott Adams

"Just once maybe there should be a story about an athlete who did steroids and didn't set a world record and hump his way through the entire Victoria Secrets model list. Otherwise you have what I call a mixed message." —Scott Adams

"Men live in a fantasy world. I know this because I am one, and I actually receive my mail there." —Scott Adams

"I go through life like Helen Keller in a room full of Rubik's cubes." —Scott Adams

"Sure, the government has a few lucky successes, such as building highways and schools and dams and reducing pollution and eradicating polio and encouraging the Internet and winning World Wars I and II. But a broken clock is right twice a day, too." —Scott Adams

"As a human being you are a collection of many things: skin, bones, brains, experience, and emotion. But more than all of that, you are your expectations. That's why I choose to be optimistic." —Scott Adams

"In case you ever consider getting off caffeine yourself, let me explain the process. You begin by sitting motionlessly in a desk chair. Then you just keep doing that forever because life has no meaning." —Scott Adams

"I'd rather staple a skunk to my forehead and go to a trade show for banjo makers." —Scott Adams

"There are many methods for predicting the future. For example, you can read horoscopes, tea leaves, tarot cards, or crystal balls. Collectively, these methods are known as 'nutty methods.' Or you can put well-researched facts into sophisticated computer models, more commonly referred to as 'a complete waste of time.'" —Scott Adams

"I recently attended a school open house for the kids. The first thing I noticed was that our kids produced spectacular works of art whereas all the other kids produced utter crap." —Scott Adams

"... a cross between a Chia Pet and a douche bag." —Scott Adams, commenting on North Korea's Kim Jong II

"I'm not the only guy whose underpants sometimes go mongoose on his snake." —Scott Adams, commenting on the design of men's undergarments

"The pope is in a tricky situation. He can either say that he believes Muslims picked the wrong religion, thereby triggering massive violence. Or he can be a liar with a funny hat." —Scott Adams

"As I write this, my Internet connection has been down for a day. I don't want to sound as if I'm starting to panic or anything, but I'd be lying if I said I hadn't given some thought to binge drinking." —Scott Adams

"If you think there's an easy way to explain to your wife why you were thinking of Vladimir Putin while she is telling you about her feelings, you would be totally wrong." —Scott Adams

"All your example shows is that other people can do other things." —Dilbert, explaining to his boss why an analogy isn't an argument

"It's like panning for gold, except the gold is cat poop. That inconvenient fact doesn't detract from the thrill of the find as much as you'd think." —Scott Adams, on cleaning the cat box

"My favorite conspiracy theory is the one that says the world is being run by a handful of ultra-rich capitalists, and that our elected governments are mere puppets. I sure hope it's true. Otherwise my survival depends on hordes of clueless goobers electing competent leaders. That's about as likely as a dog pissing the Mona Lisa *into a snowbank."* —Scott Adams

"I need to contribute to the world to feel good about myself." —Scott Adams

"Maybe we should educate the morons of tomorrow so they'll stop believing the leaders of tomorrow." —Scott Adams

"Try stuffing fewer groceries down your maw." —Dogbert, on his diet plan

"I've never seen anyone change his mind because of the power of a superior argument or the acquisition of new facts, but I've seen plenty of people change behavior to avoid being mocked." —Scott Adams

"Adams's rule of self-defeating prophecies: Any doom that can be predicted won't happen." —Scott Adams

"I think you should live your life so that the maximum number of people will attend your funeral." —Scott Adams

"You probably think Stephen Hawking is in that wheelchair because of a motor neuron disease. But if you got as much barely legal student poontang as The Hawkster, you'd be in a wheelchair, too." —Scott Adams

"I was in my thirties before someone told me that eating is not a speed sport." —Scott Adams

"I'm not convinced that oil is the problem in the Middle East. I'm pretty sure we could fly over the Middle East and drop bags of money and they'd still want to kill us for blocking the view." —Scott Adams

"My thinking is that if a bully punches you, you should run away. Later, when he's asleep, put a bullet in his head and leave the gun in his little brother's crib so it looks like a sibling squabble." —Scott Adams

"I keep hearing the argument that some things are constitutional while other things are not. The idea is that we should be in favor of all the things that were decided over two hundred years ago by a bunch of slave-owning cross-dressers who pooped in holes." —Scott Adams

"I sprang into action like a cheetah on a trampoline." —Dilbert

"I might be dumb, but I'm not dumb enough to express my true opinion about anything important. The one thing I've learned about freedom of expression is that you really ought to keep that sort of thing to yourself." —Scott Adams

"Everyone says there's a lack of leadership in the world these days. I think we should all be thankful, because the only reason for leadership is to convince people to do things that are either dangerous (like invading another country) or stupid (working extra hard without extra pay)." —Scott Adams

"There are two essential rules of management: one: the customer is always right; two: they must be punished for their arrogance!" —Scott Adams

"Dumber than a Yugo full of anvils." —Scott Adams

"I can't bring myself to believe in a God with a personality like my own. I base that on the paucity of lightning attacks on people who deserve it." —Scott Adams

"I asked how many guys would have sex with a robot if it was indistinguishable from a hot human woman. About 95 percent of the hetero guys said they would. The other 5 percent expressed a strong preference for lying." —Scott Adams

"There's no such thing as good ideas and bad ideas. There are only your own ideas and other people's. If you want someone to like your idea, tell him he said it first last week and you just remembered it." —Scott Adams

"The world isn't fair, but as long as it's tilting in my direction, I find that there's a natural cap to my righteous indignation." —Scott Adams

"Car singers believe they have an inalienable right to sing along with the music even if it does make other people feel as if squirrel-banshees have crawled inside their skulls to eat the parts of their brains that control joy." —Scott Adams

"The best any human can do is to pick a delusion that helps him get through the day. This is why people of different religions can generally live in peace. At some level, we all suspect that other people don't believe their own religion any more than we believe ours." —Scott Adams

"When it comes to handling delicate matters affecting the survival of the planet, you want to send in the seventy-nine-year-old German guy with a Marge Simpson hat, a history of talking directly to God, and seven decades of sperm backup. I don't see how that could go wrong." —Scott Adams, on the pope

"Next week, a doctor with a flashlight shows us where sales projections come from." —Dilbert

"It's like fifteen drunken monkeys with a jigsaw puzzle." —Dilbert, on his project status

"The first time you see something that you have never seen before, you almost always know right away if you should eat it or run away from it." —Scott Adams

"Looks like it was done by a drunken monkey as a practical joke on all the other drunken monkeys." —Dilbert, commenting on someone's work

"As a rule, I don't like to laugh at the misfortune of others. The exception to that rule is if it's really, really funny." —Scott Adams

"A rental car is basically an ashtray on wheels." —Scott Adams

"Give a man a fish, and you'll feed him for a day. Teach a man to fish, and he'll buy a funny hat. Talk to a hungry man about fish, and you're a consultant." —Scott Adams

"It's called a 'concept car' because that sounds better than 'something we pulled out of our ass and hope to someday shove up yours.'" —Scott Adams

"The human population is 90 percent gullible, violence-prone dipshits." —Scott Adams

"Great ideas often look identical to stupid ones right up until the moment they work." —Scott Adams

"The bottom line is that your existence is the sum of invisible forces operating on matter that is only probably there." —Scott Adams

"A retarded chimpanzee can drink a case of beer and still perform most management functions." —Scott Adams

"I'm certain that the fans of Shakespeare will tell me I would enjoy his work if only I took the time to understand it. But that's like saying I would love polka

music if I took the time to translate it in my head into the sound of a band I like." —Scott Adams

"If there is one thing that our role models in this election have taught us, it's that omitting important information is completely different from lying." —Scott Adams

"The difference between Christianity and Islam is that some people think a guy walked on water and other people think a horse can fly." —Scott Adams

"When did ignorance become a point of view?" —Scott Adams

"Stem cells are like toenail clippings with a better career plan." —Scott Adams

"Science is a good thing. News reporters are good things, too. But it's never a good idea to put them in the same room." —Scott Adams

"The government runs the Bureau of Alcohol, Tobacco and Firearms, so they must know a thing or two about satisfying women." —Scott Adams

"For the record, I am not a nut. I am an optimist. That's exactly like a nut except with a better attitude." —Scott Adams

"You're thinking I'm one of those wise-ass California vegetarians who is going to tell you that eating a few strips of bacon is bad for your health. I'm not. I say it's a free country and you should be able to kill yourself at any rate you choose, as long as your cold, dead body is not blocking my driveway." —Scott Adams

"I believe everybody in the world should have guns. I also believe that only I should have ammunition. Because frankly, I wouldn't trust the rest of you goobers with anything more dangerous than string." —Scott Adams

"My critics are self-important, humorless, autofellating, ass hats." —Scott Adams

"The creator of the universe works in mysterious ways. But he uses a base ten counting system and likes big round numbers." —Scott Adams

"I was happier than a kitten with a Q-tip." —Scott Adams

"He was deader than a shrunken head at a hacky sack festival." —Scott Adams

"I was busier than a beaver in a coffee lake." —Scott Adams

"He changed more times than a baby in a beer-drinking contest." —Scott Adams

"I was more nervous than a fan store owner with a comb-over." —Scott Adams